In Defense of Reading

In Defense of Reading

Sarah E. Worth

ROWMAN & LITTLEFIELD
INTERNATIONAL
London • New York

Published by Rowman & Littlefield International Ltd
Unit A, Whitacre Mews, 26-34 Stannary Street, London SE11 4AB
www.rowmaninternational.com

Rowman & Littlefield International Ltd.is an affiliate of Rowman & Littlefield
4501 Forbes Boulevard, Suite 200, Lanham, Maryland 20706, USA
With additional offices in Boulder, New York, Toronto (Canada), and Plymouth (UK)
www.rowman.com

British Library Cataloguing in Publication Data

A catalogue record for this book is available from the British Library

ISBN: HB 978-1-7834-8318-1
        PB 978-1-7834-8319-8

Library of Congress Cataloging-in-Publication Data Available

ISBN 978-1-78348-318-1 (cloth : alk. paper)
ISBN 978-1-78348-319-8 (pbk. : alk. paper)
ISBN 978-1-78348-320-4 (electronic)

♾™ The paper used in this publication meets the minimum requirements of
American National Standard for Information Sciences—Permanence of Paper for
Printed Library Materials, ANSI/NISO Z39.48-1992.

Printed in the United States of America

Contents

Acknowledgments

Books often have trajectories that their authors cannot predict. This book is no different. I didn't know I was going to write *this* book until it was finished, because so much changed and developed during the writing process. I am grateful to my philosopher friend and cheerleader Eva Dadlez for suggesting that I should write this in the first place. She had watched me for years give papers on a central topic, and it seemed clear to her that I had a book in the making. Only I needed to be convinced. Part of my struggle was that I want this book to be accessible to readers outside of philosophy. But I have only ever written for specialists in philosophy. So my ideas and my prose had to be constantly revised and smoothed. Thus I am grateful to those who have read drafts along the way, Eva and Jim Edwards in particular, and Sandi Annone for meticulously proofreading and making suggestions about clarity, as well. I have also been greatly benefitted by a summer research program at Furman University called the Furman Advantage. For the last three summers I have had a research student who helped me with individual chapters. I choose my students carefully based on their expertise, and each has helped me research outside of my comfort zone quite proficiently. Rachel MacAlister was a biology major and helped with the research about the brain. Sean McBratnie was an English major who helped me research genre. Kieran Cook was a psychology major who helped research the chapter about evidence. All of them were also philosophy majors who had grounding in philosophical questioning and method. I am thankful to each of them for teaching me to trust

x   *Acknowledgments*

my students and our ability to learn together. My student assistant, Samantha Menapace, helped with the painstaking job of editing the footnotes and bibliography.

I have the great advantage as a philosopher of having a steady job at a university I love. It is because of this job that I can teach what I am interested in, engage with bright and capable students, and write what I want. I thank Furman University in particular for my last sabbatical, in which I had the mental space to read literature and hatch the formal plan for this book. And it is with the utmost thanks that I acknowledge my husband Bill and my children, William and Charles, for indulging me in discussions of novels, prisons, reading on electronic devices, whether or not narrative nonfiction is really a thing, Common Core, what counts as real, and storytelling in general. I am sure that these kinds of conversations are more than two nine-year-olds should be expected to endure.

This book is dedicated to the two most influential women in my life. RoseAnna Tendler Worth, my mother, taught me to read, ask questions, relentlessly search for answers, and to delight in that search. Her sister, my aunt Judith Tendler, served as an incredible role model and showed me that a career in academia was not only attainable for women but gratifying and important. I regret that neither of them were able to see this book come to fruition.

Some of the essays in this book appeared in slightly different forms in the following articles: "In Defense of Genreblending," co-authored with Sean McBratnie, *Aesthetic Investigations*, vol. 1 (2015): 33–48; "Fact, Fiction, and Fraud: From Frey to Wilkomirski," *Southwest Philosophy Review*, vol. 26, no. 1 (2010): 27–33; "Story-Telling and Narrative Knowing," *Journal of Aesthetic Education*, vol. 42, no. 3 (2008): 42–55; "Narration, Representation, Memoir, Truth, and Lies: How We Diminish the Art of Narrative with Simple Truths," in *How to Make Believe: The Fictional Truths of the Representational Arts,* Alexander Bareis and Lene Nordrum, eds. (Berlin, New York: DeGruyter, 2015); and "Nonfiction and Narration," *Fiction as an Aesthetic Concept* (Westport, CT: Praeger Publishers, 2015).

Preface

The question of whether or how it is that art or literature could possibly improve us is an old one. Plato believed the literary arts were especially dangerous and subversive because they appealed to the basest part of us: our emotions. Aristotle believed the opposite and thought that enjoying an emotional catharsis would cleanse us in such a way that we might become more balanced and thus more rational. But now we live in a time in which we do not necessarily believe that the emotions always necessarily work in opposition to reason. In fact, many believe reason and emotion work together quite well on different kinds of problems, from basic decision-making to feelings of injustice.[1] But the question of how reading literature or narrative might really benefit is still very much alive. I believe that it can benefit us in a number of ways, specifically morally, cognitively, and socially. Arguments depend, however, on one's starting position, so I want to be clear about mine. I am an aesthetic cognitivist because I believe that a large part of the value of the arts is that they can teach us about the world. But it is not "facts" or "truisms" about the world that I am particularly interested in, and I do not think that literature or narrative give us propositional knowledge. What we gain from engaging with the arts, and with narrative in particular, is a certain way of making sense of the world. By giving meaning to our lived experiences, we learn how best to interpret information given to us from outside our own experience and how to make meaningful insights about our own lives as well as

xi

the lives of others. I do not believe that all knowledge is quantifiable or testable, which is an assumption that I assume is relatively controversial. Specifically, I do not believe that much of the knowledge we gain from reading is quantifiable in very many meaningful ways. I worry, however, that the public education system argues for the need to test and assess learning to justify the time and expense spent on public education. This suggests that we can and must quantify, through assessment, the knowledge developed from reading. But the tests leave out and devalue skills not found on standardized exams, such as empathy, creativity, compassion, storytelling, reading for pleasure, recreational exercise, and finding meaning in experiences and relationships. The assumption is that reading is goal oriented and that the goal is comprehension of facts, the division of genres (so we know how to gauge our expectations properly) and content acquisition. Maybe a secondary goal is vocabulary building. If we become a generation obsessed with test scores, we become obsessed with testable information. The intangibles and untestables are left to chance. Many of these intangibles are qualities that I will argue can be gained from reading: losing yourself in a book, focusing on distant places and characters, practicing making connections between events and details when you do not know how or when they will be relevant, being able to practice decision-making, and prediction of outcomes and counterfactuals. I believe there is significant benefit to focusing and sitting still for long periods of time while we are awake. Perhaps most importantly, reading helps us to feel empathy.

I am also a social constructivist. I believe that the understanding and creation of meaning is benefitted by collaborative forums. Solitary reading is one way to read, but for me that is only the beginning of the work of reading. I believe that reading can be an inherently social experience, as shown with book clubs, online forums about books, and reading groups with prisoners. If you think about it, our middle and high school literature classes are the primary way that we come to understand much of the literature we are exposed to formally. And even if you did not read the book, you understood what was going on through the discussions (hopefully). Talking about literature helps readers to understand not just the plot, but the meaning, and the ways in which it might help one to see the world and oneself a little differently.

Philosopher Gregory Currie suggests there is a general consensus that people believe reading is good for us but that we do not have any empirical evidence to show how or why it is good for us.[2] I will take Currie's skepticism as a challenge, because I believe that we do, in fact, have quite a bit of evidence that reading benefits us greatly. So this book is a defense of reading in relatively broad terms. I will look at what is quantifiable and what is not, I will argue for ways to accept that which is not traditionally quantifiable (like empathy or meaning construction) and I will borrow from some fields philosophers do not traditionally use, like education, sociology, prison studies, and neuroscience. I will also challenge what counts as evidence. Is it psychological experiments, sociological data, or neuroimaging? Or do we need to expand our notion of evidence even further than that? As a philosopher, I make arguments that are backed by evidence, justification, and examples.

We read less than we have in previous generations, and we read less deeply. Because of that we are losing what some might call soft skills. We are also losing the sense that we might do something purely for the pleasure of those skills, and we might be approaching a time in history where all pleasure has become guilty pleasure. We measure nutrients in carefully measured proportions to achieve optimal health. We exercise to expend an exact number of calories. We measure the sum total of our children's achievement (beginning in kindergarten) with numerical indices, and we justify our own and our children's activities with practical considerations like exercise, leadership, and skill development. I take reading to be something that can be and should be pleasurable, but valuable, real world skills accompany that pleasure. These hard won skills rarely manifest themselves without attendant pleasure. I worry that something will be lost in a future that does not value or teach deep reading and does not value reading for pleasure. With the ubiquity of the internet and all of the amazing resources at our hands, we often fall into googling information and chasing information down internet rabbit holes rather than focusing on one thing. I worry also about the internet, and social media in particular, not because they are bad but because they fill all available time and attention with things that do not require focus or cognition. They fill our heads with images unconnected to information or context and sound bites of other people's perceptions. Reading literature allows, but also forces, a reader to focus on one thing, make long-term connections, practice identifying with some characters, empathizing with some characters, and feeling dismay and disgust for those who act reprehensibly. We rarely get the depth of that feeling from the internet and social media.

This book is intended to be a very general philosophical defense of reading. Philosophers grapple regularly and often with the question of the ways in which fiction might be something from which we can either benefit or acquire knowledge. Philosophers tend to frame queries specifically around the question of what constitutes fiction, how we might learn from fiction, and how it is that we get emotionally engaged with fiction. I will take this research into account, but my focus will be more on the act of reading itself, and not just on fiction or nonfiction and what possible impacts they might have on readers. I will approach reading as a skill that needs to be developed over time, over a lifetime even. I do not think an analysis of the question of whether and what we can learn from reading can exclude consideration of the reader, her skills, her reading experience, her capacity to make literary connections, and the exposure she has had to texts that vary in quality and complexity. Whether one can learn or benefit from reading has a lot to do with the reader. This book will, I hope, appeal to philosophers, taking into consideration research in the field. But should also help to shed light on some issues in which readers outside philosophy might be interested. In particular, I hope that educators and language instructors might find my analysis helpful and that the philosophy is accessible enough to enlighten some issues that plague other disciplines. I also hope that this book will be timely, in that it will deal with some very practical matters having to do with the shift from print media to more online reading. It is also timely because we need to better understand the way we teach school-age students to read based on the ways in which they are relentlessly tested. The student improvement is then more about the teacher and the school than useful feedback for the students themselves.

I intend to do a number of things in this book, but the main focus is to defend the value of reading fictional literature. I see the need for such an argument now for two main reasons. First, I see reading, and the teaching of fiction in particular, quietly being diminished within school curricula. In the US, the new Common Core State Standards (CCSS) minimizes the teaching of fiction in high school so that English classes can teach the more highly valued lessons of so-called "instructional literature," which goes beyond simple narrative nonfiction but is in some powerful sense considered "true." The second indication that a book of this kind is necessary is derived from certain arguments I see being made, in very public places, that reading literature is not that important. Arguments in *The New*

York Times, as well as at academic conferences, are often indicative of arguments and sentiments that are felt much more widely. In the attempt philosophers have made to account abstractly for the ways in which we understand literature, some have discounted its benefits because we do not have enough scientific evidence to demonstrate them (which I also question). Others have argued that questionable moral aspects of a work also deeply inform the reading we can have, without giving specifics of what is better or worse to read. Martha Nussbaum argues that reading *good* literature, Dickens she suggests,[3] can help us substantially in becoming better citizens, but she does not account for the way in which readers who are fundamentally ill-equipped to read Dickens might benefit from reading other kinds of texts. I hope to address a number of these kinds of weaknesses in the philosophical accounts. It is a concern of mine that, simultaneously, academics question the comprehensive benefits of reading, fiction is being diminished in the public school curriculum, and the kind of reading opportunities that the internet provides and encourages (distracted reading at best) do not help us to develop real literacy. I have long believed that reading needs a more comprehensive and robust defense, and I hope to do that in what follows.

I want to make the argument that we should read more. We should read more deeply and read more widely. And we should read for pleasure. Philosophical questions about the effects of reading literature are well-trodden, but I think that philosophers have been too myopic about their own arguments. Firstly, most of the arguments about what we might or might not gain from reading literature are focused on the text itself and not the reader. What I am interested in is the reader, the text, and the kinds of likely and possible interactions between the two. I am also interested in the ways in which reading regularly, over time, might impact the way one thinks, organizes information, and uses literary references to connect to other people. Secondly, philosophers have ignored the evidence or have chosen to be willfully blind to kinds of evidence that may actually be helpful to defending their arguments. That is, philosophers can make arguments that are not solely dependent upon empirical data. But there is a current trend that calls upon us to do just that. This is the all-important data that only scientists and social scientists can give us, because they are the ones who ask questions in forms that will produce data points. Philosophers do not tend to ask questions with answers that polls, tests, and statistics address.

We ask questions that require reflection and are often questions not answered by science, like whether or not reading betters us as human beings and how reading more extended narratives can help each one of us organize the barrage of experiences we encounter every day. And the arguments we provide produce a different kind of knowledge. It goes against all of my instincts as a philosopher to have to appeal to data at all, but it further fuels my worry to imagine that all philosophical questions can be resolved with data.[4] The accusation that reading literature is without cognitive benefit is misguided. Nothing could be *more* misguided than a search for an explanation of the benefits of reading literature, other than reducing the whole search to the question of which facts people learn when they read. Literature is not about facts. It should not be about facts, and it could be argued that facts are gained only (at best) as a side benefit of reading. When facts are highlighted as the primary benefits of reading, *of course* we will fall short in defending them in the context of literature. I think, however, that this misses the point entirely. The benefits we gain from reading, and more importantly the benefits we gain from being literate, extend well into the moral realm, the intellectual realm, the realm of memory and mental organization, as well as the civic realm. I will talk about all of these, in turn, throughout the rest of the book.

I was compelled to write this book because another philosopher suggested that there really is no evidence that reading benefits its readers. I really did take this on as a personal challenge. It seemed inconceivable to me that his claim could be true. So in what follows I will argue that evidence goes beyond what we traditionally count as evidence and that reading for pleasure is a skill that is worth making time for and saving for future generations. I have two children whom I want to be readers, and I see everything in our culture work against them. From school curricula to TV to the constant desire for gaming, it seems to me that reading is always presented as a chore. I believe that the context that surrounds us and offers us constant instant gratification works against deep reading, and we need to be aware of the contexts we provide for our children and our adult selves. Deep reading will be lost to Facebook, Instagram, and Snapchat unless we recognize its value and fight for the time and mental space to indulge. Many say they do not have the time, but we have plenty of time for TV, smartphones, and video games. We make time for what we value. I implore you to value reading.

The plan of this book is to tackle a number of different aspects of reading narrative literature in isolation first, so that I can provide a more comprehensive picture of the ways in which reading narrative might benefit us. I look at reading, fiction, genre, memoir, narrative, knowledge, belief, and then what counts as evidence. Throughout the book I build the case that we should value reading, that understanding how our expectations of what we read changes the impact of what we read, and that some of the strategies we employ to make sense of literature might not ultimately be all that helpful. I argue that reading impacts the reader more than we might have thought initially and that a loss of reading culture is something to be deeply lamented.

NOTES

1. See especially Jonah Lehrer, a neuroscientist who gives ample descriptions of the ways in which emotions and reason work quite well together and why reason alone is rarely a productive thing.

2. See Gregory Currie. "Does Great Literature Make us Better?" *The New York Times Opinionator,* June 1, 2013. Accessed January 29, 2015. http://opinionator. blogs.nytimes.com/2013/06/01/does-great-literature-make-us-better.

3. See Martha Nussbaum, *Poetic Justice* (Boston: Beacon Press, 1995).

4. There is a recent and ugly debate about the problem of whether all philosophical problems can really be solved by science. The question of whether something can come from nothing is one of the founding questions of Western philosophy, asked first by pre-Socratic Parmenides. Lawrence Krauss, a physicist at Arizona State University, published a book in 2012 called *A Universe From Nothing: Why There Is Something Rather Than Nothing.* In it he argues that physics can resolve the entire question of cosmology and gives an explanation of the beginning of the universe. Philosopher David Albert of Columbia University, who has a PhD in physics, wrote a review of the book for *The New York Times* pointing out many of the inaccuracies and limitations of Krauss's argument. Krauss, in turn, called Albert "moronic" in an interview in *The Atlantic,* denying that philosophy had much to do with the discussion of science at all. He asserted that "Philosophy used to be a field that had content, but then 'natural philosophy' became physics, and physics has only continued to make inroads. Every time there's a leap in physics, it encroaches on these areas that philosophers have carefully sequestered away to themselves, and so then you have this natural resentment on the part of philosophers" (Andersen, 2012). The implication is, of course, that all philosophical

questions will be eventually answered with scientific explanations. The public accusations got ugly, and Krauss eventually apologized, but the question seems still to be unanswered as to whether or not science can resolve philosophical questions. I take scientific questions and philosophical questions to be very different in kind, and philosophical questions cannot be answered with scientific data.

Chapter One

The Benefits of Reading

1. THE CURRENT STATE OF READING

You might be wondering why reading needs a defense. Reading certainly seems to be taught in the schools, it has very practical uses, and book sales are not dwindling too badly, even with the advent of e-books and e-readers. But there are some other statistics that worry me and make me think that reading is in need of a proper defense. People read less than they used to. This is, of course, a contested claim, but it is one that is worth examining. Some studies say that people just read less.[1] Several studies have looked into our changing reading habits and how these changes affect us. Some studies suggest that our abundant internet reading has led us to become less focused and more shallow readers.[2] Others have found that, because we read less fiction, our capacity for empathy has diminished significantly.[3] Some, however, argue that nothing important has changed about our reading habits over the last several decades besides the shift from reading print to reading online. Whichever one of these is true, these studies have clearly shown that, with the advent and ubiquity of the internet, especially in the lives of our youngest readers, our reading habits have shifted significantly. What I am interested in here is making an argument that has to do with the benefits of reading in a very general way. I am less interested in the effects of a single book or even a single genre than I am in the overall benefits that being a reader and living in a community of readers can provide. This has to do both with deep reading and an extended view of the power of literacy. I am not particularly interested in just the minimal capacity to read, but in what the extended benefits are of practicing the skill of engaging with narrative prose on a regular basis with a variety of different kinds of reading materials. How might we actually benefit from being a reader and engaging with narrative on a regular basis? Why should we keep this as an important value?

I also want to address the ways in which we make sense of narrative prose (especially in the way it is different from fiction, specifically), but I want my arguments to serve a more practical end. I want this book to address some of the perennial puzzles people grapple with concerning literature, and at the same time I want to address some of the specific problems that the reality of the twenty-first century brings us. That is, we read on the internet, we are regularly asked to multi-task as we take in information and narrative, and the values of the society are being clearly reflected in the values of our educational curricula. The utility of *reading for pleasure* is under attack in a number of settings because it is perceived as impractical. The value of *reading fiction* is under attack because it presumably does not teach us anything true or useful and, therefore, is not something that school curricula should waste time teaching. The primary purpose of this book is to build a defense against both of these claims. Reading fiction and reading for pleasure may not provide a particular or singular outcome, but they can help to develop many useful human character traits that we consistently find very valuable, like empathy, cognitive skills that have to do with the organization of information (especially the kind of information that is either temporal or causal), and the way we make sense of our lived experience. Reading and literacy are skills that take years to develop. Reading should not always be about content or information acquisition. Behavior modification should also not be the main goal of reading, but is often a constructive side benefit. Reading, and a well-developed literacy, should not be held to be good for one purpose only. We read to escape, to understand, to empathize, and to learn. We read to understand how others organize knowledge and how to organize our own human experiences. Reading is a human experience that is largely different for individual readers, and so I will try to be very careful about the kinds of claims I make about the universality of its benefits. Ultimately, I want to defend the notion that reading is good for us in a number of ways and that all kinds of programs that encourage literacy and reading in general are worthwhile. This seems like an obvious claim to defend, that reading is good for us, but it is also a notion that is under attack in both subtle and obvious ways. Easier forms of entertainment fill our days *via* our electronic gadgets. Schools have begun to reduce the time given to reading deeply, and some of the moral and cognitive benefits of reading have been called into question. I want to defend the notion that deep reading benefits us greatly. I also wish to provide an extended explanation of the ways in which I believe that well-developed literacy, a strong community of readers, and a well-developed competence with extended narrative can help us to live more fulfilling lives and become better at all kinds of skills not generally associated with reading.

2. THE GATEWAY TO LITERACY

Mikita Brottman very subtly describes some of the ways in which reading is what she calls a "solitary vice."[4] She reminds us that reading is often solitary and done in bed, just before you fall asleep. Reading, she says, is best enjoyed at leisure and commands one's fullest attention. It cannot be rushed, and it involves the use of the imagination and fantasy. Some people get addicted to the practice. People learn the habit early in life, and often it takes one well into adulthood. Many people learn it in school but practice it at home, in private.[5] You might be wondering whether or not I am still talking about reading. Brottman explains that "the solitary vice" was a well-known euphemism for masturbation in the nineteenth century, and it was something that could cause physical difficulties, moral collapse, and even eternal damnation. Such a simple pleasure could cause all of these problems. Well, reading is said to cause a few problems of its own. Reading isolates, it takes precious time, and it exposes its reader to worlds unknowable and impossible to experience. It presents moral situations and asks its reader to sympathize with unfamiliar people who might have values different from the reader's own. But it is the pleasure that we derive from reading that can make it addictive, and this is exactly what we might need in order to become a habitual reader.

Academics talk about reading in two common ways. Either they talk about it as isolated incidents or as abstract generalizations. (How much more boring this is than a metaphor for masturbation). We isolate individual reading instances by talking about how we make sense of a single text when we talk about reader-response theory, or New Criticism, or when we appeal to neurological studies about which brain areas light up when one reads. We also tend to talk about reading as though all of the work of reading is finished when we set the book down. That is, there might be more to reading than just me interacting with the text as I read it by myself. Conversations and writing help develop and concretize ideas, reasons, and applications of the stories we read. We talk about reading as an abstraction by posing philosophical problems about phenomena that readers frequently experience. For example, philosophers spend vast amounts of time trying to understand why readers get emotionally bound up with fictional characters or the ways in which characters who make bad moral choices influence readers. They talk about reading as a huge phenomenon that is largely the same for most people. Philosophers like being able to make claims that apply universally. This is what we do. But the kinds of claims that I will make about readers are not going to be universally applicable. They will come in the form of an argument that suggests that more reading is better for us than less and specifically why that is so. As far as I know, philosophers have not examined the impact of being literate in a broad sense. Literacy includes the skill level a reader has, the frequency of exposure a reader has, the kinds of genres one tends to read, and the level of distraction one allows oneself while reading. Reading is a process where readers must actively engage with a text in order to create meaning. Literacy and increased literacy are how we describe the mastery of the skill of reading. Literacy is not only understanding the words and sentences but being able to make sense of the text and understand it well enough to apply it to a situation that is not exactly the same as one described in the text. Literacy begins with comprehension but moves quickly to describing a skill that allows readers to *use* the ideas, descriptions, reference points, structures, causes and effects, and narrative structure to think about situations other than the one at hand. Being able to apply parables or morality tales to other situations is just the beginning. Reading should be an activity that provides a cognitive framework for better ways to imagine and understand the world and other people.

British author Neil Gaiman calls fiction a "gateway drug" to reading.[6] He says that reading "forces you to learn new words, to think new thoughts, to keep going. To discover that reading *per se* is pleasurable."[7]

The correlation between reading fiction, especially what we might judge to be easy or shallow fiction, and a gateway drug is very powerful and is a particularly apt analogy. This suggests that reading might be subversive and perhaps even dangerous in ways that we may not have thought about before. There is a clear implication that it will likely lead to wanting more and more, like an addiction. Whether it is thought of as risky or not, it is appealing to regard reading popular fiction as a precursor to reading more complex narratives. Often, reading easy and enjoyable literature leads to reading more complex texts. The *Twilight* books, for instance, contain literary allusions to classic works like *Romeo and Juliet.* Such references often bring readers into contact with more demanding narratives. Parents often take the attitude that "all reading is good reading" and encourage their young children to read comic books, graphic novels and even books like *Captain Underpants.* The moral content of such books is likely not something parents want their children to imitate, but the books are fun and silly and use many phonetic spellings, which are particularly good for very young readers. (The *Captain Underpants* series is also filled with potty humor, which young boys love in particular.) Developing not only the skills but also the interest and the pleasure is essential to being a reader who can actually benefit from reading.

But literacy takes time to develop, time much beyond just learning to read. The development of literacy, which I take to be not just the basic ability to read but a real capacity to engage with a text, is something that takes years and decades to develop fully. This is not something one does once or in isolation, but it is a form of communication that we develop over time with the practice that comes with understanding the construction of narrative. Literacy, as Kylene Beers suggests, is the "capacity to deal with the conception of human possibilities formulated in language."[8] Literacy, she says, "is more about the person than the page, more about using written and spoken language to help us understand who we are, who we aren't, where we fit, how we work together."[9] Literacy, in other words, has to do with our facility with language, our capacity to make meaning out of language, and is something that takes years to develop. This kind of literacy is not just the base ability to make sense of the linguistic code. One can speak a language without ever developing this kind of literacy. Literacy also covers a broad range of skills. One might be considered literate when one can read a language. But deciphering the words on a page is just the beginning. A well-developed literacy provides the means for one to be transformed by a text, and it is a skill that allows a reader to find meaning beyond a text. A literary constructivist might suggest that the possibility of *meaning* happens only through the interaction between the text and the reader. In this view, the text alone has very little value. It is only when a reader grapples with it and makes sense of it that it comes alive. A literate reader can make appropriate inferences within a text but can also abstract parts of a narrative and treat it as having relevance and application to his or her own life. This kind of interaction between text and reader is key because the kind of impact reading has the potential to have cannot come from a mere deciphering of words. One who is truly literate holds the prospect of creating something new with every text he or she encounters.

One of the other important concepts I will be working with throughout this book is literature. What I mean when I talk about literature is generally any kind of extended narrative, which most often will take the form of a story with a plot, some discernable characters, temporal indications, some perceptible cause and effect, and usually a unified subject matter.[10] Literature is often used as an honorific title, distinguishing it from some lower forms of popular or genre fiction like horror, mystery, or romance. I will not assume that kind of distinction here. Rather, literature functions as an extended narrative that takes time and attention to comprehend. Although quality, length, and subject matter are all important, for now I just want to focus on the category of novels. In general, literature is described as always falling into one of two categories: fiction and nonfiction. As I will explain later, the strict dichotomy between fiction and nonfiction is problematic to me, but I think both are equally fruitful categories when it comes to our engagement with narrative. That is, I do not think it important that a narrative is believed to be either fictional or nonfictional in order for us to gain the same benefit from deciphering it. The narrative structure is the essential element, not the perception of truth or falsity. Fictional or nonfictional, false or true, constructed or veritable, well-constructed narrative can produce positive effects when readers engage regularly.

I am also particularly interested in literary *fiction*, that is, literature specifically fictional in nature. I will explain in detail some of the subtleties of distinction between fiction and nonfiction in the next chapter, but for now this category refers to literature that describes events that are not considered strictly "true" and are not necessarily connected to historical facts or persons. Literature has to do with the complexity of the narrative by means of which it is constructed.

What I take to be currently under scrutiny is the *value of reading literary fiction.* Its importance is being questioned for two primary reasons: The first is because, culturally, we say we value truth, as if truth is some sort of static notion that we can construct our own realities around. In fact, however, truth has very little to do with the positive effects of understanding narrative, narrative structure, developing a sense of how cause and effect work, and the ways in which storytelling functions so widely in our culture as a form of explanation. I do not believe that fiction cannot provide truth, nor do I believe that nonfiction always produces truth. Fiction and nonfiction are not direct or simple correlates for falsity and truth, but they are the easy default assumptions about what constitutes those genres. I think that an appeal to an overly simplistic notion of truth has diminished the cultural value of reading fiction and reading for pleasure. The second reason the importance of reading literary fiction is being called into question is that it is said not to have any practical consequence. Especially in the case of what we tell our children about learning, we want them to develop practical skills that they can turn into high-paying jobs. We do not want them to develop time-wasting skills that eat into the practical skills that might one day pay off with a high-paying job. In reality, however, we allow our children and ourselves all kinds of time to play video games; read Facebook, Twitter, and blogs; watch YouTube videos; and toy with Yik Yak, Instagram, and Snapchat. Although all of these media have some useful purposes, presumably, they have replaced the time that many children and adults used to spend reading, or could spend reading. These media are also largely nonnarrative. They are never very long (Twitter limits its users to only 140 characters) and do not require much in terms of one's attention span. Many social media platforms are also inherently visual, like Instagram, and do not allow any verbal associations with the images. Twenty-first-century social media encourages the belief that one can constantly multi-task, despite the fact that multiple studies have shown that people (adults and teenagers alike) are very bad at multi-tasking and that these new media encourage us to constantly expose ourselves to the mindless, not very well thought out, conventional wisdom and gossip of the day.[11] These media invite us to immerse ourselves in the minutiae of everyone else's lives, without encouraging us to engage in any real self-reflection. I do not want to sound like an antiquated schoolmarm here, but I think that the brevity of these communications, the thoughtlessness of many of them, and the extensive time and focus that we give to them all change the nature of our ability to concentrate on extended narrative and to immerse ourselves for any length of time in anything. They decrease the likelihood that we will engage in more meaningful conversations or stories. I do not want to denigrate these platforms, either. But I worry about the ways in which they fill in the empty spaces in our time and how, bit by bit, we are reading less actively and watching more passively.

Another challenge I want to address is the changing nature of public educational standards. In much of the West, the underlying assumption about educational curricula and strict testing that begins as early as the first grade is that students need to learn more information but do not have time for more general critical thinking and reading skills. As we train our children, particularly in the science, technology, engineering, and mathematics (STEM) fields, it is important not to forget to teach them in ways that will develop their ability to do some critical self-reflection and self-exploration. We want them to foster empathy with others and allow them to enjoy and find pleasure in literature, which has a direct link to literacy, more broadly conceived, and to facility with language. Perhaps even more importantly, literacy helps to develop creativity and personal skills, both of which help in the global economy. But maybe *everything* we do might not have to feed into our success in that global economy. Perhaps this just feeds us as humans. A well-developed literacy allows us to engage with others in ways that we might never encounter independent of it. It allows us to imagine possibilities that we might never have come across in our own experience, and it gives us access to other cultures and historical periods that we could never experience firsthand. In short, literacy opens both real and imaginary possibilities that we would never have otherwise. Diminishing any emphasis on reading, or even letting it go by the wayside because we forgot to pay attention, will allow us less access to a full, meaningful life. As a philosopher, I think a lot about how we construct or make meaning of our own life experiences, and I also think about the ways in which we can get the most happiness out of life. Reading literature can benefit us greatly in both of those realms.

3. READING AND THE INTERNET

There is some cultural worry about the transition from a written culture to a digital one. Whereas we have valued the written word, in book form, letters, documents, and declarations, we are now moving away from this. We still read, but we are moving away from paper and words that appear in tangible form to words that are ephemeral, whose existence is fleeting and can disappear with a single swipe.

In ancient Greece, the beginnings of Western philosophy, there was the beginning of a shift from an oral culture and oral knowledge to a written culture. Of course, the written culture did not become abundant until the fifteenth century with the advent of the printing press, but as far back as ancient Greece scholars debated the relative merits of the written word. For Socrates, all knowledge was of right and good behavior, and right behavior never came about because one was blindly following a rule or a dictum. Right behavior came about because of understanding, and understanding came only from dialogue, questioning, examining assumptions, and articulating answers.

Books cannot question their readers, nor can they retort back. They are immobile and unresponsive. Socrates questioned whether any real knowledge could come from these lifeless texts. Plato talks about Socrates' concerns about the written word (Socrates, relevantly, never wrote anything down) in a couple of different dialogues, the *Phaedrus* and the *Seventh Letter*, in particular. Plato Describes Socrates' concerns in the *Phaedrus* by saying that "if men learn [to write], it will implant forgetfulness in their souls; they will cease to exercise memory because they rely on that which is written, calling things to remembrance no longer from within themselves, but by means of external marks. What you have discovered is a recipe not for memory, but for reminder. And it is no true wisdom that you offer your disciples, but only its semblance, for by telling them of many things without teaching them you will make them seem to know much, while for the most part they know nothing, and as men filled, not with wisdom, but with the conceit of wisdom, they will be a burden to their fellows."[12] Conversations and dialogue require one to respond immediately; they require one to think through ideas and assumptions while engaging with another person. One must be present and engaged in order to participate in a dialogue. But the written word also serves as a reminder, as a commitment, or as a form of witness; one that can be copied, researched, and used as evidence for historians, legal issues, or documentation. The way Socrates describes written language is that it allows one to externalize one's memory to the paper, and one does not need to hold onto it oneself. He believed that this would weaken the memory. One exercises memory by remembering, but more importantly, one cannot really do philosophy if one is constantly referencing other people's ideas, citing other texts, or looking things up. This is the antithesis of philosophical engagement. It was also the basis of the argument against moving from an oral culture to a written one.

Socrates was primarily concerned with the development of moral behavior but, more importantly, moral understanding. And no one behaves morally by accident. One only succeeds at moral behavior through dialogue, assessment, and reassessment. No one, according to Socrates, behaves morally because they read about it in a book. But Socrates was obviously fighting a losing battle with this. Plato *wrote* about Socrates' concerns in dialogue form. He is cited throughout Plato's writings endlessly, in print. But more than that, after Plato, even the philosophical dialogue or conversation went by the wayside. Aristotle shifted philosophy singlehandedly into a completely different kind of philosophical prose. Whereas all of Plato's works were in dialogue form and dialectic tension was represented throughout, Aristotle wrote philosophical treatises. Knowledge came in the form of a written lecture. Ever since Aristotle we have assumed that this is how information, knowledge, and understanding arrive: in a written text that we are to make sense of. We have theories about how we best relate to written texts, but we do not question that the text is the primary source of knowledge.

It seems to me, however, that we now share some similar concerns about our shift to a digital culture. What do we make of texts that contain abbreviations and lack grammar completely? Or emails that contain no greetings or salutations? Or Wikipedia entries that have no author but are definitions and collected knowledge contributed by anyone who cares to log on? Wikipedia is knowledge at its most democratic but with no particular expert who has researched or might give explanations and context that others cannot. What do we make of comment and review options populated by anyone, even anonymous comments no one is held responsible for? Digital culture allows us to make threats, slurs, and incessant commentary on pretty much anything we want without expertise or reflection. Anyone with access to a computer can post musings on Facebook, Twitter, or whatever comment section they find.

Digital culture also allows us access to a billion things we did not have access to before, but we have not been trained to differentiate good information from bad, good argument from bad, or reliable information from the untrustworthy sources. We have no etiquette around our phones that might make us resist taking calls at all hours of the day and night, stop scrolling mindlessly rather than paying attention to those with whom we are physically present. We also reinforce our own beliefs by consuming content we already agree with and limiting our "friends." I imagine Socrates would be horrified at our ability to post on Facebook and merely hope for as many thumbs up of approval we can generate. No engagement no dialogue, no challenges, no new understanding. Just posting ideas that pop into our heads in an incredibly public forum.

So what does this shift to a digital culture mean for reading? Well, we have been reading widely on screens since the 1990s. Most of the studies in the 1990s claimed that there was no difference between reading on a screen and reading a paper book.[13] But many of the studies since then have shown that, for purposes of retention and comprehension, readers of paper books fare modestly better.[14,15] When reading paper books, we read in a linear way. That is, our brain tracks words and is able to comprehend in a sequential motion. But when we read from a screen our eyes have a tendency to jump around, skim, or read text in a way similar to scanning a webpage.

Deep reading, according to Sven Birkerts, is the "the slow and meditative possession of a book. We don't just read the words, we dream our lives in their vicinity. The printed page becomes a kind of wrought-iron fence we crawl through, returning, once we have wandered, to the very place we started."[16] Deep reading is understood in opposition to horizontal reading, which is what we do with the internet. We scan and sift and gloss over many different words, ideas, and images. Birkerts notes that, before the printing press, only a very few people owned books. These rare books (most likely including a Bible) were poured over for hours on end, day after day. The stories were powerful in the imagination of the reader, and the lessons were profound. But with the proliferation of books and now the explosion of the internet and screen reading, we have become bi-literate and can do both deep reading and horizontal reading. The problem is that if we do not practice deep reading, we will lose that skill.

Digital natives, those born into a culture of digital screens and media from a very early age, run the serious risk of not being able to do any deep reading at all. If one can do horizontal reading, scanning, and taking in information, then words, and sentences, and even paragraphs only function for the transmission of information. They lose their capacity for facilitating presence of mind, deep reflection, and the transportation that is allowed by reading deeply. I do not think that we should do away with the internet or screens, but I do think that, like with many things important in life, we should find a balance with the screens and paper.

4. PLATONIC TRADITIONS

Before philosophy was systematically developed, it was the poets who were given credit for explaining traditional wisdom, understanding religious beliefs and rituals, and the transmission of myths of their own and other cultures. One of the things that differentiated philosophy from these other traditional forms of wisdom was the way it went about gaining reliable knowledge. Philosophers, as opposed to the poets before them, believed that knowledge was the product of an accurate and direct reflection of the world as it really is. Philosophy became the systematic study of the various ways to explain and describe the world around us and our experience in it. Poets were more likely to insert personal per-, spectives, individual explanations, and underlying cultural mores within their stories. Philosophers thus distinguished themselves by knowing and justifying differently and, hopefully, more reliably. Socrates felt he needed to establish the dominance of philosophical dialogue that he thought demanded more meaningful and reliable truths. Plato (Socrates' student) declared in his notorious *Republic* that there had been "from old a quarrel between philosophy and poetry,"[17] between truth and art. According to Plato, poets and painters create things that are "inferior to reality,"[18] their works appeal to "the inferior part of the soul,"[19] and the poets "set up in each individual soul a vicious constitution by fashioning phantoms far removed from reality, and by carrying favor with the senseless element that cannot distinguish the greater from the less."[20] Plato barred the poets from his ideal republic because their works were dangerous to the goal of training its citizens to maximize their capacity for reason. He also wanted to mark a clear distinction between the kinds of knowledge poetry could provide and the kinds of knowledge that philosophy could provide. Philosophy generates true, reliable knowledge, he said, which could potentially improve one's character. One of his famous maxims was that "If you know the good then you do the good. If you don't do the good then you don't know the good." This is a clear indication that knowledge is what one needs to be able to behave properly, and without true knowledge one would never quite know why one is doing things properly or not. Only reasoned argument (philosophy, he would say) can produce that kind of knowledge. The arts, as he argued throughout the *Republic*, could *not* improve character. They distracted one from the truth, they distorted reality, they encouraged people to stir up dangerous and potentially unrestrained emotions, they had the potential to corrupt the soul since they appealed to the basest and most easily manipulated part of us (our emotions), and they led people to behave immorally—in ways they would never behave when they were rational and seeking to understand abstract forms of the virtues using unadulterated reason. Philosophy, on the other hand, led one to true knowledge, good government, and right behavior. Plato's student, Aristotle, argued against this position, and so have countless scholars since.

At least in this one way, Plato has had a profound impact on our contemporary world. He clearly articulated this opposition between the arts and the kinds of works they produce on the one hand, and truth on the other. Ever since their inauspicious beginnings in Plato's *Republic*, artists and art theorists have been trying to prove the value of the arts in this debate. But as it stands (arts vs. truth), the arts will never win. Art is rarely seen as a powerful reality in and of itself, neither containing the capacity to produce insight not otherwise available, nor as something that can illuminate truths that are not mere facts about the physical world. But art provides descriptions of particular worldviews, explanations of all kinds of phenomena, and insights into human behavior. The arts, largely due to Plato's denigration of them, are seen as not only separate from reality but, even worse, as a pale reflection of reality. As long as the arts are seen as separate, distanced, imitative of the real, and inferior to real life and thereby truth, it will be impossible to show how we can learn from them or be improved by them in any meaningful way. In this dichotomous system where art and reality are pitted against each other, the arts are necessarily inferior, and it is impossible to gain insight from them. If they are not real, and not true, they cannot be useful.

Currie

This ancient quarrel, however, is still alive and well. The quarrel has once again reared its ugly head, and the legitimacy and necessity of the arts, of literature in particular, is being called into question. Literature is a legitimate source of knowledge but not one that produces the *same kind* of knowledge as teaching subject matter content would. Philosopher Gregory Currie has very publically questioned the empirical validity of the evidence that reading literature is good for us. He even goes so far as to suggest that what we get from literature is "pretend learning."[21] There is no such thing as pretend learning, though. What we gain from reading is not something that has to do with content acquisition and cannot be measured easily on a test. And what we get from reading is real learning or real knowledge, but it does not arrive in a convenient testable form. It is also not wise to turn what it is that we get from literature into something that can be measured quantitatively. Rather, literature, and increased literacy, should help us to broaden the scope of what we consider knowledge and what it is to be educated. Reading literature, in fact, increases literacy, which in turn allows us a broader base of understanding of language and better access to the ways in which meaning is constructed by ourselves and others.

Plato, in another dialogue called the *Theaetetus*, supposes that knowledge is a form of acquisition. He says that our minds are like containers. He asks his reader to imagine that each piece of knowledge we have is represented by a single bird. The mind is then like an aviary, filled with different kinds of birds that have been acquired over a lifetime of education. He says, "whenever a person acquires any piece of knowledge and shuts it up in his enclosure, we must say he has learned or discovered the thing of which this is the knowledge, and that is what 'knowing' means."[22] It cannot be considered knowledge, however, if one cannot *retrieve* the right bird at the right time. The retrieval system is at least as important as housing the birds. But I would like to take this analogy a step further. Having knowledge, even if one can retrieve the relevant pieces at the right time, is not useful if you cannot *apply* the knowledge in a meaningful way. Being literate, understanding how stories organize and apply in all kinds of ways, helps us organize our own experiences. With less literacy and without good stories, we would be significantly less capable of organizing information.

Plato suggests that we *do* learn from stories, but what we learn is of no real use. He says that often what we get from stories are lessons that distract us from learning and thinking about the most important of abstract truths, like justice, beauty, and courage. He banned the poets from the ideal republic so they would not distract citizens from seeking truth through abstract reasoning. But he did not ban them because we could not learn from their stories. It was quite the opposite; he did not trust people to be able to differentiate truth from story. He said that we could, in fact, learn quite a lot from stories, poems, and plays. And what we learned could be subversive. It could teach us to be selfish and confused about what was really important. It could obscure truth and falsity. According to Plato, children were more susceptible to the dangers of stories than adults, and so poetry was not to be part of the school curriculum in his ideal republic.

Aristotle, on the other hand, argued that stories and our emotional responses to them could engender an emotional catharsis that is cleansing in such a way as to clear one's mind for rational thought to develop more fully. He said his was particularly true of the theater. Part of the catharsis also had to do with the way in which we could rehearse our own emotional dispositions so that we would be more likely to respond in the right ways to the right things outside of the theater, in our real lives. He did not worry that people could not differentiate between truth and story, because our engagement with narrative produced primarily emotional impacts, not cognitive ones. Aristotle praised poetry and drama and wrote quite extensively in the *Poetics* and the *Rhetoric* about the positive learning outcomes of stories and narratives. It is not clear to me whether either one of these positions is accurate or whether one or the other clearly reflects current thinking about the role of stories for me, but they do represent two of the most influential historical positions that have impacted the way generations of people have seen the role of stories. If you think that violent video games cause their users to act more aggressively or violently in real life, then you advocate a Platonic position. If you think that going to the movies to have a good cry might make you feel better and produce a nice catharsis, then you advocate an Aristotelian position. These two ways of looking at stories are still very much with us.

5. AMERICA'S COMMON CORE

Ever since this early debate, scholars have continued to argue about what exactly we gain or lose from reading stories, narrative, and fiction.

In the twenty-first century, the debate continues not just among scholars but also among religious groups, educators, publishers, libraries, and parents. There is no clear consensus about what impact reading fiction has on a developing mind, and victory in the debate often falls to our current set of so-called experts. The experts are educators, religious leaders, decision-makers in the government, people in the business or publishing world, those who determine school curricula, and even psychologists who can work out the actual benefits of all kinds of things we do and say. Unlike Currie's accusation that there is no evidence that reading literature helps us in any way, people make decisions about the role it will play in school and home curricula all the time. People often work on assumptions about what will most benefit them, their children, and their society. There has been a long-standing assumption that reading literature does do something beneficial for us—beyond just providing basic literacy. It would not have stayed in the school curricula this long if it had not had some good effect, I hope. But this assumption is under attack. It is under attack by those who dictate the new educational curricula as well as those who implement it. The new educational experts say that, as it turns out, being able to read and analyze fictional literature is not a very practical skill. Literary analysis is not a marketable skill that employers are looking for on a resume. Literacy, on the other hand, *is* in large demand. The problem is understanding how the two are distinct, if they are at all.

In the US, the benefits of reading literary fiction are being heartily questioned with what are called the Common Core State Standards (CCSS): new academic benchmarks implemented in 2013 by most states. The Common Core document states that reading *fiction* is not as *productive* as reading so-called "instructional literature," which loosely falls into a category of discursive prose (not just nonfiction but a category that also includes nonnarrative and discursive language), the intention of which is to teach about the natural and social world. One of the clearly articulated assumptions about the Common Core is that it teaches and tests that which is more directly relevant to success in both college and the work world (called "College and Career Readiness"). This seems like a nice goal, but it also assumes that preparation for both college and career are the same, and it assumes that readiness for both is something measurable by a standardized test. I take issue with both assumptions. The larger assumption I take issue with beyond these is that K–12 primary education prepares students for adult life only by teaching them content or information, rather than skills or enrichment or rather than exposing students to ideas or practices that they might just enjoy or that might make their lives better. Common Core exemplifies the idea that school is only for learning "facts." Beginning in first grade, students are told they are being trained for college or career readiness. They are not told that learning is a skill that takes a lifetime to develop, and that developing and mastering the skill might just be fun and enjoyable.

The language used in the Common Core documents is that students should be trained and tested in such a way that the "measures of text complexity must be aligned with college and career readiness expectations for all students."[23] Of course, it is problematic to assume that college and career readiness adhere to some single standard, but it is even more concerning to think that the replacement of fictional literature with "instructional literature" will somehow better prepare students for life after high school. Common Core suggests that the emphasis should be shifted from English Literature courses to what is called English Language Arts and Literacy. In middle school there should be approximately 50 percent fiction and 50 percent "informational text." Then, in high school, there should be only 30 percent fiction and 70 percent informational texts. This shift in emphasis allows for a more natural focus on the *content* of a reading, which is more easily tested with standardized tests, according to the Common Core document. Emphasis should also be placed on writing across the curriculum, so writing instruction will happen, presumably, outside the English classroom, as well, which should be very beneficial, they say.

According to the Common Core document, narrative prose is "less complex" than "informational texts," and acquiring the ability to comprehend increasingly complex texts is one of the main goals of the new standards. In addition to this, the standards say that fiction and literature should be downplayed "because college and career readiness overwhelmingly focus on complex texts outside of literature."[24] Presumably, most colleges and most careers do not expect their students and employees to read and analyze literature all day. I am not sure, however, if that is a reason to remove serious emphasis on and training in this kind of literary competence. (If this is the case, I think they should start by cutting calculus, not literature!) I think it a stretch and probably a mistake to argue that fiction is not something worth teaching in school because it is not "useful" or "practical." This seems to be a very

frightening trend that started long ago, with cutting the other unneces-
sary and impractical subjects: music, art, and physical education, for
example. As these become nonessential, they are the first to go when
budget cuts hit. It seems that we have gotten to the point with literature
classes that music and art classes faced several years ago. They are just
not *useful*. They are not *practical*. The skills they teach cannot be tested
and so cannot be given over to accountability rubrics. Students gain no
practical skills in these classes, and we cannot afford to pay for nonessential education. Career and college readiness does not require skills in
music, art, physical fitness, or the ability to sit and leisurely read novels
all day. College and career readiness requires graduating students to
know facts. Mr. Gradgrind, the strict but very practical teacher from
Charles Dickens' novel *Hard Times*, could not have structured this curriculum better himself. "Facts, facts, facts!" says Mr. Gradgrind, who
has no time for frivolous novels or emotional outbursts. Not only has
literary fiction become nonessential in the new curriculum, it seems that
it is so considered primarily because it cannot be tested and it is not
something that can be content-beneficial (likely because it is merely just
false). I disagree heartily with this assessment of literature. Not only is
literary analysis something worth preserving in the school curriculum,
but I believe it is something that is worth encouraging both children
and adults to do for fun. It is a skill worth developing, like many other
cognitive skills that bring readers intellectual pleasure. It can help us
in very particular ways that increase the moral imagination, help us to
empathize with others, and enable us to make particular sense of the
problems of which we learn only in abstract ways in political science,
economics, and sociology.

One of the primary reasons for the reduction of fictional literature in
the Common Core is that it is particularly difficult to quantify and measure that which literature or narrative offers. According to the Common
Core, "many current quantitative measures underestimate the challenge
posed by complex narrative fiction."[25] For instance, on the quantitative
scales used by the Common Core (Flesch-Kincaid Grade Level test and
the Lexile Framework for Reading), John Steinbeck's *The Grapes of
Wrath*, a Pulitzer Prize–winning novel from 1939, is rated as appropriate reading for second and third grade. This is because the language in
The Grapes of Wrath is relatively straightforward and commonplace,
using "familiar words and simple syntax"[26] that takes the form of a
simple dialogue that "mimics everyday speech."[27] The explanation

continues by saying that "until widely available quantitative tools can better account for factors recognized as making such texts challenging, including multiple levels of meaning and mature themes, preference should be given to qualitative measures of text complexity when evaluating narrative fiction intended for students in grade 6 or above."[28] What that means is that, in terms of complexity, the computer says that *The Grapes of Wrath* is appropriate for second- and third-grade readers. But because of the content inappropriateness, it should not be given to elementary school children. Thus, because the qualitative aspects of a narrative work of literature are too difficult to measure with a standardized measure, *it is preferable not to use works that cannot be quantitatively assessed.* Mature themes and inappropriate levels of violence, aggression, or war are all deemed appropriate for elementary school children if the language is simple enough for them to understand. The Lexile rating system gives a point score to each book that can then be correlated with particular grade levels. (Scores are conveniently generated by a computer program.) The Lexile Test Measure "indicates the reading demand of the text in terms of semantic difficulty (word frequency) and semantic complexity (sentence length)."[29] According to the Lexile website, "the text complexity of K–12 textbooks has become increasingly 'easier' over the last 50 years," based on research indicating "steep declines in average sentence length and vocabulary level in reading textbooks." At the same time, "the text demands of college and careers have remained consistent or increased over the same time period." So teaching the skills to read fictional literature are downplayed to more "practical skills," while we simultaneously lament that students are not as good at reading more complex texts.

The Lexile Company claims that there is a literacy gap equivalent to four grades that college freshmen currently face. The Common Core is structured to help minimize that gap. My concern, however, is that word frequency and sentence length are not the only, and certainly not the most important, aspects of reading literature or narrative. They are, however, the aspects that can be measured by a computer and easily counted and tested. If works cannot be assessed in terms primarily concerning content or information acquisition, then they need to be left out of the curriculum. Presumably, this makes perfect sense in a test-driven educational system. If it is not testable, then we should not bother teaching it. And as the standards say, if a better assessment model were to be developed that could account for the complexities and subtleties of *The Grapes of Wrath,* then perhaps the focus could be shifted back to fictional literature. Thankfully, these experts recognize that *The Grapes of Wrath* is not appropriate for second- and third-grade readers, but it does not seem reasonable to me to remove it from the curriculum to solve the problem. Perhaps not everything worth teaching is testable or measurable.

My guess is that no such assessment tool to measure the subtleties of complex narrative fiction will be developed, nor *could* it be, nor *should* it be. The benefits of reading literary fiction should not be primarily about content acquisition or the complexity of sentence structures. Instead, the benefits of reading literary fiction have to do with much more abstract notions of the moral imagination, cognitive organization, understanding linguistic structures that go well beyond simple chronological narrative descriptions. Most importantly, narrative literature allows for *multiple meaningful interpretations*. This is one of the things that differentiates it from math and science. Learning to analyze literature and understanding how to discern multiple interpretations allows readers to develop a sense of the world where there is not merely one right answer but, instead, multiple better and worse answers and explanations for complex narrative descriptions. I cannot imagine better preparation for "college and career readiness" than an understanding that right answers do not always manifest themselves as bubbles on a score card, class rankings, and standardized test scores. It also seems that very few of life's problems come with answers that are straightforward or correct. Adult life is very much about interpreting what is going on around you and trying to make sense of it given what you choose to make important, how you make inferences between causes and events, how you make sense of what happens to you, and how all of that influences the choices you make. This all seems much more like a meaning-making strategy than a straightforward calculation.

6. SHOULD PRISONERS READ?

Bruno Bettleheim suggested in his 1976 book *The Uses of Enchantment* that prisoners and criminals were often not read to as children as much as the general population and were specifically not exposed to a standard set of moralizing fairy tales. Ironically, he offers no real evidence for this claim but merely uses it as an explanation for their bad behavior, their indifference toward severely negative consequences, and their lack of empathy toward others. He might just be right, despite his own lack of evidence. Convicted prisoners presumably are characterized as moral failures. Likely, they would need some kind of re-education to become moral experts or even morally competent. I am hesitant, however, to use the terminology of such extremes as experts and failures. One who is called a failure seems to have failed completely—not just morally, perhaps, but also in terms of their use of logic and reason—and has failed significantly in achieving what society expects of its members. I do not think that reading a single book will change any of that in any meaningful way. I will *not* concede that a more literate community is in no way better than a less literate one, however, nor will I concede that the capacity to comprehend narrative in no way helps us to become better citizens and better humans—particularly in the way that someone like Aristotle suggests human excellence functions in the development of persons and character. There is no "moral expertise" in the form of perfection, but there is certainly a continuum of moral behaviors that we deem acceptable, and there are a plethora of ways to nurture and develop moral capacity. One of the many ways in which moral capacity grows is with exposure to narrative literature, and this is well documented.

Philosopher Ludwig Wittgenstein claimed that "the limits of my language mean the limits of my world."[30] He was not talking about literacy *per se* but rather the absolute possibility that we either have or might not have to express propositions clearly in or through language. I am interested in the ways in which this claim might be applied to literacy. If the limits of my language are the limits of my world, then if my language is restricted or minimal, the possibility of what I might be able to think would be limited, too. The less vocabulary I have, the fewer complex sentences and thoughts I am able to put together. The more language I have, the more subtle distinctions I am able to make, the more discriminating I can be, and presumably the more I might be able to express my thoughts to others. There is a large history of scholarship about the way language informs and influences the way we construct personal identity—the way we define ourselves, think of ourselves, portray ourselves to others, make sense of ourselves over time, and make sense of potentially very disparate experiences that we have over the course of a day and the course of a lifetime. All kinds of theorists have argued that there is a myriad of ways in which we make connections in order to make sense of our lives. To my knowledge, there has not been anything written about what happens to one whose linguistic lacunae have undermined or eroded personal identity. If Wittgenstein's dictum is right, and the limits of my language are the limits of my world, then my world and my possibility and likelihood of creating meaning for myself are limited, too.

The correlation between low literacy (here just meaning the ability to read, but it has many more implications) and the likelihood that one will go to prison is extremely high. Educators call this correlation the "pipeline to prison." Achieving a third-grade reading level is considered significant by literacy experts, because that is around the time when students generally transition from learning to read to reading to learn. According to the National Adult Literacy Survey, 70 percent of all US prison inmates scored below a fourth-grade literacy level, and 75 percent of all inmates function below a twelfth-grade level.[31] As much as 68 percent never receive a high school diploma, and 19 percent are completely illiterate. The United States also has a significantly higher incarceration rate than any other country in the world. The US has a rate of 500 prisoners per 100,000 citizens, whereas in other first-world nations the rate is closer to 100 prisoners per 100,000 citizens. As the population grows, so does the number of prisoners.

Journalist Eric Schlosser has written widely about what he calls the prison-industrial complex, or the increase of the US inmate population that has largely been given over to private industry so that they can make bigger and bigger profits. Given that the prison system is a profit-making business, it is in the best interest of the shareholders for prisoners to stay for long periods of time and for those who leave to eventually return. As Elizabeth Kleinfeld argues, "illiteracy serves to produce a permanent prisoner class, solidifying and stabilizing the power and control of the prison-industrial complex."[32] Opponents of the ideology that supports the prison-industrial complex question whether increased imprisonment, especially for less violent offenders, is an effective solution to larger social problems. One of the arguments that Schlosser makes is that the prison-industrial complex, the one that makes a profit off of the prison system, *wants* prisoners to stay illiterate, since the likelihood of their returning to prison if they are illiterate is considerably higher. This means more recurrent business. One of the stunning statistics about the prison population is the connection between illiteracy and rates of incarceration. According to the National

Assessment of Adult Literacy, 85 percent of all juveniles who interface with the juvenile court system are functionally illiterate.[33] Court records indicate, however, that inmates who become literate in prison have only a 16 percent chance of returning to prison (a recidivism rate) as opposed to a 70 percent recidivism rate for inmates who receive no literacy training while incarcerated. According to the Department of Justice, "the link between academic failure and delinquency, violence and crime is *welded to reading failure.*"[34] It seems clear that the high correlation between illiteracy and delinquency is not coincidental, and it is not entirely clear which came first, an inability to read or a disinterest in learning on the part of the offenders. Although not all children who are illiterate will go to jail, 70 percent of inmates are illiterate. Being functionally illiterate means one cannot fill out a form, read a bus schedule, submit an appeal, or apply for a job. Prisoners who commit felonies (four times more black than white) will never be able to vote again and so are even less able to change or improve the system.

This extremely high correlation between illiteracy and incarceration leads me to some additional arguments about the benefits of reading. I take Wittgenstein to be right about the limits of one's language and the limits of one's world being one and the same. When language is restricted, so is one's ability to maneuver within one's world, especially in a literate society. Sadly, the best predictor of the prison space we will need in 15 years is the percentage of 10- and 11-year-olds who cannot read. With one simple algorithm we can predict with almost complete accuracy how many prisoners there will be 15 years from now.[35] Further, the amount of money spent on literacy training for struggling students is a fraction of what it costs to keep someone in prison for a year. Schlosser may be right about the prison-industrial complex wanting to keep the prisoners illiterate, because it would be so much easier to educate them than to keep them in prison. But if the limits of my language are the limits of my world, then my world stays small when I remain illiterate. Lower literacy means fewer grievances and fewer appeals. Lower literacy means less capacity for rational thought, less likelihood of the understanding of rights, opportunities, and organization. Lower literacy means prisoners are more easily manipulated and controlled.

So why would it be important to spend time and money on literacy programs in prisons? Well, first of all, because if we teach prisoners to read then there is a lower recidivism rate. This has been shown consistently.[36] They will return to prison less often if they can function more effectively in a literate society. But I suggest that there is more to it that just the practical aspects of being able to read a bus schedule and fill out a job application. Many prisoners, especially the ones who are illiterate, suffer from decreased reasoning skills and a lack of a moral imagination. These are two skills that might develop from a child being read a set of moralizing fairy tales, but educational opportunities in prison communities are extremely limited and very inconsistent. Usually, the number of books a prisoner is allowed to have in his or her cell is limited, and all written materials are censored for content. The environment itself is often not conducive to focused study. There are constant interruptions and often very poor lighting. But literature can provide prisoners with some much-needed relief from what can be an extremely stressful existence. Poet Jimmy Santiago Baca writes about his first experience being incarcerated:

> With shocking speed I found myself handcuffed to a chain gang of inmates and bused to a holding facility to await trial. There I met men, prisoners, who read aloud to each other the works of Neruda, Paz, Sabines, Nemerov, and Hemmingway. Never had I felt such freedom as in that dormitory. Listening to the works of these writers, I felt that invisible threat from without lessen—my sense of teetering on a rotting plank over swamp water where famished alligators clapped their horny snouts for my blood. While I listened to the works of the poets, the alligators slumbered powerless in their liars. Their language was the magic that could liberate me from myself, transform me into another person, transport me to others places far away.[37]

Had he not been with the prisoners he was with, he might not have had the opportunity to enter this world of words and, more importantly, this world of expression.

Tracking prisoners and collecting consistent data is notoriously difficult. Prisons are run differently from state to state and country to country. Facilities that are government-funded function differently from the private prisons. Educational programs vary depending on who is in charge, who is willing to volunteer to teach, and whether there are any resources available to be given over to the education of the incarcerated. But consistently, it seems, educators try to run programs in prisons to help educate and to minimize recidivism. Although I cannot talk about all of them here, I will talk about two specific programs in order to discuss the ways in which the prisoners have been helped.

Chang lives through literature [handwritten]

Robert Waxler, a literature professor from the University of Massachusetts, runs a program called Changing Lives Through Literature that helps prisoners understand the concept of personal responsibility through reading and analyzing novels.[38] The recidivism rate for the prisoners who take this class is dramatically lower than it is for the general prison population.[39] But this is not a literacy class. This is a combination of book club, modern literary interpretation class, support group, and a bit of bibliotherapy (the practice of using various texts as part of therapy). The idea for the class was hatched between Waxler and his friend, Judge Robert Kane, who was at the time a Massachusetts District Court Justice. Kane lamented that the criminal justice system did very little to actually help the inmates, and he was frustrated seeing the cycle of incarceration and repeat offenders. Waxler, being an English professor, was completely convinced by the idea that learning to analyze literature would be helpful to the inmates. Participants were chosen by the judges, but not all inmates were eligible. Rapists and murderers were automatically excluded, and participants needed at least an eighth-grade education to be allowed into the program. Initially, groups were strictly divided by gender. The groups met regularly and talked about modern short stories and novels carefully picked by Waxler himself. In addition to a small group of participants (usually no more than 12) a judge, a professor, and a probation officer would also actively participate. It is key to the program that all of the represented voices are equally democratic. Inmates and "experts" are all allowed insight and equal time voicing their understanding of the texts. At the end of every class, a graduation ceremony is held in the same courtroom in which they were sentenced, and praise is showered upon the graduates. This graduation is symbolic of change for the inmates. The program has blossomed in the last 20 years and is now held across the US, Canada, and England.[40]

The Changing Lives Through Literature program is based upon the assumption that "literature has the power to transform."[41] But it is different from the way literature is traditionally taught in the classroom. This program is dependent upon its equity among participants and its encouragement to identify with the characters and their struggles. Inmates are encouraged repeatedly to imagine the perspectives of others and to reimagine their own worldview. Waxler says that "when we talk about literature, we are not just talking about the words on a page or about a book sitting peacefully on a shelf. It is the material that engages us deeply and enables us to be part of the tale. This way of relating to literature is active. It takes imagination and a willingness to participate. But it does not necessarily require advanced reading skills or a college degree."[42] One participant made this list of accomplishments after completing the program:

1. Read and completed a book
2. Comprehended others' point of view on same literature
3. Read books with uncomfortable subject matter
4. Related to characters in book
5. Read for pleasure
6. Expressed my opinions with less fear each time
7. Learned how to take time to focus
8. Different way of life other than AA program and parenting.[43]

This program is an excellent example of the ways in which people who may not have been taught to empathize with others or to see the world from multiple perspectives can learn to do both of these things through narrative fiction. This is, perhaps, one of the most effective rehabilitation programs available for the prison population.

Laura Bates, an English professor from Indiana State University, decided that she was going to teach Shakespeare not only to prisoners with the hope of rehabilitation but to prisoners who were in solitary confinement for long periods of time and had no hope of appeal. They would never leave the prison. The prisoners she chose were literate already but had not had much exposure to formal literature instruction. Each week she taught 10 prisoners who all stayed in their cells, with only a small opening in the door through which she could communicate with them. She sat in the hallway in between the locked cell doors and talked about Shakespearian plays, themes, characters, and the analogies with which the inmates best understood the plays. She would give each participant a small stack of papers each week with the assigned reading on it, because they were not allowed to have books. The prisoners poured over these papers with the time and attention no college or graduate student has ever had. They worked through whole Shakespearian plays reading only pages per week. The inmates loved the class. It began with only four inmates participating but quickly grew to eight, and soon there was a waiting list.

Bates worked with one inmate, Larry Newton,[44] very closely and formed a trusting relationship with him over several years. He is the

main focus of her memoir called *Shakespeare Saved My Life: Ten Years in Solitary with the Bard*. He explained to her one day that Shakespeare really did save his life, both literally and figuratively. He said, "for so many years, I had been really self-destructive, on the razor's edge every day. I'm confident that I would've done something drastic and ended up on death row. Or I would've one day found the courage to take my own life. So literally, he saved my life."[45] But he continued that he also meant that Shakespeare had saved his life figuratively. He said, "Shakespeare offered me the opportunity to develop new ways of thinking through these plays. I was trying to figure out what motivated Macbeth, why his wife was able to make him do a deed that he said he didn't want to do just by attacking his ego: 'what, are you soft? Ain't you man enough to do it?' as a consequence of that, I had to ask myself what was motivating me in my deeds, and I came face to face with the realization that I was fake, that I was motivated by this need to impress those around me, that none of my choices were truly my own. And as bad as that sounds, it was the most liberating thing I'd ever experienced because that meant that I had control of my life. I could be anybody I wanted to be. I didn't have to be some fake guy that my buddies wanted me to be."[46] Bates worked with Larry for years, through his changed circumstances of solitary and less solitary confinement and through his development of thought about Shakespeare. Although Larry will never leave prison, he and Bates have written together and have published commentaries on several Shakespearian plays. Some time and attention and Shakespeare helped Larry Newton expand his language, expand his world, do some self-reflection, and provide some insights that he would not have had otherwise.

7. BOOK CLUBS

As I focus on reading and different kinds of practices of reading, I want to address some of the aspects of book clubs, which offer a different kind of reading experience than the solitary reader has. Although book clubs are not often taken very seriously by academics, I think there might be something interesting about the conversations that emerge from group book discussions. When we think about reading, we likely think about the solitary reader curled up on the couch alone with a book. Lots of reading might start this way, but it is often not the end result of the reading.

When children are in school they read for their classes, and in those classes they learn how to analyze the literature they read. They talk about genre, plots, characters, themes, tension, and resolution. But book clubs seem to be an entirely different way of understanding and using literature. Solitary readers, who do not read for a class or a book club, are able to benefit from reading in a number of ways, but what book clubs offer is a very social way of allowing literature to impact us as readers.

Book clubs might, in fact, be a challenge to the valued notion of a solitary reader. As Elizabeth Long notes, academics have had a really hard time taking seriously the notion of a female amateur reader, who is the primary participant in a book club.[47] Long even goes so far as to say that book clubs cause a certain discomfort for academics and those of us who take literature very seriously, because they challenge two long-held values of academic study. First, book clubs are absolutely influenced by the commercial side of publishing. Books are advertised as excellent book club books, published with book club guides and lists of questions in the back, and of course we cannot forget Oprah's Book Club, which can make any book an overnight best seller. But perhaps more importantly, as Long points out, book clubs challenge "the scholar's position of authority in the world of reading."[48] She explains that "academics tend to repress consideration of variety in reading practices because of our assumption that everyone reads (or ought to) as we do professionally, which usually involves a cognitive and analytic approach to texts."[49] Her use of "our assumption" about the proper way to read emphasizes the authority with which academics tend to think of themselves as the experts who own the best uses for literature. Not reading for "cognitive and analytic reasons" is what might be left for housewives who indulgently consume romance novels. As Long points out, the indulgent pleasure of reading novels is regularly associated with eating bon bons, as well—two indulgences at once. But academics do not own reading. Nor do solitary readers. Book clubs challenge the academic notion of literary expertise and put the interpretation of literary works back into the hands of amateur readers.

Not only do academics tend not to take the work of book clubs very seriously, they also do not really study them very widely. Catherine Burwell, who has studied book clubs, notes that "almost all the studies suggest that these groups eschew formal literary-critical concepts and ways of addressing the text. Instead, literature is viewed, in the words of Edmund Burke, as 'equipment for living' and addressed through modes of identification and empathy."[50] Most book club conversations focus on characters, actions, motivations, the relative moral perceptions of various actions, and the ways in which the stories relate to the lives of the readers. Book clubs, because they are so often centered on understanding the books through the platform of the participant's lives, can become a bit like philosophical counseling or even talk therapy when people tell, retell, and change the stories that they tell about themselves, given a different story framework that might make better sense to them. She says that by looking at book clubs "one can see people in the process of creating new connections, new meanings, and new relationships—to the characters in books or their authors, to themselves, to the other members of the group, to the society and culture in which they live. In other words, they are in the process of remaking themselves in dialogue with others and with literary texts."[51] I might go so far as to say that the focus of book club work is as at least as much on the participant as it is on the text itself.

Academic classroom instruction is typically about understanding a text and only secondarily about understanding ourselves, if at all. It is about learning how to read more and more complex literature as well as exposing students to a canon of works that are culturally significant. Classrooms have a teacher who presents or teaches a book and who often gives specific guidance for understanding the context in which the book is best understood. The teacher is the perceived expert. Often, the teacher has read the book multiple times and has well-informed ideas about the way it would best be taught, the most important parts of the book to emphasize, and the standard analyses. Any *conversations* about the book end when the teacher speaks, because the teacher is the authority and the expert. The teacher has the right answer.[52] In book clubs, however, there is general equity among the members. No one there is the designated expert, and no one's reading is supposed to be more "accurate" than anyone else's.

Book clubs, however, unlike classrooms, are comprised primarily of people who choose to be there but whose purpose is not primarily about literary analysis. Groups might assign a rotating discussion leader, but generally there is an equality among group members, who feel free to express their thoughts. Book club members regularly and often talk about books in a very personal way. They do not talk about the text, alone, but how they understand the text in relation to themselves. Book club members have a special opportunity to gain

insights into their peers and how they understand themselves in reference to the texts. Michael Smith, who analyzed the conversations of
two different adult book clubs (one of men and one of women), had one
participant who said about his group that he "enjoys hearing his friends
expound upon moral or ethical views that they might not have occa-
sion to cover in our general friendship."[53] Another participant says, "I
guess I learn how other people see the world through books in ways
that are different from the way I see the world."[54] Smith notes three
important aspects of book clubs that traditional classroom instruction
do not have: the social aspect, equality among members, and the spirit
of cooperation.[55] Smith was able to see clearly how these groups func-
tioned differently from a traditional classroom setting where a piece
of literature was being discussed. The social aspect seems to be one
of the main reasons participants enjoy going to book clubs so much.
Not only do people have a focused reason to get together, but they
have opportunities to do a bit of self-reflection about the books. One
of Smith's participants said, "I think what's beautiful about this group
is that it doesn't become a therapy session and yet people are fairly
open in showing how they relate to the book and how their experience
has been similar to it without it becoming a bleeding-heart session."[56]
Smith also notes that one of the primary characteristics of book clubs is
that members regularly feel perfectly comfortable using their own lives
as a source of knowledge in their discussions. According to Smith's
analysis, adult book club participants used their own lives as a source
for informative statements 27.5 percent of the time, whereas students
in a classroom only used personal reference points 9.1 percent of the
time and classroom teachers only 5.6 percent of the time.

People have been reading in groups for quite a long time. Because
our storytelling traditions all started as oral traditions, stories were
sometimes traded among folks like commodities but more often passed
down from generation to generation in the form of wisdom from the
elders; practical advice about cooking, farming, and child rearing; and
applicable morality tales that members of a community could apply in
different situations. But once stories had become so commonly written
down and one did not need a crowd to tell a story, the work of reading
became more solitary. The stories became much longer when they could
be committed to paper, and it would be almost impossible to convey
them to a crowd (think *War and Peace*).

In one formal psychological study, Zazie Todd looked at the way a conversation about a book went and analyzed it in terms of different kinds of emotions identified by the readers, as well as some of the expectations readers had about the novels they read. Her goal was to look at the ways people actually talk about books they have read with one another. Previous to this there had been no studies on conversations about whole novels (only short stories and excerpts), so she was interested to see if she could identify any particular patterns in the emotional valence of the book club dialogues. Todd used 64 participants, most of whom were women (which is consistent with most actual book clubs). Groups were broken up into groups of seven participants each, about the average book club size. Each group was assigned a novel and given one month to read it. Todd filmed the discussion so that she could analyze the kinds of conversations that were had about the book without having her presence be an influencing factor. She identifies what she calls narrative feelings as "expressions of sympathy for the characters, or empathy with them."[57] These kinds of narrative feelings are standard for novel readers, but in book clubs they become even more pronounced when members have conversations about a novel. Todd also found that "a lack of empathy for the characters was sometimes given as a reason for disliking a book."[58] Readers often have particular expectations of novels that the books' perceived aesthetic qualities will have to do with the readers' own abilities to identify or feel empathy with the characters. Todd suggests the two most important factors allowing for identification with a character are the novel's realism and the character's similarity to the reader. Some characters are just not as relatable as others, but readers want to connect with them all the same.

The other thing Todd looked at in her study is the way in which feelings about a book can be modified through group discussion. Sometimes a portion of a book can be explained by an analogy to a readers own life, but sometimes the experiences found in a novel are so inconsistent with or so distant from the reader's own life that the reader has trouble identifying with the characters. The reader's search for meaning or insight is thwarted if they cannot relate at all. Most participants in the study reported finding (or hoping to find) some deeper meaning within the novel through the conversation with those in their group. And it was particularly gratifying when they could find meaning that "would give them some new understanding of the world."[59] This study, which is really an extended observation of the ways in which book clubs might extract reading behavior, brings to light three aspects that are important to know about readers. First, readers desire to feel empathy with the characters they read about. Second, readers use their own experiences to relate to a story. And third, readers look for a specific message or truth within novels that group discussion can often help to illuminate. None of these three things seem like surprising insights into what readers want. It does seem noteworthy that, at least for the first two aspects, readers want to feel empathy and use their own experiences to relate to a story. These are things that we want in "real" life, as well. We make connections with both real and fictional characters in similar ways, and this is something that reading can help us develop more fully. Book clubs can help us to develop this capacity for empathy and can provide some of the practice that we might need to understand our own situations in reference to another's story.

8. CONCLUSION

I want to return to Greg Currie's accusation that there is no evidence that reading literary fiction can do us any good. Currie cites the lack of moral experts, but I would like to call as witness the moral failures who are so highly correlated with illiteracy. Moral failures may be a harsh characterization of our prison population, but it seems apt here. Those who are moral are able to follow basic social rules and customs. They are concerned, for whatever reason, be it internally or externally motivated, with the principles of right and wrong behavior and the goodness or badness of character. Philosophy takes up the question of ethics as one of its primary branches. Why should we be moral? Where do standards of morality come from? Are moral standards absolute or relative? Figuring out what it means to be moral has historically been considered to have a lot to do with our capacity to reason and reflect. We cannot be moral purely by accident. It also has historically had a lot to do with our capacity for empathy. Without our ability to empathize with others, we would not necessarily be concerned with the plight of others and thus would have no obligation to act morally.

Reading fiction may not necessarily make us more moral, but as it turns out, it is one of the best ways to help develop a sense of empathy, especially for others who are not like us in significant ways: racially, religiously, socially, culturally, economically, and historically. Reading fiction can help us to develop a healthy theory of mind. Assuming that it is uncontroversial that we have mental states, like knowing, wishing, wanting, and feeling, for example, a theory of mind is something that can regularly attribute how others might be thinking or feeling about a certain event. Folk psychology, or common sense psychology, is the natural ability that most people have to predict or explain the mental states of others. Some people are better at this than others. Autistic people are often cited as the prime example of those who are particularly ill equipped to read emotions on the faces of others and who, thereby, do not have a particularly good theory of mind. Thus, as we become socialized, we learn to anticipate and guess at what others are thinking and feeling. In real-life situations as we are given visual, behavioral, and situational cues to guess at what is going on inside another's mind, but we are not privy to the actual inner dialogue or inner monologue. What literary narrative gives us, on the other hand, is no visual cues but lots of inside information, so to speak. Not all narrative, but most narrative fiction, allows us direct access to the inner motivation and understanding of others. Lots of narrative fiction also gives us considerably better insight than any real person might, just because of the particular kind of narrative construction that most fictional literature employs, making direct connections between particular events and characters' feelings about those events.

Currie dismisses literary fiction as helping to develop theory of mind because so many fiction writers were unstable (subject to various kinds of psychoses) and did not have healthy theory of mind themselves. On my account, theory of mind is less dependent on the author of a text than it is on the quality of his or her narrative. Great writers or "creative types," as Currie calls them, do not need to have the greatest amount of insight into their own motivations or the best guesses at the motivations of others. What they do need and doubtless are able to produce, if they do indeed produce quality literature, is the capacity to express mental states in a convincing way and the capacity to convey an appealing or authentic feeling theory of mind for their characters. It strikes me that this would be one of the most rewarding or most attractive reasons for reading literature in the first place. As human beings we function better, are more able to adapt, and are better able to form close bonds with people we feel we understand. Literary fiction provides us with one of the most reliable inroads to understanding the motivations and mental states of others, even though they are fictional others. Fictional others often have more transparency and coherency because of both the form of the writing and the construction of the narrative arc. That is, literary fiction is often written in a way that makes motivations transparent, or at least understandable, given requisite context. Presumably this is why readers often miss fictional characters when a book ends or are reluctant to finish a book once they are close to the end. Readers become emotionally invested in the characters themselves but also in the access to the inner motivations that they rarely, if ever, have to those of their real-life contemporaries.

When academics talk about "literature" as an abstract category, this does individual works a huge disservice by overlooking the particulars of what makes the individual books powerful in and of themselves. It overlooks the possibility that different works mean different things to different people, and they mean different things to different times and cultures. Most importantly, different works can be interpreted in multiple meaningful ways. The sheer possibility of interpretive plasticity is not a quality that diminishes literature, but rather it is one of its finest defining qualities. The fact that no one owns the premier interpretation of a work means that "literature" as a category verges on the edge of meaningless itself. I think that we should value reading because it can make us more empathetic. It can give us perspective we might not be able to gain otherwise, and it can prompt self-reflection. When we ask for evidence for this sort of thing, we are most likely wanting something that includes statistics and a double blind study. But our desire only for evidence that comes in the form of a psychological study with statistically significant data points leads me to think that we have been caught up in a culture that demands the instant gratification of having immediate and perceptible change after every discrete event. This is also the culture which produces a school system that desires accountability for the teachers and so gives standardized tests to its students multiple times per year, even to its youngest students (first grade), many of whom cannot even read yet.

The analogy to smoking is fitting here, I believe. I would not run a test to have a subject chain smoke for 10 hours and then see if he has any statistically significant increase in the number of cancer cells in his body. Similarly, reading one book will not change a person with one reading. What will change a reader is developing the skills of a reader and practicing those skills on a regular basis. Being a reader allows one to develop and practice a multitude of skills at one time. Sometimes paying attention well enough and deeply enough to a long and complicated narrative helps us to hold many things in our minds at once. Sometimes understanding what motivates the characters we read about helps us to understand our own motivations and behaviors. Sometimes seeing how a fictional character is treated unjustly prompts a reader to change their own behavior toward one of their real life contemporaries. But sometimes none of these things happen, or other ones happen, or nothing happens other than that I have practiced my skill. So I take being a reader to be more akin to being a runner than a smoker. Many of the exercises that a runner does are not significant by themselves, but they all build competence and strength so that she can run a race. Runners do not just train to finish one race but to continue to push themselves run after run, or race after race. Being a reader works similarly. Readers develop basic skills and practice them in different ways in different contexts. No one reading changes me in the same way that no one run changes my ability as an athlete. If we think of reading and literacy as a skill set to be developed and not something to be finally achieved, then reading might just be good for us, not because it makes us more moral or cognitively superior, but because it is a part of a practice that can build empathy and can help readers develop the habit of making meaning out of lived experience.

NOTES

1. To Read or Not to Read: A Question of national Consequence. The National Endowment for the Arts. Research Report #47, 2007.

2. Jamil Zaki, "What, Me Care? Young Are Less Empathetic," *Scientific American*, December 23, 2010, http://www.scientificamerican.com/article/what-me-care/ (accessed January 29, 2015). Also see Nicholas Carr, *The Shallows: What the Internet Is Doing to Our Brains* (New York: W. W. Norton & Co., 2011).

3. Sarah Konrath, Edward H. O'Brien, and Courtney Hsing, "Changes in Dispositional Empathy in American College Students Over Time: A Meta-Analysis," *Personality and Social Psychology Review* 30 (2010): 1–19.

4. Mikita Brottman. *The Solitary Vice: Against Reading* (Berkeley, CA: Counterpoint Publishers, 2008).

5. Brottman, *Solitary Vice*, 3.

6. Neil Gaiman, "Why Our Future Depends on Libraries, Reading and Daydreaming," http://www.theguardian.com/books/2013/oct/15/neil-gaiman-future-libraries-reading-daydreaming (accessed January 27, 2015)

7. Gaiman, "Why Our Future Depends on Libraries."

8. Kylene Beers, "Literature: Our Way In," *Voices from the Middle* 7 (1999), 12.

9. Beers, "Literature: Our Way In," 12.

10. I am drawing upon Noël Carroll's work on what he calls the narrative connection. In attempting to define the basic necessary and sufficient conditions of what constitutes a narrative, he describes these five elements as the building blocks of what we generally accept as narratives but says that none of them are necessary or jointly sufficient. The more you have, the more likely it will resemble what is generally accepted as a narrative. It is also a useful way of identifying the main characteristics even when one isn't attempting to identify necessary and sufficient conditions. Noël Carroll. "On the Narrative Connection," in *New Perspectives on Narrative Perspective*, ed. Willie Van Peer and Seymour Chatman (Albany: State University of New York Press, 2001).

11. Laura Bowman, Laura E. Levine, Bradley M. Waite, and Michael Gendron, "Can Students Really Multitask: An Experimental Study of Instant Messaging," *Computers and Education* 54 (2010): 927–31.

12. Plato. *Phaedrus* 275 a–b.

13. A. Mangen, P. Robinet, G. Olivier, and J.-L. Velay, "Mystery Story Reading in Pocket Print Book and on Kindle: Possible Impact on Chronological Events Memory," Conference paper presentation, IGEL (The International Society for the Empirical Study of Literature and Media), Turin, Italy, July 21–25.

14. Jeff Duntemann, "Pages in Peril: What We May Lose as Ebooks Go Mainstream," *The Indexer*, 26 (2008): 148–51.

15. Luanne Freund, Richard W. Kopak, and Heather O'Brien, "The Effects of Textual Environment on Reading Comprehension: Implications for Searching as Learning," *Journal of Information Science* 42 (2016): 79–93.

16. Sven Birkerts, *The Gutenberg Elegies: The Fate of Reading in an Electronic Age* (New York: Fawcett Columbine, 1995), 146.

17. Plato, "Republic," in *Collected Dialogues*, ed. Edith Hamilton and Huntington Cairns (Princeton, NJ: Princeton University Press, 1961), 607 b5–6.

18. Plato, "Republic," 605 b1.

19. Plato, "Republic," 605 b2.

20. Plato, "Republic," 605 b8–c2.

21. Gregory Currie, "Literature and the Psychology Lab," *The Times Literary Supplement*, August 31, 2011, http://www.the-tls.co.uk/tls/public/article765921.ece (accessed January 29, 2015)

22. Plato, *Collected Dialogues*, ed. Edith Hamilton and Huntington Cairns (Princeton, NJ: Princeton University Press, 1961), *Theaetetus*. 199e.

23. Common Core State Standards (CCSS). www.corestandards.org (accessed March 11, 2015)

24. CCSS.

25. CCSS.

26. CCSS.

27. CCSS.

28. CCSS.

29. "The Lexile Framework for Reading: Matching Students with Texts," www.Lexile.com (accessed March 11, 2015)

30. Ludwig Wittgenstein, *Tractatus Logico-Philosophicus*, trans. D.F. Pears and B.F. McGuinness (London: Routledge & Kegan Paul, 1961), 115.

31. Sandra Greenway, "Library Services Behind Bars," *Bookmobile Outreach Service* 10 (2007): 44.

32. Elizabeth Kleinfeld, "Growing Up Incarcerated," in *Growing Up Postmodern: Neroliberalism and the War on the Young* (2002), 89.

33. National Assessment of Adult Literacy, *A Nationally Representative and Continuing Assessment of English Language Literary skills of American Adults,* http://nces.ed.gov/naal/kf_demographics.asp (accessed March 11, 2015)

34. Bureau of Justice Statistics, http://www.bjs.gov/index.cfm?ty=pbdetail&iid=1345 (accessed March 11, 2015)

35. Neil Gaiman,"Why Our Future Depends on Libraries, Reading and Daydreaming," http://www.theguardian.com/books/2013/oct/15/neil-gaiman-future-libraries-reading-daydreaming (accessed January 27, 2015)

36. Dennis Stevens and Charles Ward, "College Education and Recidivism: Educating Criminals Is Meritorious," *Journal of Correctional Education* 48, no. 3 (1997): 108. See also James Vacca, "Educated Prisoners Are Less Likely to Return to Prison," *Journal of Correctional Education* 55, no. 4 (2004): 297–305.

37. Jimmy Santiago Baca, *Working in the Dark: Reflections of a Poet of the Barrio* (Santa Fe: Red Crane Press, 1992), 4.

38. Robert Waxler and Jean Trounstein, *Changing Lives through Literature* (Notre Dame, IN: University of Notre Dame Press, 1999).

39. William Bole, "A Novel Approach to Sentencing Criminals," *Village Life Magazine*, January 20, 1997, http.villagelife.org (accessed June 23, 2016). See also Jean Trounstine and Robert Waxler, *Finding a Voice: The Practice of Changing Lives through Literature* (Ann Arbor, MI: University of Michigan Press, 2005).

40. Trounstine and Waxler, *Finding a Voice*, 4.

41. Trounstine and Waxler, *Finding a Voice*, 5.

42. Trounstine and Waxler, *Finding a Voice*, 5.

43. Trounstine and Waxler, *Finding a Voice*, 3.

44. Name is changed, but Larry Newton is the name she uses for him in her book.

45. Laura Bates, *Shakespeare Saved My Life: Ten Years in Solitary with the Bard* (Naperville, IL: Sourcebooks, 2013), 173.

46. Bates, *Shakespeare Saved My Life*, 173–4.

47. Elizabeth Long, *Book Clubs: Women and the Uses of Reading in Everyday Life* (Chicago: University of Chicago Press, 2003), 11.

48. Long, *Book Clubs*, 11.

49. Long, *Book Clubs*, 11.

50. Catherine Burwell, "Reading Lolita in Times of War: Women's Book Clubs and the Politics of Reception," *Intercultural Education* 18, no. 4 (2007), 285.

51. Long, *Book Clubs*, 22.

52. Michael Smith, "Conversations about Literature outside Classrooms: How Adults Talk about Books in Their Book Clubs, *Journal of Adolescent & Adult Literacy* 40, no. 3 (1996), 184.

53. Smith, "Conversations about Literature," 183.

54. Smith, "Conversations about Literature," 183.

55. Smith, "Conversations about Literature," 180.

56. Smith, "Conversations about Literature," 182–3.

57. Zazie Todd, "Talking about Books: A Reading Group Study," *Psychology of Aesthetics Creativity and the Arts* 2, no. 4 (2008), 259.

58. Todd, "Talking about Books," 259.

59. Todd, "Talking about Books," 262.

Chapter Two

Fiction and Nonfiction

As a philosopher, I have a tendency to problematize distinctions and definitions that most people do not see as problematic. My son asked me recently if a story we were reading was real or not. I asked him what he meant by real. He said "real, mom, like real." I basically could not answer his question. The appropriate answer for a six-year-old could have been one of several options: "I don't know"; "yes, it happened"; or "no, this particular story did not happen." I got stuck on what the relationship was between story and reality because it is not a relationship that can be easily mapped one onto the other. This relationship is one that has been discussed largely in reference to fiction and reality, primarily in terms of how or what we might learn from fiction or why we might have emotional responses to things we know to be fictional, but it has not been discussed specifically in reference to narrative or story and its relationship to reality regardless of whether the story is fictional or nonfictional.

My son wanted to know if the story was true or false, if it had happened or had not happened, if it was real or pretend. He wanted to know how to map this story onto his experience. Unfortunately for him, all of these dichotomies are loaded for his philosopher mom. Initially, a number of the sets of opposites we use to describe our everyday experiences are obvious and clear. They are also mutually exclusive. Propositional statements are said to be true or false, and they do not cross borders. Real and fake describe fundamentally different kinds of objects and experiences. Truths and lies involve different intentions on the part of

those who utter them. And fiction and nonfiction are two different sections in the bookstore and in the library, used to indicate true stories
and made-up stories, respectively. They must be easily distinguishable
from one another, because one is described as the mere negation of the
other. If fiction and nonfiction are taken merely as genre distinctions or
aisles in the bookstore, things might remain relatively simple. But fiction and nonfiction are not *merely* genre descriptions, they are used to
describe the ways we *should* approach and respond to a text. Fiction and
nonfiction are normative terms. That is, they set a norm or a standard
for which we should understand those categories. All of these pairs are
much more loaded than they initially seem, and none of the pairs are as
mutually exclusive as we would like to think.

The pair of opposites I want to look at is fiction and nonfiction.
Although my focus will be on the ways in which we distinguish
between them and whether there can be a mutually exclusive category
distinction applied, the other pairs of opposites will continue to inform
my investigation into the ways in which we use, understand, confuse,
and misuse the tenuous distinction that we make between fiction and
nonfiction. Our understanding of both genre descriptions is in fact
largely dependent upon another distinction: narrative and nonnarrative,
and in significant ways the negation of fiction (nonfiction) cannot fall
into a mutually excluded category at all. Also, the association of truth
with nonfiction and falsity with fiction is doubly wrong, since the ways
in which we talk about something being true or false refers to a kind of
statement of fact that a narrative description could never offer us.

1. THEORIES OF FICTION

In order to understand how we understand what it means to be fictional,
I want to first define what it means for a work to count as fiction and
talk a bit about held theories of fiction or larger explanations about the
way we understand the concept. Something *fictional* is created or made,
not an undirected, naturally occurring event. Fictions can be made up
entirely or partially, or they can be abstractions that emphasize a particular meaning or interpretation of an event. Fictions are not merely
the same as lies, but they do have the connotation that they are not
just stories about true events. Whereas lies are intended to undermine
the truth, fictions are not. Though fictions are *stories* about things that
have been created, imagined, speculated about, or made up, many have

largely true events and/or details woven into them as well, such as historical fiction that uses historically accurate contexts to stage fictitious plots. When I read fictional stories, I need comprehensive cognitive organization to understand the linguistic elements of the narrative, but often I also have the added dimension of emotional affect that contributes to my understanding. Philosophers have questioned the authority of this emotional response because of its seeming irrationality. Why would I respond emotionally to something I know not to be the case? If I were told that I fictionally won the lottery, I would not be *really* excited, but I might feel something if it were told in a really good fictional story! I would not go out and run up my credit card because I do not *believe* that I have really won. In this case, the truth *acting* on or constraining my life does not correspond with the fictional one.

But what we describe as fictional can be taken in a number of ways; it can be something that is made up (fabricated) or simply that which does not correspond with reality. Fictionality can be dictated by the author's intentions, or something can be made fictional by use. Presumably, fiction could be dictated merely by the Library of Congress designation printed on the back of a book jacket. However, what is *fictional* is not merely what is *not true*. Fictionality is not simply aligned with lying or falsehood; nor can nonfiction simply be aligned with truth or fact. What is fictional is not based on subject matter alone, and it is not based only on truth value or reference failure. Lies are not what become fiction and fictions are not mere lies. Fiction is not a conglomeration of false sentences. It cannot be seen *only* as a negation of truth. It is an intentional construction of a certain kind. Things described in fictions can and often do correspond to real places, persons, and events, but fictions are not *necessarily* about real places, persons, and events. Fiction is a literary genre that is to be read in a particular way. Stories or narratives are a form of *explanation* and, as explanations, are used as *justification* in ways corresponding to those in which we validate truth claims.

Conversely, nonfiction is also a literary genre that we are taught to read in a particular way and is dependent upon certain social and literary conventions for us to understand properly. It is not merely that which is true, *simpliciter.* One of the preconditions of nonfiction is that it is both true and something that can be documented. What is true also goes well beyond just "what happened" or what corresponds to "reality." Nonfictional literature does not just appeal to a simplistic version of truth as "what *really* happened." Narratives written about true events, events that really happened, are still largely *constructed* into stories by editing time, event, setting, tone, character, and emotion, and often by constructing or inventing causation. Narratives are also always written from a particular perspective. Nonfiction does not and cannot embrace only true accounts of an omniscient narrator. Nonfictional literature is a genre of storytelling that *includes* true events, but it can include much more also, like emotionally laden perspectives that could never be derived from "facts alone" or "true events." Moreover, nonfiction includes a descriptive aspect that is necessarily inserted by a narrator. This perspective alone distances narrated stories from propositional sentences and propositional knowledge.

The seeming difference between fiction and nonfiction is, most significantly, that one is *false* and the other is *true* or, likewise, that I *do not believe* that what is fictional happened, but I *do believe* that what is nonfictional happened. It seems reasonable to me that we should respond in emotionally appropriate ways to one and not the other, especially considering the fact that we do not tend to respond emotionally to things we do not believe to be the case. But the fact remains that, as readers, we respond emotionally to both fiction and nonfiction in consistent ways. To understand both requires very similar cognitive mechanisms. That is, what it takes to understand the mechanics of a narrative, whether it be fiction or nonfiction, is largely the same—plot construction, character development, being able to locate characters in time and space, and being able to make sense of cause and effect relationships, to name a few. We use memory and imagination to make sense of narratives. The truth status or the reference status matters very little when it comes to the mechanics of narrative comprehension.

Philosopher John Searle argues that it is a general convention for us to distinguish between true stories and fictional stories and claims that we function easily with two categories of discourse: fictional discourse and serious discourse. For Searle, serious discourse is a specific kind of illocutionary act (what is meant but not necessarily what is said) that includes making assertions, and these assertions are tied to certain kinds of rules to which fiction does not have to adhere. Serious discourse commits the speaker to the *truth* of the assertion and what the speaker *believes* to be the truth about the assertion. Fictional discourse, on the other hand, does not have to abide by the rules of belief or truth, but we suspend the normal rules of reference to the real world and work with what we take to be "pretend assertions."[1] Pretend assertions then allow us to still use the language and normal linguistic references to objects in the real world, but as a reader I understand that because the author's intention is not for me to take the text "seriously," the rules binding me to the actual world do not hold in this case. This seems reasonable, but as it stands, the reader must always know in advance of reading what was intended by the author and only knows whether to take a text as serious or fictional with prior instruction. Words within a text cannot differentiate the "seriousness" of the story at all. Although this seems reasonable, I think it relies too heavily on knowing in advance the intentions of the speaker and a strict binary that goes between belief and unbelief or belief and imagination. If foreknowledge determines all outcomes about the way we should take all utterances, we cannot rely on our own meaning-making at all as part of the process. Although this does accurately describe a general convention, I do not think that it can account for a complete explanation of the ways in which we make sense of narrative broadly. Searle's account is useful but also partial.

For clarity's sake I should also add that we refer to fiction in one other ambiguous way; we refer to "fictional characters" or "fictional events" but also to the *genre* of "fiction" as a literary category. When philosophers speak of the ontological status of fictional characters or events, they refer to a specific nonexistent being, someone who does not refer to anyone who really exists. But the genre of fiction is not about this kind of reference failure. We also refer to the truth status of something being "fictional," or made up in this case. I take some of our confusion about the concept to result from our multiple uses of the term. When philosophers concern themselves with questions about the legitimacy of the emotions that result from engagement with fictional intentional objects, "fictionality" is used primarily in reference to the truth status or lack-of-belief status of the *whole* narrative. But when we give examples of fictional intentional objects, we are more likely to give singular examples, like that of Anna Karenina or the Lilliputians, as opposed to any meaningful reference to a complete fictional world—one that is meaningfully narrativized or storied.

2. FROM DEFINITION TO THEORY

Philosophers have worked hard to develop a theory of fiction or a general explanation of what it is and how it functions. We need a theory, something that goes beyond a mere definition, not only so we know how to organize books in the bookstore and the library but also so that we can distinguish meaningfully between fiction and nonfiction and so we can better understand our responses—emotional, cognitive, and moral—to both kinds of narrative. Understanding our responses to both fictional and nonfictional narrative can in turn help us to understand appropriate kinds of responses more generally. As I explained above, nonfiction cannot be a mere negation of fiction, and a theory of nonfiction cannot be applied in an intuitive way by assuming structural similarities between fiction and nonfiction.

a. Fiction as Make-Believe

Although fiction is addressed widely as a topic, only a handful of theorists prescribe a "theory of fiction" proper. Kendall Walton, for instance, argues that something is made fictional when it is used as a prop in a game of make-believe.[2] For Walton, something is made fictional when an object, any kind of object really—a stump, a teddy bear, a work of art, or a sentence—is used in certain kinds of games of make believe. I will refer to this as the "use theory" since something is fictional when it is used that way. Walton's explanation is about the representational arts broadly, but he extends it to narrative and fictional literature. Walton says that we can distinguish fiction from nonfiction by noting the fact that "works of fiction are simply representations in our special sense, whose function is to serve as props in games of make believe."[3] So that which is *fictional* is that which is *treated as fictional*. "It is fictional that" is a kind of invisible pretense claim that prefaces whole works but also individual instances (claims, utterances, sentences, etc.) so that we know how to take the instance. When something is treated as fictional in this way, it does not have existential belief associated with it. Walton's account of fictionality prescribes a particular kind of imagining, which invites those who engage to *imagine seeing* what the prop (or the prompt) represents. He suggests that when we read about the Lilliputians we *imagine seeing* Lilliputians. We do not believe they exist, but being fictional we *imagine* them in a particular way. Being fictional prescribes a certain kind of imagining of the intentional object.

Something's being fictional for Walton can also provide a kind of internal consistency, one in which it makes sense to make truth claims. For instance, it is logical to say that "it is true in the fiction" that Anna Karenina is torn between two loves. It is true in the story that Gulliver is taken hostage by a race of tiny people. "It is true in the story that" is code for "it is made fictional that," which is the equivalent of "making-believe that." These propositional statements (Gulliver is taken hostage by a race of tiny people) then have a fictional modifier (it is fictional that) attached to them so that being fictional *parallels* a nonfictional account but is held apart in Walton's special sense of making-believe or pretense. In some ways, this allows Walton's pretense account to be a particular kind of alternative universe in which the "fictional world" is one that has the same kind of internal consistency, rules, and coherence as a "nonfictional world." For my purposes, speaking of fictional worlds makes a lot more sense than just speaking of individual fictional sentences.

On the surface, fictional texts are ones that are considered "unreal." They did not happen. When we look deeper, however, it is not that simple. Part of what it means to understand or appreciate something as fictional is to be able to turn the fictional descriptions into conceptual mappings that we know how to make sense of. That is, although what happens in a fiction did not *actually* happen, the events described in most fictional literature do happen in familiar kinds of places, with descriptions of plausible relationships; they are about familiar kinds of situations, and they involve recognizable motivations, feelings, and resolutions. We are able to make sense of fictional descriptions because they are often not so different from descriptions of real events, people, and places. Events narrated in a fictional work differ from nonfictional narrated events only in that the events in the fiction presumably did not happen. The story form or narrative structure is the same, but I am not invited to believe the events in a fiction as I am with nonfiction.

Philosophers often use fiction as a technical term that has to do with the way we can meaningfully interact with a work of art, whether it be a painting, novel, or any other kind of representational work. This generalized attitude is primarily because of Kendall Walton's seminal account in *Mimesis as Make-Believe.*[4] Although Walton focuses on the representational arts in general, I focus primarily on the literary and narrative. I will call this generalized form of fictionality "Walt-fiction,"[5] named so in his honor. Walt-fiction is the kind of fiction that is both imaginative and prop-generated and has to do with the ways in which fiction invites us to imagine in certain ways. Others use fictionality differently and focus more on the ways in which the work refers semantically and the resulting category distinction that places a particular literary genre. That is, fictional works do not refer to real objects in the same way that nonfictional works do. That which is fictional refers to the events, characters, and storylines that are made up, imaginary, invented, or just not real. It also includes traditional genre limitations: that it may not be true (or if it is it is only incidentally so)[6] and that it has a certain kind of narrative structure that allows readers to make sense of a text as a narrated storyline with a discernible structure. Presumably, readers do not have a very hard time figuring out what is real and what is not or what is fictional and what is nonfictional, but this division is potentially problematic because of the myriad of cases that involve the blending of the two genres. Philosophers have spent vast amounts of energy in an ongoing discussion about the best way to describe the interaction with fictions that we have emotionally, cognitively, and morally, but we have not spent nearly as much time thinking about how to engage most fruitfully with nonfictions or how literary nonfictions need to be accounted for in a fundamentally different way. I will begin here with an explanation of the development of the ways in which I deal with fiction, not as a genre, but as a means of interaction.

Walton suggests that when we engage with a fiction we are simply engaging in a game of make-believe. With any game of make-believe we need "props" as a starting point for the game.[7] This follows from what Walton calls the principals of generation, which are contextual clues required for things to be imagined.[8] That is, in the act or process of reading, the fictional text acts as the prop and we, as readers, are simply the players of the game. Walton explains that the props "give fictional worlds and their contents a kind of objectivity, and independence from cognizers and their experiences which contributes much to the excitement of our adventures with them."[9] Taking into consideration the principals of generation and the need to use props, I can make the assumption that the key to entering a fictional world is also based upon our typical interactions with the real world. Thus Walt-fiction is what is to be imagined, in a parallel way as what is true is to be believed.[10] Fictionality then is incited in certain ways by certain kinds of prompts. For Walton, they can be stumps (as in a children's game of "bears"), paintings that provoke imagining certain kinds of pictorial worlds, or the prompts described in literary narratives.

But Walton's account is really only concerned with fictionality as an abstract concept that has to do with particular ways of imagining. He does not deal with nonfiction as a literary genre but only nonfiction, as it is not fictional. He actually has a whole chapter in his book called

"Fiction and Nonfiction," but here Walton specifies that "for the sake of clarity I will mean by 'nonfiction' simply 'not fiction'. Any work with the function of serving as a prop in games of make-believe however minor or peripheral or instrumental this function might be qualified as 'fiction'; only what lacks this function entirely will be called nonfiction."[11] He talks very meaningfully about the category of fiction but not of nonfiction as a theoretical construct. I want to have a better sense of how nonfiction functions specifically as a literary genre, because I believe that the way readers comprehend *narrative* as a particular kind of construction is very similar with both fiction and nonfiction.

b. Fiction as Intention

The other way of approaching a *theory* of fiction is taking it to be a fictional utterance. Most generally, the utterance argument is one based in philosophy of language (and Searle's *Speech Acts* in particular)—that is, if one *intends* something to be taken *as* fictional then it *is* fictional. I'll call this the intention theory. Peter Lamarque and Stein Haugom Olsen, who are the primary advocates of this approach, explain that "the fictive dimension of stories (or narratives) is explicable only in terms of a rule governed practice, central to which are a certain modes of utterance (fictive utterance) and a certain complex of attitudes (the fictive stance)."[12] Fiction then is a particular kind of language game that only exists within a certain practice of storytelling. Lamarque and Olsen explain that the "central focus is not on the structural or semantic properties of sentences but on the conditions under which they are uttered, the attitudes they invoke, and the role that they play in social interactions."[13] That which is fictional is only fictional when used in a particular kind of storytelling community. For Lamarque and Olsen, however, "fictive utterance is ultimately a [particular] kind of communication, involving an interaction between speaker (writer) and audience (reader)" since the intention is always that of the speaker or writer.[14] This differs significantly from Walton in that his theory focuses on how something is *used* as opposed to the way it is *intended for use* by Lamarque and Olsen.

Gregory Currie, also of the intention camp, adds that a fictive utterance can be no more than *accidentally true*. That is, true and fictional utterances cannot be equally said to incite the proper kind of imaginings that fiction should incite. So belief, according to Currie, is necessarily something that should *not* be associated with a fictional utterance. For

Currie, belief/nonbelief may be the guiding principle that divides non-fiction and fiction, rather than advocating for a particular kind of imagining, as Walton suggests. Further, Currie argues that fictionality is not located in the text itself (as there are no essential features of fictional writing that a nonfictional text might not have), and fictionality also cannot lie in the understanding of the audience, (I might misread the morning newspaper as fiction, but that does not make it fictional.) For Currie, fictionality develops out of the stated or implied intentions of the author of the fictional utterance. He explains that "what the author of a fiction does intend is that the reader take a certain attitude toward the propositions uttered in the course of his performance. This is the attitude of 'imaginative involvement' or (better) 'make-believe'. We are intended by the author to make believe that the story uttered is true."[15] A work can only be taken as fictional if it is intended to be taken as fictional, and the fictional utterance advocates a certain kind of imaginative stance toward the work.

c. Fiction as Context

Stacie Friend addresses nonfiction as a literary genre by approaching it specifically as a genre that is a potential compliment to fiction but claims that fiction and nonfiction are, at base, of two fundamentally different kinds. Yet even she admits that it is not clear how fiction and nonfiction are related to one another. One genre (nonfiction) is not merely the negation of the other (fiction), nor are they really compliments *per se*. She argues for what she calls a contextualist account of genre as the best way to distinguish between fiction and nonfiction. She claims that this account "focuses attention, not on how the parts of a work add up to the whole, but instead how the whole work is embedded in a larger context, and specifically in certain practices of reading, writing, criticizing, and so on."[16] Friend has worries, however, about the ways in which the intentionalist approach to categorizing fiction, as well as the make-believe theory, both tend to end up being reductionist accounts of cataloguing and appreciating fiction.

Friend suggests that we not use fiction and nonfiction as categories needing necessary and sufficient conditions to define but rather that we think of fiction and nonfiction *primarily* and merely as (relatively messy) genre distinctions, "categories whose membership is determined by a cluster of non-essential criteria, and which play a role—or rather, a variety of roles—in the appreciation of particular works."[17]

She suggests this because of the plethora of examples and counter examples that arise with the use and intention theories. She further suggests, rightly I think, that fiction and nonfiction cannot usefully function in mutually exclusive or jointly exhaustive categories. If we take the two categories to describe reading practices (genres), but not much more, presumably a text cannot be in both categories at once but could potentially be in both categories at different times or in different storytelling traditions. For example, Rigoberta Menchu, a Guatemalan activist, wrote a memoir about her horrific experiences as a refugee of the Guatemalan Civil War, which began in 1960. Initially, it was believed to be a straightforward memoir with accounts of her own experiences. Subsequently, however, evidence surfaced that her memoir is not merely reflective of her own experiences but was a compilation of many people's experiences. So, at one point, it was believed to be a memoir (and presumably true or nonfictional) but now is considered more reflective of the South American tradition of *testimonio* or testimonial narrative. In this case the narrative changed from one genre to another. It might even be said to have moved from nonfiction to fiction. Another kind of example would be the way that many Biblical narratives can be taken both literally and metaphorically by different people. The same text in this case prompts both belief and imagination. Further, as Friend notes, fiction and nonfiction do not conveniently fit into the genre/compliment genre description either, as one would be hard-pressed to figure out which one, fiction or nonfiction, would serve as the primary genre.

I agree with Friend's concerns about the reductionist tendency to assess genre and want to continue to avoid this reductionism, as well. The problem is that when the discussion stays at the abstract level of fiction and nonfiction in terms of what we are either intended to imagine or believe, it sells short all of the subgenres of actual literary works. This should also be a larger concern. Fiction and nonfiction are not merely genres of literary works; they are also conceptual categories that apply to the broadest way of approaching the understanding and appreciation of literature. When philosophers talk about what it is for something to be a fiction or what it is to be considered fictional, we take this to be an entirely abstract category with which to make sense of our experiences. When literary critics (or even most everyday readers) hear mention of fiction, they think of a particular category of literature or go so far as to even equate it with novels. So there is a disconnect between fiction as intention and fiction as literary genre.

What I want to talk about is fiction as a literary genre, but through a distinctively philosophical framework. I also take it that fiction as intentional stance and fiction as genre both have ways to inform the other. Discussions of fiction and nonfiction certainly have their place in the philosophical literature, but I want to focus more on the discussions that are required to understand the way in which narrative comprehension is possible at all and the way that the work of comprehension is coextensive with making sense of genre. What this means, however, is that the work of the reader must function not only at the abstract level of understanding the genres but also dealing with a number of particular examples and thinking seriously about the way in which comprehension works at the micro level (sentence structure), the macro level (story comprehension), and how various works form the network of relationships that make Friend's contextualist account of genre make sense.

The use and intention theories make up the two primary approaches in the literature. I take issue with two aspects of these, which will help me outline my own position. First, I mentioned briefly the notion of fictional worlds. In the discussion of fictionality, it is dangerous to rely primarily on individual fictional utterances, sentences, or small examples. When small or singular examples are used, which both the use and intention theories do, the literary work is reduced to something that fictional worlds cannot be reduced to. Fictional or true sentences refer *only* to the truth status, *not* to the fictional world status. A theory of fiction must, I think, encompass not only imagining or taking individual sentences in a certain way, but a coherent system that is what narrative describes, not just that which is true or false. Narrative and narration, which are produced by both fiction and nonfiction, should not be evaluated at the level of the sentence but rather by the description they evoke and the world they create. When narrative is addressed at the sentence level, with the fictional modifier ("it is true in the fiction that" or "it is make-believe that"), all one focuses on is the truth status rather than the context in which the sentence fits—the way it fits into the greater fictional world. If the truth status of the sentence is what is held to be the defining characteristic, then I think we are missing the forest for the trees. The truth status of particular instances is not what make stories themselves fictional or nonfictional, even though truth status may be accurately used. The "truth" of nonfiction remains secondary for me, second to the narration, the descriptions it evokes, and the well-fleshed-out imaginative worlds that are developed.

So a big part of the problem is the size of the examples that are talked about. For example, *Anna Karenina* is the most popular example to which everyone refers, presumably because this is the example used in the first important article about the paradox of fiction.[18] But the way the example is used just involves a theoretical supposition about why readers might feel pity for the fictional Anna at all, given that we know she is fictional. Anna herself is incidental to the conceptual problem. She is a convenient placeholder for the question, "Why are we moved by characters we don't believe really exist?" But we are never really challenged by the particulars of her situation, the success or failure of Tolstoy's descriptions of her character, her failing marriage, how compelling or attractive Vronsky is, how restrictive Russian culture was at the time, or whether we think her situation really warranted suicide. It seems to me that all of these concerns, and probably many more, are relevant to the question of whether and why we should pity Anna. The quality of prose must be taken into consideration and not just the fact that Anna is fictional. Better prose and more compelling characters are more likely to evoke feelings in a reader, but that is never part of the supposition about the paradox of fiction, which never really questions any specific text but questions only the apparent inconsistency or irrationality of having seemingly real emotions about events or characters we do not believe exist.

The second issue I take with both the use and intention approaches is the relatively simple notion of belief that is utilized—a notion that has only to do with belief about existence. It is assumed (especially largely by the paradox of fiction) that a reader either clearly believes or clearly disbelieves a narrative to be true. Presumably, this belief is informed primarily by the back jacket of the book we are reading. That is, genre classifications help to guide our expectations about what we read and whether or not we *believe* what is going on in the narrative. Our beliefs dictate, or at least heavily influence, the ways in which we are supposed to imagine elements of a story. Belief, however, is created in more than one way. Whether a story is true or fictional is not something we can know simplistically in advance. Belief is something that can be created and cultivated simultaneously along with plausibility, emotional cadence, and imagination. The lack of plausibility is something that will degrade belief even if we are told the story is "true." Belief is not always a simple result of something being clearly true or clearly false in advance. In most cases, belief is reasonable when it matches up with some set of circumstances for which we have reasonable evidence.

Evidence comes in a multitude of forms—direct sensory evidence, first-person testimony, evidence that comes from a secondary but generally trusted source, or descriptions of causes that generate into something reasonable and plausible. Evidence and conclusions that result from reliable syllogisms as well as compelling arguments should be given a lot of credit. But that certainly is not the only kind of belief that is generated or evidence accepted when engaging with narrative. Belief *can* result from a correspondence-type theory of truth—a direct correspondence between "reality" and one's own representation of that reality—but belief can also be constructed in more complex and subtle ways as we become convinced of things. Belief is also not just about existence. I do not *only* have beliefs that an event or person has existence, current or historical. Rather, I can also have evaluative and dispositional beliefs, which are often underlying my comprehension of many different kinds of narratives. For instance, I may have evaluative or moral beliefs concerning the relationship between Humbert and Lolita[19] that have nothing to do with the relationship described in the text. Those evaluative beliefs guide my enjoyment and appreciation of the narrative, but they do not have anything to do with whether I believe the characters exist. I believe that Humbert acts inappropriately toward Lolita because of their ages. (He is 38 and she is 12.) He becomes obsessed with her and engages her in a sexual relationship that is clearly inappropriate for a 12-year-old girl and one that is absolutely inappropriate for a stepfather. As a reader, I maintain these evaluative beliefs about their relationship, and at the same time I am not confused at all about the fact that neither of them exist. If beliefs can be other than just existential, then it seems reasonable to me to consider the roles that belief plays in our explanations of the ways in which we interact imaginatively and emotionally, not just with fiction but fictional *and* nonfictional literature.

3. BELIEF, IMAGINATION, AND NARRATION

In Derek Matravers' recent book *Fiction and Narrative*, he points out that most of the argument about fiction starts with the basic assumption that the primary way of distinguishing between fiction and nonfiction has to do with their respective relationships to imagination and belief. The view is said to be ubiquitous among the use theorists as well as the intention theorists and dozens of others who have worked on the problem of fictionality. Matravers actually refers to it as the "consensus view."[20] The consensus is that fiction is associated with imagination, and nonfiction is associated with belief. If this is so, then it does not matter whether fictionality is prescribed by either use or intention. According to Matravers, there is no *necessary connection* between fiction and imagination *that is exclusive of nonfiction.* That is, nonfiction can and often does require the imagination in order for the reader to understand, conceive of, and make the necessary connections between events. Matravers explains that "the consensus view holds that what goes on in reading nonfiction differs from what goes on in reading fiction and that the difference [has] to do with the difference between belief and imagination."[21] What Matravers then argues is that fiction and nonfiction are not the primary category distinctions we should use to determine the difference between the way that we interpret different kinds of stories. In fact, both fiction and nonfiction share the essential element of narration. It is *narrative* that requires the imagination, not merely fiction.

Although nonfiction includes a plethora of different kinds of texts, including textbooks, scientific papers, user manuals, photographs, and biographies, it also includes narrative prose like essays, personal journals, memoirs, and most importantly, what might be called literary or creative nonfiction. While it is generally agreed that nonfiction functionally reports about persons, places, and events in the real world, literary nonfiction employs prose techniques that are normally associated with literary fiction. These works resemble the format of the (fictional) novel, for example, except that they are narrative explanations of real people, places, and events. The category of narrative or creative nonfiction would include books like Truman Capote's *In Cold Blood*, and Erik Larson's *Devil in the White City*. Both of these books read like (fictional) novels. If it was not stated on the cover that they were nonfiction, a reader would probably assume they were fictional. But, as Matravers points out, the kinds of imaginings that nonfiction can incite tend to be no less vivid than those provoked by fictional prompts. It is the narrative nature of these texts that prompts us to imagine certain kinds of scenarios. In the case of *In Cold Blood*, readers imagine more than just a news report, say, of the murder of a Kansas farmer, his wife, and two of his four children. The narrative provides the reader with extensive descriptions and accounts of causation, requiring the reader to make certain kinds of inferences about why various events happened and encouraging the reader to imagine the events in a particular way and not in some other way. Capote is even credited with creating a new genre: journalism that exists in the language and structure of fictional literature. It was possibly the first "nonfiction novel" that required its readers to make sense of the text in similar ways as one would a fictional novel, by learning about characters, making inferences, and connecting together the relevant pieces to make sense of a plot. (One of the most powerful inferences in the story is the way that the smell of cigarette smoke lingered in the Clutter household. The daughter who returned home to discover the murder knew something was gravely wrong just because she knew that under no normal circumstance would her parents allow anyone to smoke in their house.) Thus, with *In Cold Blood*, which is ostensibly nonfiction, the reader is supposed to approach it with an attitude of belief while, at the same time, it is written in such a way as to stimulate imagination. For the consensus view this would be problematic, because those two attitudes are mutually exclusive. For Matravers, however, one can easily approach this with an attitude of both belief and imagination. They are not mutually exclusive.

It is relevant here that the kinds of imaginings prompted by narrative are not connected to belief or non-belief or the particular existence of certain events, places, or people, and it does not matter what the intention of the speaker is. The kinds of imaginings prompted by narrative have to do with the kinds of connections between events that allow the story to make sense. What is significant about Lilliputians is not that it is fictional that they are a race of tiny people but that they do things in a particular way that makes coherent sense. Lilliputians contribute to a story line. What is significant about *In Cold Blood* is not that it is true but that it is told in a compelling way that allows the reader to imagine the events in the book as harrowing, gruesome, and described in a way that is convincing, compelling, and coherent. Of course we imagine things we also believe, but what stimulates imagination really well, more often than not, is well-told stories.

4. FICTION AS SUBVERSIVE

I started this chapter with a query about whether or not a children's story was real or not. So how do I move closer to finding a satisfactory answer to my son's question about his book? Having addressed various approaches to fiction and nonfiction, I can now move on to some of the resulting queries about why this matters. What seems to be at stake here could be as insignificant as how we catalogue our books (although that does not really seem all that insignificant), but I believe that there is a larger problem here, as well. The way we define fiction is at the root of several bigger questions. For example, the paradox of fiction hinges on the ways in which we *define* fiction. Discussions of the ontological status of fictional characters depend on how we *define* fiction. And all of the epistemological and moral questions, such as whether or not we can learn from fiction (and if so *what* we can learn), hinge on the definition. Fictionality also plays an integral part in the way in which we approach the question, "Can we be benefited or harmed by reading literature?," as well as the question of whether we can ever make sense of truth *in* fiction or truth *through* fiction. All of these questions necessarily begin with a particular view of fiction on which all their answers depend. But if one changes what it means to be fictional, then the findings prompted by these queries change, too. In order to develop a sense of what constitutes fiction for contemporary readers, I want to look back a bit historically.

Plato introduced us to the question of the subversiveness of narration with his concern about stories being disallowed in the *Republic*, along with his distrust of storytellers more generally. Although he had no notion of fiction per se (he only spoke of falsehoods or lies), he knew of their potentially persuasive powers over both reason and emotion. But at the same time that he warned against the dangers of storytellers, he conveyed his own arguments through story. Socrates did so through dialogue, and Plato did so through both story and parable. What Plato feared was that the narrative elements of a story would entice one away from Truth, or the Forms, and would make a reader more emotional and more likely to be persuaded by manipulation, rhetoric, and nontruths. But he was a rationalist and argued not only that our capacity for reason was the best part of us but also that it was the only means to abstracted Truth. The Truth he describes is one available only to the most abstracting minds and cannot be accessed by those who indulge in representations and *mis*representations of the physical world.

Although Plato did not, in fact, work with our distinction between fiction and nonfiction, had he been familiar with it I think he would have rejected it. He would have argued that all narrative is fiction and that narrative nonfiction as a literary category cannot exist at all. If it is too presumptuous of me to make arguments for Plato, then I will use his inclinations to make my own speculative suggestion: There is no such thing as narrative nonfiction *except* as a genre distinction. In other words, it may be the case that because of the artificially constructed and potentially manipulative nature of the content of such works, the category is essentially meaningless. Worse possibly is that it is just a largely misleading category.

5. TYPES OF TRUTHS

Nonfiction implies a direct relationship with truth: some might say belief. But to what does truth in this context refer? Correspondence truth? Coherence truth? Pragmatic truth? Most people generally only mean correspondence truth when they talk about nonfiction and the way it refers. Nonfiction claims a direct, accurate, truthful relationship between what the text describes and reality. But this is, in any meaningful way, unlikely since reality is not storied in the way narrative nonfiction is. Reality, for lack of a better term, arrives in relatively static pieces to our necessarily perspectival minds. *One* of the ways in which we make sense of reality is to construct stories about it. We impose a temporal structure (often eliminating seemingly irrelevant *events*), we eliminate *causes* that we believe not to be important or relevant (or that we choose not to credit), and we *create* plot, drama, narrative arc, suspense, humor, self-serving perspectives, and intention where there may or may not have been any. Nonfictional narratives are often said to be governed by what David Davies calls the "fidelity constraint." As he explains, "the author is presumed to have included only events he or she believes to have occurred."[22] "Having occurred" is here meant to be the same as "true" or "truth." But this goes back to being entirely dependent upon the intention of the author and the likelihood that there is (or can be) a significant or direct correspondence between the narrative and "reality." As nonfictional *narrative* prioritizes narrative and description over correspondence truth claims, narrative aspects end up at a real disadvantage. The narrative aspects, which are not incidental, in a way invalidate the nonfictional status. The relationship between nonfiction and narration is then inherently problematic if nonfiction is assumed to be in some relatively straightforward sense true or accurate, but what is narrated necessarily includes perspective, the inclusion of some facts and the exclusion of others, and the imposition of some sort of narrative structure onto a series of events and descriptions. So the fidelity constraint really has a very limited use in that the narration itself distorts any sort of direct correspondence truth claims. Nonfiction then is, in reality, not just a set of true descriptions, but aims for some sort of true-ish descriptions, or as descriptions accurate as can be, or something entirely different in kind from "fact."

a. Correspondence Truth

One of the ways in which these distinctions get confused is through the simple ways in which we refer to events or sentences being true. It seems a simple matter to say that something is true in the sense only that it "really happened" or in the way in which it corresponds with "reality." Accordingly, the correspondence theory of truth is our most general default theory of truth. According to the correspondence theory, a claim is true if and only if it corresponds to the facts or reality of a situation. It is false if it does not correspond. It then follows that I have true beliefs about a situation if the correspondence holds and false beliefs if the correspondence does not hold. Alternately, the coherence theory of truth states that a statement is true if it is logically consistent with other beliefs that are considered true, and a belief is false if it contradicts beliefs that are considered true. This theory of truth is more useful when more than one state of affairs is involved. For example, if I have a set of beliefs that form the basis of my religious convictions, any single belief that contradicts my other set of beliefs has to be evaluated as being false based on its lack of coherence with my other beliefs, not based on its lack of correspondence with states of affairs in the world. Correspondence theory works well for single and simple propositions that form the basis of what I claim to be true or those beliefs with which others align. For instance, "the cat is on the mat," "the sun is shining," "the month is March" are all easy examples of correspondence-type truths that can easily be checked. Correspondence theory is the default theory that most people use when they talk about truth in reference to the news, history, and science.

b. Coherence Truth

The correspondence theory is a bit loaded though, since the way in which we evaluate our beliefs (or potentially new beliefs) is most often to insist that our beliefs already correspond with the facts of reality. To say about a *narrative* that it is either true or false assumes that we make correspondence-type claims when really we are often making *coherence* claims, thinking (or believing) that we are making straightforward correspondence claims. Coherence can refer to the internal coherence of a narrative, the plot, but it can also refer to the many "truths" that connect it to our other beliefs that we can have about a text. For instance, although I have a correspondence belief about the existence of a woman named Anna Karenina, the belief is that she does not exist. That *kind* of belief is not really that interesting or productive. Much more potentially interesting, I also have *coherence* beliefs about Anna's character and her actions in the novel by the same name. These beliefs include my understanding of how various aspects of the plot are developed, how time is constructed for her, and how she eventually comes to the incredibly painful decision to end her own life. I also have beliefs about what is said to be "true in the fiction," like that Anna was torn between two lives of which she wanted both very badly.

With the basic components of correspondence and coherence models laid out, I would like to unpack these a bit to see how they might help us to address some of the issues with fiction. If I take these two theories of truth also to involve different theories of meaning (and possibly use), I can show that I use both kinds of explanations in different ways to describe the ways in which I interact with our world. For my purposes here I will refer to correspondence and coherence as theoretical *models* rather than mutually exclusive theories of truth. I do not see it as problematic to suggest that we use correspondence and coherence models for complementary purposes, and since this is not a strict epistemological argument, the form of *models* is more descriptive of what I am actually trying to describe. A problem arises, however, when I unknowingly mistake correspondence for coherence truth claims and justify our beliefs as such. The correspondence model does more than merely connect a belief about the truth of something to some external situation that may or may not be the case. In addition, it allows us to posit an externalist account such that there is a clear distinction between what is "in here" in my mind and "out there" in reality. The correspondence model forms a relationship between my belief in some truth and a specific state of events in the physical world. The correspondence model allows us to be able to make clear dichotomies between true and false, fiction and nonfiction, and accurate and inaccurate statements. It is this model that gives rise to other kinds of strict dichotomies that in turn produce paradoxes such as the paradox of fiction. When the correspondence model is used as the default model in common language it forces us into these dualistic ways of thinking about our beliefs and reality. Using this kind of framework, of course, the affective element of engaging with fiction certainly looks inconsistent, incoherent, and irrational. If I respond emotionally to things that I do not have correspondence beliefs about, then that external world we are trying to match our beliefs to is not really there in any meaningful sense and does not react to *us*.

What a coherence model does, on the other hand, is to get rid of the need for an absolute metaphysical and ontological distinction and offers some possible blurring of the lines between truth and falsity and fiction and nonfiction. The coherence model of truth nicely accords with the narrative connection and the narrative-type grammars that many fictions follow. When I read narrative fiction I do not merely think about what is the case, such as whether it is "in here" (story) and "out there" (external reality). I think about not only the ways in which the story makes consistent sense internally but also the ways in which I make sense of our own storied, narrativized worlds of explanations. In order to do this, I can recognize the real possibility of our own sense of "self" being deeply narrative.[23] If I can do this, then the fact that I respond emotionally to narrative fiction is not surprising or irrational. Instead, it is a natural extension of the ways in which I create a sense of self through the stories we tell of ourselves and how we understand ourselves in terms of temporality and relation. Hearing and telling stories about ourselves relates directly to reading the stories about fictional others. Although the fictional others do not have existential reality, the narrative explanations that are involved in both processes are hard to deny.

6. A THEORY OF NONFICTION

Up to this point, I have laid out some of the problems with the ways in which we characterized our engagement with fictions. In particular, I have criticized a very reductionist trend that tends to characterize that which is fictional only, or primarily, in terms of fictional sentences or single propositions. I am also very critical of the reductionist tendency to make what is "fictional" into that which is "false" or merely "not true." The reality of the situation, however, could not be further from the ways in which we have set up the problem. What I want to do next is build a case that accounts for the legitimacy of our engagement with fictional *and* nonfictional literature, based on a more subjective interpretation of what counts as true and a broader explanation of the ways in which we construct belief and worldview—a case that argues that the ways in which we construct and thereby understand fiction is mutually determined by the ways in which we construct and understand nonfiction. I want to outline what a "theory of nonfiction" might look like.

If I were to describe a theory of nonfiction that looks like a complimentary account to the theories of fiction, it might look like this: Parallel to Walton's theory would be a "reality theory" as opposed to a pretense theory. The modifier "it is fictional that" becomes "it is true that." It is a *truth* modifier rather than a *fiction* modifier. Or the modifier might be "it is nonfictional that" or "it is verifiable that" or "it really happened that." But none of these modifiers sound all that appealing since none of them capture an alternate attitude to pretense. Rather, they all focus on the *truth* aspect of the *content* of the narrative. I could go with the intention approach—that which is nonfictional is anything intended to be nonfictional. But that does not sound right, either. My intentions in this case must measure somewhat reliably between narrative and reality. Intending something to be true can likely fail in all sorts of ways, intentionally or unintentionally. More generally, the fictional utterance model could be applied to nonfiction by maintaining nonfiction in a particular storytelling tradition. The boundaries of nonfictional literature would then be anything, perhaps, that worked as nonfiction or was accepted as nonfiction. Both of these accounts, seen primarily as counterparts to theories of fiction, are unsatisfactory because neither of them addresses the truth status of the actual story. A theory of nonfiction must address the relationship between story and reality as being one of strong veracity and reliability. A theory of nonfiction says that nonfiction starts in a particular storytelling tradition, it fits into a particular standardized genre, but it also goes beyond that. The narrative must align with reality in some verifiable ways. Nonfictional narrative is riveted to reality in ways not only that are reasonable even if we never fact-check but also in ways that we *can* fact-check. It should be plausible or believable. It must *aspire* to be true, but not in the way that propositional statements can be true, since propositional statements rely primarily on their correspondence character. Facts are always true in context—in relationship to other facts and in relationship to time and place. Stories are true and stories are nonfictional in context, as well. Nonfiction must not just be "supposed that" or "imagined that" or even "believed that." Nonfictional literature must "advance that" or "claim that" or "attest that" or say "it happened that." Nonfictional literature must convince its readers that "it happened this way" and not some other way. Nonfictional literature makes arguments for its particular view of "what happened." The author and the work must jointly testify that the story maps onto reality in ways that can be substantiated. This is no easy task for narration, since I take the narration itself to make stories opaque. But literary nonfiction is not just about *retelling* "what happened." We have journalism and history for that.

Nonfiction as a genre is relevantly *literary*. Martha Nussbaum has shown us how "with respect to any text carefully written and fully imagined, an organic connection [exists] between its form and its content."[24] While she is primarily concerned with the style differences between philosophy and fiction, she rightly points out that different styles are often associated with different kinds of contents and that form and content cannot easily be separated. Thus, since fiction and nonfiction both adhere to generally the same literary style (they do not necessarily, but they share it at least more commonly than with philosophical prose, poetry, or history, presumably), the content might be relevantly similar. Perhaps this is accurate, but not necessarily. What does happen necessarily with nonfiction is that our expectations as readers are changed. The standards are different. We desire transparency where we may never find it. The genre of nonfiction promises something it can never deliver in full but only with verisimilitude. Whereas we expect fiction to be constructed intentionally, with the story elements applied in ways in which we make sense of the form we are accustomed to, nonfiction struggles with this a bit more. If we take Nussbaum's explanation of the relationship between form and content to be one that holds, I might have to return to the claim that literary nonfiction is not a category distinction we can defend at all. It might be said to be an oxymoron, reducible to something like "assembled truth." *Nonfictional content* cannot have a *literary form,* because the ways in which we develop story are contrary to the ways in which we describe truth or reality. But whether or not I am philosophically opposed to the category designation, it remains a meaningful designation for cataloguing, and it is one that is appealing to readers.

7. TRUE STORIES

So what do I tell my son about his book? Is the story of *Stone Soup* real or not? I do not think it happened, but that is not to say that it couldn't have happened. Hopefully, in many places, events like that happen, where communities come together and individuals contribute to make big communal pots of soup. But that is not really satisfactory and not really the point. Indeed we may never have a satisfactory answer to the question "Is the story true?" because *truth* cannot be a modifier of *story* in the ways that we want it to be. Stories are constructions, and even the ones that are connected to reality in part cannot be said to be true in the sense in which we might seriously employ the notion of truth.

Aestheticians are interested in this notion of fiction and our interest in fictional literature as a phenomenon. How is it different from truth? How do our beliefs about it differ from our beliefs about real events? How do our emotions in response to fictional intentional objects compare with emotional responses to real events, whether those emotions are real, genuine, as if, quasi, or the same as our responses to so-called real events? We wonder whether or not there are any real epistemic benefits or whether there is nonpropositional knowledge that we might gain from reading fiction. But it strikes me that while we have spent much time thinking about what makes something fictional and how we respond to things presented *as fiction*, we have spent less time looking at the ways in which we understand and respond to nonfiction, in particular literary nonfiction. When we talk about the ways in which we understand, comprehend, or respond to a work, we assume that the norm is that we only respond to what we believe to be true. As we write about our responses to fiction and the fictionalized we assume that this is *not* normative—that our responses to the fictional are an aberration of some sort. It is as if, when we respond to fiction, we are doing something irrational or incoherent, as Colin Radford has famously argued.[25] But for those outside of the realm of philosophy, and often those who are outside of the realm of aesthetics, the fact that we respond emotionally to fiction is hardly a paradox and hardly even all that curious. It is certainly not characterized as irrational—it is just part of our everyday experience. We have turned a seemingly normal response into a philosophical puzzle that is really only puzzling to us. But in fact, although philosophers have spent decades trying to disprove this claim by explaining (and explaining away) our seemingly irrational or odd responses to fiction, I do not take our responses to fictional works to be all that odd or irrational, primarily because we are engaged cognitively and emotionally in reading both fiction and nonfiction through narrative constructions. Narrativized events are necessarily understood in different ways than singular or individual events, and the narrativization trumps, in most cases, the truth status of the story. If one is asked outright if they *believe* the fictional characters that they are moved by are *real* or if the story is *true*, most readers would readily admit that they do not *believe* and the story is not *true*. But belief and truth are hardly the most relevant factors when one engages with a *story.*

8. IS THERE A PARADOX OF FICTION?

With the standard theories of fictionality, as well as many of the accounts that attempt to resolve the paradox of fiction, many have appealed to a reductionist theory of fiction (one that in practice equates fiction with falsity or lies) as well as a reductionist theory of existential belief. What we end up with is an account that reduces our emotional responses to engaging with fictional literature into a *reductio ad absurdum* argument. The emotion that we experience as a result of engaging with fiction, or the knowledge we might gain from engaging with fictional literature, has been treated as if it is merely an aberration from what should happen under *normal* circumstances. The question the paradox presumes is that there are correct ways in which to engage with literature, which I question myself.

As the paradox of fiction has been classically constructed and discussed, the reductionist version has condensed our enjoyment of literature, of reading, of engagement with well-constructed and interesting fictional worlds. So the paradox as it is constructed is a paradox of the singular fictional sentence or proposition (or utterance), which almost has to be taken as a mere falsehood or lie (as constructed) or as a proposition of nonbelief. As it is typically stated, the paradox of fiction reduces extended narratives into individual lies and falsehoods, and then we attempt to resolve the paradox, defending our own intuitive sense that engaging with fiction is not irrational or inconsistent. For example, the paradox of fiction is generally presented as three ostensibly reasonable but internally inconsistent premises:

1. In order to have real emotional responses we must believe that the people and situations in question really do exist or did exist at one time.
2. When we engage with fictional texts, we do not believe that the events or characters really do exist or did exist.
3. Fictional characters and situations do incite (seemingly) real emotional responses.

Those who attempt to resolve the paradox generally approach it as having to take the premises as they are, and they try to show how one of the three premises is false. What I want to suggest is that the terms "fictional" and "belief" are both being used in overly simplistic ways, ways that have little or nothing to do with the ways in which we engage with narrative. The paradox forces us to make incoherent arguments. As I said above, it makes the issue of our responses to fiction (aka here, "lies" or "objects of nonbelief") into something curious and potentially irrational. The paradox really resembles something more like this:

1. Real emotions must be prompted by existential belief or real intentional objects.
2. The definition of what is fictional depends on the lack of existential belief or in fictional intentional objects.
3. Fictional characters are things we do not have existential beliefs about.

It is no wonder that we cannot seem to justify our emotional responses to fiction when things are defined this way. According to this, it would be "inconsistent, incoherent and irrational" for us to have emotional responses to fictional intentional objects.[26] But we do not need to define fiction merely or predominantly in terms of our lack of existential belief. Narratives have more to them than just belief or disbelief.

When philosophers address the question of how it is that we can reasonably have real emotional responses to stories we know are fictional, they tend to focus only on the fiction/nonfiction or truth/false distinction. The underlying premise of the paradox of fiction lies with the assumption that there is a clear distinction between what is true and what is false within the context of a storied narrative. There is another underlying assumption that there is some sort of clear ontological distinction between what is real and what is fictional, when in fact the constructed plots of both true and fictionalized stories invalidate that clear distinction. The problem with this is that, in understanding the ways in which I perceive our emotional responses to narrative, the focus should not simply be on what is true or false but on the conceptual ways in which I come to comprehend the constructed narrative itself. That is, the fiction/nonfiction distinction is significantly less important than the distinction of narrative/nonnarrative. The ways in which I understand narrative complicate the fiction/nonfiction distinction such that the two issues cannot be easily disconnected.

What we think of when we think of nonfiction is truth, but truth is never all that direct or clear. The question "what *is* truth?" begs an answer in the form "truth is X," but at the same time no answers in that form have ever really been found to explain the nature of truth or what we really want to express with the term. No answer has been able to successfully evade circularity or counterexamples. Philosophers have described truth as that which corresponds to the facts of a situation, that which is provable, that which has practical utility, or that which has some sort of stable consensus. Some philosophers have suggested that absolute truth is impossible to attain or comprehend, and others say that the only way to make meaning of it is to insist that it fits one of the common definitions. But as philosophers sometimes miss the trees while looking for the forest, we also ignore the ways in which people actually use the term. There is no denying that people speak meaningfully of literary truth, journalistic truth, emotional truth, religious truth, and many others. Presumably, these varied kinds of truth all appeal to some meaningfully relevant set of standards. Presumably, although the standards for each kind of truth are different, the appeals to the notion of truth should be the same. So I ask a very Socratic kind of question: If all of these are indeed *kinds* of truth, then what is that essential nature that underlies all of them? Certainly the term refers to some kind of static relationship or ideal. Hopefully, this ideal is somewhere involved in my question about nonfiction.

In this chapter I have tried to lay some of the groundwork for an explanation about the current state of the philosophical literature concerning fiction and nonfiction. What I hope I have provided is not so much a clear conclusion about it, but rather a demonstration of the ways in which fiction is treated as something too abstract about which to make definitive claims and of how narrative nonfiction, or literary non-fiction, is inherently problematic because of its necessarily perspectival and constructed nature. The philosophical literature has, to this point, abstracted the idea of fiction to such an extreme that it is completely separated from the process of reading. "Fiction" does not even refer to a particular text *per se* but to an abstract notion of something merely imaginary. These issues pose problems for aestheticians dealing with abstract issues concerning our relationship with fiction. I am more interested in the way the act of reading itself allows one to literally make sense of a fictional world, how reading skills and fluency change the possibilities of the impact of a certain text, and how habitual reading develops the ways in which one sees the construction of meaning inside and outside of a text.

NOTES

1. John Searle, "The Logical Status of Fictional Discourse," in *Expression and Meaning: Studies in the Theory of Speech Acts* (Cambridge: Cambridge University Press, 1979), 70–73.

2. Kendall Walton, *Mimesis as Make Believe: On the Foundations of the Representational Arts* (Cambridge, MA: Harvard University Press, 1990), 70–73.

3. Walton, *Mimesis as Make Believe*, 72.

4. Walton, *Mimesis as Make Believe.*

5. Thanks to Stacie Friend for that great terminology of "Walt-fiction."

6. Greg Currie says that a work is fiction "if (a) it is the product of a fictive intent and (b) if the work is true then it is at most accidentally true." See: Gregory Currie, *The Nature of Fiction* (Cambridge: Cambridge University Press, 1990), 46.

7. Walton, *Mimesis as Make Believe*, 11.

8. Walton, *Mimesis as Make Believe*, 38.

9. Walton, *Mimesis as Make Believe*, 42.

10. Walton, *Mimesis as Make Believe*, 40.

11. Walton, *Mimesis as Make Believe*, 72.

12. Olsen, Stein Haugom, and Peter Lamarque, *Truth, Fiction and Literature* (Oxford: Oxford University Press, 1997), 32.

13. Olsen, and Lamarque, *Truth, Fiction and Literature*, 32.

14. Olsen, and Lamarque, *Truth, Fiction and Literature*, 34.

15. Currie, *Nature of Fiction*, 18.

16. Stacie Friend, "Fiction as Genre," *Proceedings of the Aristotelian Society* 112, no. 2 (2012), 187.

17. Friend, "Fiction as Genre," 203.

18. See Colin Radford, "How Can We Be Moved by the Fate of Anna Karenina?" *Proceedings of the Aristotelian Society,* Supplementary 49 (1975): 67–93.

19. Vladimir Nabokov, *Lolita* (Vintage international: New York, 1955).

20. Although the whole book is largely a rejection of what he calls the consensus view, Matravers first mentions and defines it on page 24 of *Fiction and Narrative* (Oxford: Oxford University Press, 2014).

21. Matravers, *Fiction and Narrative*, 24.

22. David Davies, "Fiction," In Berys Gaut and Dominic McIver Lopes (Eds.), *The Routledge Companion to Aesthetics*, 2nd ed. (London: Routledge, 2002), 266.

23. There are several arguments about the ways in which personal identity and selfhood are constructed narratively. Of particular import see Charles Taylor, *Sources of the Self: The Making of the Modern Identity* (Cambridge, MA: Harvard University Press, 1989) and Alasdair MacIntyre, *After Virtue: A Study in Moral Theory*, 3rd ed. (Notre Dame, IN: University of Notre Dame Press, 2007).

24. Martha Nussbaum, *Love's Knowledge* (Oxford: Oxford University Press, 1990), 4.

25. Radford, "How Can We Be Moved by the Fate of Anna Karenina?," 67–93.

26. Radford, "How Can We Be Moved by the Fate of Anna Karenina?," 75.

Chapter Three

The Boundaries of Genre

Readers often care about one primary distinction before they read—is it fiction or nonfiction? Did it happen or didn't it? Presumably, we need to know if something we read is fiction or nonfiction in order to understand it properly. If we read *Anna Karenina* thinking it is nonfiction, we potentially have a very different reaction to it than if we go in thinking it is fiction. Likewise, if we read something like *Schindler's List* thinking it is fiction, then the reaction we have might not be as emotionally impactful as it would be if we believed it were true. Further, when we read something like the Dr. Seuss book *The Sneetches* (which nicely outlines the dangers of obsessive consumerism and greed), if we know it falls into the genre of moralizing children's fiction, we can take the important moral lesson to heart, have fun reading the book, and simultaneously teach our children the dangers of the need to have stars on our bellies (or whatever manufactured consumer need they beg of that day). As it turns out, cognitively, we do make sense of events we believe happened in a different way than we make sense of the ones that we do not believe happened, and we have different kinds of beliefs that follow from nonfiction than we do in relation to fiction.

As readers, we have a tendency to assume that nonfiction is simplistically true and that fiction is merely that which is false. But it is not necessarily that simple. The hazards that attend the strict binary thinking with which we tend to orient ourselves have long been heralded. But we organize our worlds hastily into black/white, male/female, mind/body, straight/gay, liberal/conservative and our literary works into fiction/

anti-binary?

nonfiction.[1] The habit of dichotomous thinking (or binary thinking) can be very dangerous, though. When we think in this way or make sense of our experiences in this way, we think not just with two distinct categories but also tend to think that one is the norm or the standard or even the good and that the other is the negation or opposite. We do this with grammar, for instance, when we use the masculine pronoun as the standard generic pronoun. When we do this, we assume that by "man" we really mean all people, but we just say man all the time. Only when we specifically say woman do we refer to women. But this makes men the standard and women the exception, or the alternate, or the other. When we think that something is *this thing*, it cannot be *that thing*. To be rational is to be not emotional. To be body is to be not mind. To be white is to be not black. And to be fiction is to be not nonfiction. But when we categorize like that we also tend to overlook any sort of nuances, subtleties, or integrated categories. To think of race, for instance, as only blackness or whiteness misses out on all of the mixed race, blended peoples who do not fit nicely into either category. We also neglect all of the aspects of race that do not have anything to do with skin color. So we do ourselves a disservice when we think in exclusive categories with no possibility for blending.

When we think about fiction and nonfiction as the primary categories with which to sort out literature, however, what we might be doing is setting up a dichotomy where there does not need to be one. It might be that fiction and nonfiction are not binaries, not opposites, but merely different genres. But when the boundaries get blurred between fiction and nonfiction, which often occurs in many contemporary works of literature, readers can become unsettled. I think that genre, and even the more broad categories of fiction and nonfiction, should not be found exclusively as properties internal to the text itself. Rather, the way we make sense of genre should be an active process of narrative comprehension. If making sense of genre is something that necessarily involves the reader, then the way in which genre is understood will shift into less strict categories and not be binary at all. I want to question how the particular binary concept of fiction and nonfiction has sold us short concerning the ways in which we make sense of literary texts and how much more fluid our notions of genre really could and should be. I also want to suggest that the reduction of the binary division of genre merely into fiction and nonfiction is a giant oversimplification of the ways in which both genres are understood as well as the ways in which both truth and reference are used with genre.

1. GENRE

In its most general terms, genre is a classification system, and it is not a classification system that has remained the same over several centuries of texts. Poetry, prose, and even Greek plays all used to be catalogued in ways that related to the theme or subject of their plots. But the classification system, almost as soon as it was put into practice, was subject to change because of the new ways in which plays and plots changed throughout history. What seems to be most important about this is that many of the genre categories that we consider most important overlap other genres. These categories rarely remain isolated. Genre can be determined by subject matter, length (as in the case of short stories, novels, or epic poems), content, structure, or methodology, among others. A genre such as horror, for example, can also have multiple and ever-changing subgenres like realist horror, psychological thriller, art horror, comedic horror, and gothic horror. There are dozens of different conceptual maps that diagram how various genres are related to one another. The primary binary idea of genre, however, only allows for two categories: fiction and nonfiction. All other genre descriptions fall under one of those two categories. The binary chart would look something like this:

Fiction	Nonfiction
Fantasy	Memoir
Romance	Creative Nonfiction
Science fiction	Travel Journals
Mystery	(Auto)biography
Thriller	True Crime
Comedy	History
Crime	Food Journal
Horror	
Satire	
Adventure	

The classification system for genre is useful in libraries, bookstores, and presumably for aspiring writers who want to write for a particular audience. Writers know what the standard conventions are of various genres, and readers come to know what to expect, especially in their favorite genres. But something happens that can be unsettling for readers whose expectations are thwarted by mixed styles, confounding structures, and potentially an overabundance of "facts" when one is expecting fiction. If fiction and nonfiction do not conform to the simple binary state that creates the foundation for the taxonomy of literature, then the whole classification system might be less stable than we had hoped. But if we think about genre less as a pure classification system for bookstores and libraries and more as a guide for readers to manage their expectations, it might make sense to make that guide more fluid, descriptive, and comprehensive.

One of the most common indicators of genre is subject matter, but according to Robert Stam, "subject matter is [in fact] the weakest criterion for generic grouping because it fails to take into account how the subject is treated."[2] Westerns, horror, and alien fictions, for example, are all so named because of the kinds of characters, subject matter, or settings they include. But then there are musicals, science fictions, thrillers, and dramas that are not dictated by subject matter but rather by style. Musicals are so called because there is singing in them, not just because they are entertaining or happy. Many musicals are not all happy. *West Side Story*, for instance, is a tragedy, and *Sweeney Todd* is horror, but both are still, at the same time, musicals. Horror fictions (in novel form), on the other hand, might be categorized as horror not because of their content or subject matter but because they are intended to produce a certain kind of emotion in their readers. Noël Carroll makes this argument extensively about horror[3] and adds that both horror and tragedy are so categorized because they evoke certain kinds of related emotions in their readers. That is, horror fictions (novels and films presumably) give audience members the emotion of feeling horror. He calls this "art-horror," as a specific kind of appropriate emotional response to horror fiction. Tragic fiction gives its readers the feeling of tragedy, sadness, or grief. These are appropriate emotional responses to tragedy. In the cases of horror and tragedy, the emotional response helps to inform the way we can talk about the genre, but that obviously does not work in all cases. Musicals, again, do not incite any particular emotion in their viewers but are clearly a meaningful genre distinction that is useful to people. So genre is useful for making general category distinctions, and it helps to align our expectations about how storylines within a text generally function. But genre is not tied to any one set of criteria that determine how all genres function. In fact, many works subscribe to multiple genre standards and then produce mixed genres, which are harder for us to make sense of, such as alien romance novels.

Carroll describes an additional category of what he calls "Junk Fiction"[4] that others before him might have called pulp fiction or genre fiction, which is primarily categorized by its ease of plot complexity and formulaic tendencies. Junk narratives, according to Carroll, are those whose "story dimension is the most important thing about them."[5] These books are plot driven and do not require a huge amount of attention to comprehend what is going on. Character development is thin and description is low, but intrigue is high. These texts mostly make us want to keep asking, "What happens next?" Think about Dan Brown's novel *The Da Vinci Code*, for instance. This is one of the top selling books of all time, but no one praises Dan Brown for descriptive prose or well-developed characters. It is, however, written in such a way that it is easy to read, the end of every chapter (which are standardly only about two or three pages) makes the reader want to jump right into the next chapter, and it is filled with enough intrigue to keep the reader engaged. It is a perfect book to take with you to the beach because it does not require serious concentration to understand the plot. Junk fiction aspires to be a whole genre of page-turning beach books. Romance novels, for instance, especially of the Harlequin variety, offer standard plot developments that include a boy-meets-girl scenario, which inevitably involves some misunderstanding between the boy and the girl. The misunderstandings are resolved, and love endures. There are also often (or always) some really steamy parts that make us want to keep reading and make us want the lovers to choose each other over whatever obstacles they might have in their way. Works like these are plot driven and not generally noted for literary qualities such as complex sentence structure, depth, detail, well-developed characters, or the basis for real textual interpretation. What junk fiction provides are reliable plots that allow us to make regular predictions and to have our predictions realized. As it turns out, being able to make these kinds of regular predictions is very cognitively satisfying to us as readers. If our expectations are frustrated too much, we tend to think the book is not very good.

2. MANAGING OUR EXPECTATIONS

Literary fiction (like novels) and expository nonfiction (like science textbooks or newspapers) can differ with respect to structure, language, topics, and use, among other things. They also differ when it comes to our expectations of fiction and nonfiction as well as our understanding, appreciation, memory retention of details, application to other knowledge we hold, and the way it may or may not alter our beliefs about the world. Fiction and nonfiction also tend to vary based on the subject matter with which they deal. This seems like a potentially problematic distinction to make, but in general fiction tends to deal with social relationships, emotions, the way people face various circumstances, and human (or anthropomorphized) interactions. Nonfiction deals with whatever it is about, whether it is poverty, economics, weight loss, or the Paleo Diet. There are interesting crossovers between these two ways of looking at what we read. Nonfiction can have descriptions of human relationships, and, more interestingly, nonfiction can be written in prose that resembles literary fiction, like in the case of Joan Didion's *The Year of Magical Thinking*. This book is a narrative account (written in narrative prose that is descriptive, emotional, and plot driven) that resembles the form and style of a novel. Didion is actually a well-respected author known for both her fiction and nonfiction writing, but in this particular book she describes only real events in her life. If one did not know they were reading nonfiction, it would be easy to believe it was fiction just because of the writing style, development, narrative arc, and general affect of the work. Thus style, or even narration, does not exclude a work from being nonfiction. In fact, narrative nonfiction, or creative nonfiction, is one of those relatively new genre categories that came about through the acceptance of works that are narrative but that rely on true events and facts.

The genre classification system is one in which we find similarities and differences among texts and categorize them based on these findings. Although genre distinctions are most commonly taught in reference to literary texts, the larger culture itself is where readers begin to learn how to use this classification system. Through our interactions with bookstores, libraries, and even as early as elementary school, genre distinctions are not only completely apparent but are also needed to help physically (and electronically) house and keep track of our books. Even when encountering the confusing world of television, young children learn to navigate through various television programs by beginning to sort programs into rudimentary genres, thus making it easier for them to interpret their shows.[6] However, once readers advance into more complex literary categorizations and are able to unpack the subtleties and nuanced distinctions between different genres, they often find that it is more and more difficult to place a text accurately within just one genre. This is a problem that can take place at the most basic level of choosing whether a text should be considered fiction or nonfiction. After all, just like in the Linnaean Taxonomy used to classify species in biology, it becomes likely that genre species begin to mix and blend. Unlike with biological categories, however, genre distinctions are literary conventions and do not exist empirically or ontologically. That is, genre distinctions do not materialize out of the text with sufficient examination. Rather, genre distinctions are social constructions, and they can change over time as literary conventions blend and adapt. This leads to some theoretical disagreements about the definitions of specific genres. The fact that genre classifications do not exist empirically can lead us to believe that our *perceptions of genres* might even be socially constructed, as well. In their primer about genre theory, Robert Hodge and Gunther Kress suggest that "genres only exist in so far as a social group declares and enforces the rules that constitute them."[7] Even though we categorize genre as a social exercise, I would like to question what the true benefits are of this constant categorization, especially with our favorite binary categories of fiction and nonfiction. Obviously, we need basic categories to help us navigate around the world, and in this case the literary world, but I wonder whether or not some of the deeply ingrained categories are doing some potential damage to our literary expectations. I am not alone in this investigation; there have been several authors known to push the boundaries of genre purposefully for those very reasons. One author who does this, for instance, is Mark Sundeen, who purposefully stretches the constraints of genre by incorporating elements of memoir, journalism, fiction, and travel log in his book *Car Camping*. He first published this story in a nonfictional magazine and then developed it into a book he marketed and sold as fiction (Reader reviews indicate many disappointed readers who thought they were buying a manual on how to go camping in your car.) But Sundeen seems to push boundaries by purposely moving from fiction to nonfiction, from journalism to memoir, and by adding a relatively misleading title. The book itself in its fiction version is a well-developed account of his experiences, written in narrative prose, but it includes many incidents that really did happen. Readers just do not know which events are true or how they were woven into the story.

Another interesting example of confounding expectations is Yann Martel's book *Self.* (Martel is also the author of the more well-known

Life of Pi.) The book reads as a relatively straightforward autobiography of the author. Given the information on the back cover, it seems that the basic facts fit the story of the author. The description on the back cover questions what the line is between autobiography and fiction and where the line is between male and female. There is no clear genre listed and there is no Library of Congress designation. The book opens with a relatively straightforward autobiography. I did not much like it, but I had picked the book up in a lending library when I was traveling, and I did not have very many other choices. Midway through the book, the narrator is all of a sudden a woman. And she was a woman who menstruated, became pregnant, and suffered sexual trauma. I became very intrigued. The experiences of the male narrator influenced the experiences of her as a woman. What was, I thought, an autobiography turned out to be very much a novel, but with no possibility for the reader to know in advance (at least without the help of the internet). I was traveling with no access to the internet, and all I had was the book to guide me. The novel grapples with the construction of sexuality, the development of the self, and the attempt the narrator makes to deal with evil (rape) and faith. Reading the novel this way, without prior knowledge, was relatively confusing to me. I did not know how to manage my expectations properly. When the narrator suddenly was speaking from the perspective of a menstruating woman, I looked back through the book looking for signs to help me make sense of things. Knowing that Martel was the son of Canadian diplomats led me to believe that he was the narrator. Part of the success of the novel is precisely that it is written (successfully) as an autobiography. But the unanticipated plot twists make it an even more successful fiction.

There are genres that seem to hover in between the so-called, clean-cut genres of fiction and nonfiction—those that might begin to blend into one another. I am thinking of works that fall loosely into categories like historical fiction, (auto)biography, memoir, essay, lyric essay, journalism, New Journalism, documentary, autofiction, faction, and other kinds of narrated works that straddle the amorphous line between nonfiction and fiction.[8] What is distinctive about these is that they all aspire to have some accurate representation of real or actual events. Presumably, the accuracy of the representation of people and events described in nonfiction is one of the key elements that allows these to be categorized as nonfiction at all, since it is not simply discursive prose. Other important elements also include specific kinds of narration and narrators, plot developments, story structure, and various kinds of descriptions of people, places, and events. But confusion can set in when the story elements or the literary elements we are most familiar with, which readers associate with fiction, are also used with true stories.

Genre is not dictated exclusively by subject or theme or content, but it does help readers to know how to interpret, evaluate, and properly manage expectations of a text. If I anticipate a horror fiction and end up reading a psychological thriller, I am bound to be disappointed and think that the work was not as successful as I might have thought otherwise. If I read something I believe is nonfictional and it turns out to be fictional, I am not merely disappointed. I feel duped, and I have to actively rework things I believed to be true into categories of fiction. This is often extremely unsettling. For example, when people found out that certain parts of James Frey's memoir, *A Million Little Pieces*, contained fabricated and exaggerated plot points, readers were so upset that they filed a class action law suit against him to get their $13.95 back (and they won!). Conversely, as with *The Da Vinci Code*, readers are upset by the fact that too many details are accurate, even though the work is classified as fiction, and the author says clearly on his website and in the preface to the book that it is a novel and a work of fiction. In this case, however, the blending of the fictional with the factual caused an outpouring of nonfictional responses to the book, debunking the so-called assertions made in *The Da Vinci Code*. Often, in cases like this, readers can become mistrusting of authors and might dismiss several works by that author. Unfortunately, this happens despite the fact that much might be gained aesthetically and literarily from reading those works.

American essayist John D'Agata, for example, has taken liberties with his work, which he plainly admits to, and has changed "facts" about what he has written that he believes betters the literary quality of his writing. D'Agata describes himself as an essayist but writes what would normally be considered both fiction and nonfiction. Other essayists dismiss his work, as they find him not as respectful to the genre as they think he should be. D'Agata wrote an essay about a teenager who committed suicide in Las Vegas by jumping off the Stratosphere Tower. He submitted it to *Harper's Magazine*, but it was rejected because it took too many liberties with the story and because the descriptions

contained in the account were *too literary*. Because of all of the questions of fact, description, and liberties that D'Agata took with the story,
he and Jim Fingal, his fact-checker, ended up publishing a whole book
that sketches out the boundaries that both of them felt (*The Lifespan of
a Fact*). The book outlines, quite literally, the fact-checking and editing
process. Each page of the book contains a small portion of D'Agata's
story surrounded by Fingal's questions of fact as well as all of the
details that he was able to confirm. For instance, D'Agata writes, "It
was Saturday and hot and the wind was blowing hard but did not come
in the house." Fingal writes "**it was Saturday** . . . Since the piece seems
to imply that the person who called John was Levi Presley and that he
did so on the day Presley dies, I can confirm that indeed this was a
Saturday."[9] Fingal continues ". . . **the wind was blowing hard but did
not come in the house**. I've already established this to be imprecise,
as there was no heavy wind that evening at the time of Levi Presley's
death, which is when John was supposedly working on the [suicide]
hotline."[10] The entire book continues in this fashion, with Fingal questioning and confirming every sentence, every claim, and every description that D'Agata makes. Some replies are about specific inaccuracies
in the story, about how many bars there are in Las Vegas, the exact
number of seconds it took for Levi Presley to fall to his death, and how
much concrete there is in Vegas. But the interesting struggle between
author and fact-checker is about style, genre, description, and how that
impacts the story, and whether it counts as nonfiction. There is also a
good bit of name-calling between the two. It is eminently clear that the
two are extremely frustrated with each other and that their expectations
of the other are out of line throughout the entire work. The question
looms through the whole book as to whether D'Agata, an essayist, is
even capable of writing something that could be classified as nonfiction. Some of the more interesting exchanges include things like Fingal
saying: "he's manipulating what this guy actually said in order to create a literary effect, which apparently is allowed among the writers of
John's non-journalistic literary genre—for which he apparently writes
all the rules."[11] D'Agata responds, "I'm not sure how I can say this so
that you understand, Jim, because it doesn't seem to be getting across
to you. But one more time for the record: I am not a journalist: I'm an
essayist. OK? And this is a genre that has existed for a few thousand
years. (Ever heard of Cicero?) So these 'rules' that I'm working under
are not mine, but rather were established by writers who recognized a

difference between the hard research of journalism and the kind inquiry of mind that characterizes the essay, an inquiry that's propelled by lots of different sources simultaneously—including science, religion, history, myth, politics, nature, and even the imagination. So there's a bit more freedom in essaying than there is in reportage."[12] Their banter is fun in parts and downright ugly elsewhere, but the book is a brilliant example of the tension that is drawn between facts and stories.

D'Agata and Fingal pose an interesting case study of the stringency of the rules surrounding journalism or perhaps even nonfiction. But this case also gives us great insight into where and why these rules exist and also where they bend and blend into other genres. If we think of fiction and nonfiction as binaries, then there can be no blending. If we take the essay to be an example of the ways in which certain genres borrow from one another, then we might be able to move away from the strict binary thinking of a two-system party. That is, if we do not assume the one-drop rule applies to fiction and nonfiction then we do not have to assume that nonfiction is the *pure* version of journalism, truth, and what really happened. It is what we associate with belief (by consensus). One drop of fiction taints the whole work. But as with race, this does not really work with genre either. It makes no sense to say that genres cannot be blended; we blend them all the time. We need a different binary.

3. CATEGORIZING AND BLENDING GENRES

If genres are not static but created at least in part by our interactions with them, then it makes even more sense to think of them as blended. My inspiration for the notion of genre-bending derives from gender-bending, where one actively resists or rebels against the standard male/female gender norms. One who is a gender-bender is someone who seeks to define gender outside of the standard, socially constructed gender-binary categories of man/woman or masculine/feminine. Men gender-bend by wearing feminine clothing or makeup or walking or sitting in more feminine ways. Women gender-bend by dressing or carrying themselves in a more traditionally masculine manner or acting out more typically masculine characteristics like being aggressive, assertive, or using harsher language than might be expected of women.

How then, do *genres* bend or blend? Genre-bending happens when one genre includes nonstandard features of that genre but does not

fundamentally transform it. An example of genre-*bending* (a less fundamental transformation than blending, I think) would be a horror movie
that has elements of science fiction but where the two genres have no
logical inconsistencies in the ways in which they are woven together.
Genre-blending, on the other hand, goes a step further, as the blended
incorporates elements that change the genre more fundamentally. The
lyric essay, for example, does this by including poetic literary elements
and style that are not traditionally found in a nonfictional essay. This
presents potential problems, however, since presumably fiction and
nonfiction cannot coexist within the same text. Fiction and nonfiction
cannot be bent or blended. Fiction and nonfiction are both generally
bound by a set of literary and appreciative conventions. My account
acknowledges that the two genres can work together without inconsistency, with the end result as a form of genre-blending.

Kendall Walton provides a nice framework that helps to identify the
appreciative categories with which we tend to identify certain kinds
of works of art. I will use it here to help explain how genre-blending
might work. In his classic article "Categories of Art," Walton argues for
an anti-intentionalist account of the way in which we best appreciate
aesthetic properties. An intentionalist might suggest that the best way to
appreciate an artwork is to understand what the artist intended the work
to mean, what the proper representational structure is, or that all of the
aesthetic properties (the qualities that make it aesthetically interesting
or important) in a work of art are discoverable through observation,
even though some observation might require specialty training to be
able to detect them. Basically, an intentionalist argues that the aesthetic
properties are *in* the work and should be discernable by an observer.
Walton argues against this form of intentionalism by positing his
account that aesthetic properties are based not merely by what is *in* the
work of art, but by properties that are gestalt, or emergent, that generate
out of the work.[13] Sentimentality, for instance, might be a descriptor of
a story, but it is not something inherent in the text, it is something that
emerges from the work as a whole.

Walton suggests that there are three nonaesthetic properties that can
help us navigate how we make sense of the categories of art that allow
us as experiencers of art to best appreciate a work. He states that "what
aesthetic effect [the artwork] has on us, how it strikes us aesthetically
often depends in part on which of its features are standard, which variable and which contra standard *for us*."[14] Walton wants to account for

proper appreciation of works in terms of different kinds of representation. He also wants to understand works and our appreciation of them as distinct from their histories as well as from any stated or implied intention that we might have from the artist about the work. He believes that people need to be able to appreciate and understand a work in different ways than just what the author intended. He also emphasizes the "for us" because all appreciation will not be the same for every observer, in different cultures, and in different historical periods. Walton explains that "a feature of a work of art is standard with respect to a (perceptually distinguishable) category just in case it is among those in virtue of which works in that category belong to that category—that is, just in case the lack of that feature would disqualify, or tend to disqualify, a work from that category."[15] With literary fiction, the standard features of a work would be that it is something to be imagined, it is intended to be imagined by the author, it is written in prose, it has a tendency to be worldbuilding, and it often gives insight into the human psyche.[16] Literary nonfiction, on the other hand, although it is also written in prose, is generally understood as something to be believed, and it is intended to represent reality. A feature is variable, Walton says, "with respect to a category just in case it has nothing to do with works' belonging to that category; the possession or lack of the feature is irrelevant to whether a work qualifies for the category."[17] A variable feature of literary fiction is that it is a Western or a romance, that it is a realist novel or an essay, that it makes allusions to other works, or that it might be postmodern in that it is self-conscious or self-referential by making reference to its own narrative structure. These features vary from work to work, but the presence of these features does not exclude the work from any particular category. Variable features of literary nonfiction might also have to do with form. The work might be a news article or a biography, it might include footnotes or it might not, but these features do not exclude the work from the category. A contra-standard feature has to do with the *absence* of a standard feature with respect to that category, that is, a feature whose presence tends to disqualify works as members of the category.[18]

The descriptions of standard, variable, and contra-standard are useful here because they help us recognize typical features of a particular kind or category (as Walton might say) or of a given genre. As readers, we need to know in some general terms what to look for and what to expect in order to make sense of the text. One of the pleasures we derive from

reading stems largely from being able to make predictions about the kind
of things that the characters will do. One of the things genre categories do
is help us to make the right kind of predictions. For instance, if I am reading a romance, I predict and anticipate certain kinds of behaviors from
the characters, especially those having to do with gender roles. I know
that women tend to get saved by men and that there will likely be some
sort of misunderstanding that will have to be sorted out. I know that most
misunderstandings do get sorted out so that there is a happy resolution in
the end. A large part of our satisfaction from making sense of narrative is
being able to make these kinds of predictions and having them satisfied
by the story. I will not be satisfied by my predictions if I come across
contra-standard features for my narrative. That is, if I am reading what
I take to be a romance, but then the inevitable misunderstanding involves
not the protagonist's best friend but rather an invading race of aliens,
I will be thrown from the story and my enjoyment will be diminished.
This contra-standard feature makes it difficult for me to comprehend,
understand, and make accurate predictions about the kind of work that
I think I am reading. The conventions of genre are neither set in stone nor
so variable that they can accept any convention. Genres bend.

Walton's categories are useful then, in helping me to show how
functional categories of genre work when talking about genre *merely* as
literary convention. What happens, however, when genre is moved to
the more abstract level of just fiction and nonfiction? It is my contention that none of the features (standard, variable, or contra-standard)
are, in fact, necessarily tied to either category of fiction or nonfiction.
The features regularly associated with the two categories are all nonessential. For example, footnotes, perhaps standard with nonfiction, can
be the variable with fiction, but they are not necessarily contra-standard,
which would eliminate a work with footnotes from the category of fiction. The one possible sticking point is when a work said to be nonfictional has too many elements that are standard with fiction, especially
that it has too many untrue parts. There are dozens of books that are
nonfictional but written in the style of a (fictional) novel. Truman
Capote's *In Cold Blood*, for example, and James Baldwin's *Notes of
a Native Son* are both examples of nonfiction, in which the prose is
essentially indistinguishable from fictional prose. The genre of literary
nonfiction indicates more of a way of approaching a text than a property
of the text itself, since the form and style of the text give no clues that it
is something fundamentally different from a fictional novel.

like Waltons Cat[egories]
a way of approaching not a feature of the work

4. BLENDING IN ACTION

I want to return here to Stacie Friend's contextual approach to understanding genre. She says that most genres "are determined by a variety of non-essential conditions, including contextual and historical conditions."[19] Before diving into particular examples, it would be prudent to take a moment to reflect on the "rules" that govern our biases in evaluating whether something is "fiction" or "nonfiction." In general, fictional works are texts in which there is the abundant use of figurative language, varied organizational styles, and character and plot development. Documentation is neither needed nor relevant, and narrators are usually found along the way. It is basically set up for the world of the imagination. Rules that dictate nonfiction include works based on what the author believes or asserts to be true. There is clarity and directness in the language that the author uses, they are usually organized in a straightforward fashion, and nonfictions provide documentation where there might be question. Although these rules appear to be clear, the reality is that they are not as clear as they appear. These general characterizations are often bent and blended and can produce texts that can easily fit into both fiction and nonfiction. Platonic forms of fiction and nonfiction would be nice, but none are forthcoming (despite the fact that Plato is granted as making the first genre discrimination between poetry, prose, and drama). Further, style and form are no longer reliable ways of determining genre.

a. Example: *The Brief Wondrous Life of Oscar Wao*

One example that straddles this fiction/nonfiction divide is Junot Díaz's fictional novel *The Brief Wondrous Life of Oscar Wao* (*Oscar*). I will show here how this text not only straddles traditional subject and style genre barriers but how it can straddle both fiction and nonfiction. On the publication page, the Library of Congress asserts (as it does with all novels): "This is a work of fiction. Names, characters, places, and incidents are either the product of the author's imagination or are used fictitiously, and any resemblance to actual persons, living or dead, business establishments, events, or locales is entirely coincidental."[20] I find this statement problematic because it contradicts what is, in fact, in this text. I understand this is a standard disclaimer, presumably given for legal purposes, but what interests me is that this particular book (and perhaps many others catalogued as fictional) contains numerous true historical accounts. This book deals directly with an important part of Dominican history and the historical, cultural, and individual identity of its citizens. It is peppered with historical accounts of the tyrannical Dominican dictator Rafael Leónidas Trujillo Molina who ruled from 1930 to 1961 when he was assassinated.

Oscar could be taken merely as fiction. Walt-fiction suggests that I can use this as a prompt for imagination, and I can focus on the ways in which I am incited to make-believe the story of Oscar. Gregory Currie might tell us that since the authorial intent (assumed on the cover) is to be taken as fictional, I can just use it to incite fictional imaginings.[21] Both of these approaches are reasonable, but it seems to do this particular book a disservice to leave it at that. Díaz uses literary techniques that mirror those of comic books, science fiction, and Caribbean literary styles (specifically magical realism). The plot line about Oscar himself is presumably fictional, as well. So I should just take it as fiction. Upon closer analysis, however, there is an abundance of accurate history as well as an attempt to rewrite Trujillo's devastating reign. This seems to me more than a coincidental insertion of incidentally true facts that many fictional works include. But this is not historical fiction. In this case it seems to change the nature of the work into something potentially genre-blended. It arrives in the package of fiction, but the essence and details of the text are, at base, nonfictional. The nonfictional elements are not incidental; they are a significant part of the work. The nonfictional elements do not merely provide a framework within which to tell a story (like much historical fiction might), but they change the nature of the story told in a more fundamental way. Because *Oscar* is about diaspora, self-identity, and national identity, the historically accurate framework of the story allows this "novel" to blend into something other than mere fiction. It carries not only the appeal and ease of a novel but also the power and impact of a survivor's testimony.

Díaz also uses multiple references to comic books as well as many comic book plot devices. This narrative is loaded page after page with thinly veiled allusions to comic books and other formulaic science fiction works. Monica Hanna, writing about historiographies in *Oscar*, goes so far as to suggest that the four main characters in this work actually mirror the Fantastic Four.[22] Given this, in line with the assumption that character and narrative are made for each other,[23] it is safe to say that the plot structure of *Oscar* could also be considered a superhero story. Instead of the final product of *Oscar* being read as what Carroll would call a "Junk Fiction," Díaz goes beyond this formulaic plot structure and incorporates other elements that make this text vastly more complex and more challenging to make narrative sense of.

Louise Rosenblatt suggests that we have what she calls a transactional approach to reading. She argues that there is a continuum, or range, of ways in which we approach reading. At one end of the continuum is what she calls the "aesthetic," which is reading for sheer pleasure. At the other end is what she calls efferent, which is reading to gain information or meaning. As there could be dozens of different kinds of reading continuums, this one seems to be particularly useful in getting at the levels of seriousness we ascribe to different kinds of reading. This scale might also account for the range of approaches we take toward fiction and nonfiction, assuming we regularly approach fiction as pleasurable and nonfiction as where we go to gain meaning or understanding. How then does this apply to my analysis of *Oscar*? Simplistically, if we take the standard attitude that books labeled fiction are there to provide pleasure, then we could miss or dismiss the insights that this novel provides having to do with historical circumstance and real and perceived options for a life.

The quick read might view *Oscar* as a story about a young man who is obsessed with science fiction and fantasy, who dreams of becoming the "Dominican Tolkien," and who plays the part of "hero" by trying to save a downtrodden girl. Read deeply, on the "efferent" side of Rosenblatt's continuum, in which one reads to gain meaning, Oscar's tale becomes one of migration and finding and creating one's identity within a new culture. More importantly, it is both history and revisionist history, difficult to disentangle for a nonspecialist. Oscar continually struggles not only to identify with his Dominican heritage but also struggles trying to figure out who he is while living in America. This is seen when the narrator, Yunior, comments on how Oscar's "nerdiness" negatively affects him in the Dominican community. Yunior says, "Anywhere else his triple-zero batting average with the ladies might have passed without comment, but this is a Dominican kid we're talking about... [He] was supposed to be pulling in the bitches with both hands."[24] In order to deal with this rejection from his own people, Oscar becomes attracted to American-styled fantasies that give him access to American culture. The key to opening up his love for fantasies derives from his Dominican culture and its implementation of magical realism, which is not only *another* genre but a prominent element that Díaz uses within the text. This plot device is what moves Oscar away from formulaic writing and causes the narrative to experiment with multiple genres, which makes it more complex for a reader to comprehend. It also allows us to work backwards as readers, with the narrative moving from the props used by superhero fiction to finding the truths they represent, just like an extension into magical realism.

Outside the world of comics and Oscar's fantasies, this text can be looked at as simply a rewriting of an unstable Dominican history, in which Díaz gives a voice to the marginalized and traumatized citizens over whom Trujillo ruled. He begins this by layering features of magical realism within the narratives of both Oscar and his family members. According to Hanna, magical realism originated in Latin American literature and was inspired by the "New World that is so different that it appears magical because it does not coincide with European conceptions of reality."[25] Although this literary feature may appear purely as another type of fiction to a Western reader, Hanna emphasizes that "magical realism is the Caribbean mode for understanding and representing history"[26]; therefore, to simply discount this as fiction that holds some aspects of truth seems to become problematic and shortsighted. Traces of magical realism begin at the start of the novel and are threaded throughout. Although there are many moments of magical realism in the novel, there is one primary form of magical realism that Díaz invokes heavily. The first form is that of the "Fukú." The fukú could be simply understood as a curse, but as it is explained in *Oscar*, it is much more than that. It "came first from Africa, carried in the screams of the enslaved . . . just as one world perished and another began; that it was a demon drawn into Creation through the nightmare door that was cracked open in the Antilles. *Fukú americanus*, or more colloquially, fukú—generally a curse or a doom of some kind; specifically the Curse and Doom of the New World."[27] It could be that Díaz uses the fukú as just a plot device (it does seem to be an invention wholly his, which sounds to me an awful lot like "fuck you"). Possibly, but it really seems to indicate a metaphor for Caribbean Diaspora and how that experience is inevitably a curse for those forced to leave their countries. Even the narrator of *Oscar* brings to light the power of fukú by saying, "the fukú ain't just ancient history, a ghost story from the past with no power to scare. In my parent's day the fukú was real as shit, something your everyday person could believe in."[28] The fukú is not just used as a plot device; it is a truthful representation of the ways in which Dominicans make sense of difficult, painful, and sometimes absolutely horrific experiences.

In some ways, *Oscar* has generally followed the rules of a fictional novel; it is imaginative, it uses figurative language, and only with the use of magical realism do I get slightly less realism. All of this changes, however, with one dominant element of nonfiction that Díaz uses: footnotes. Footnotes are traditionally found only in nonfictional texts, typically academic publications where documentation is readily needed, so it is rather curious that they are also used in this book. The footnotes also appear on the page of text, not in the back only for the most serious reader to check. The footnotes themselves denote historically accurate information, but with a twist, from the fictional narrator's bias. They are also not formal, in the sense that one might expect footnotes to be. They do not only reference outside sources using a consistent reference system (although some do). One example in particular is the footnote that describes the dictator Trujillo, "A personaje so outlandish, so perverse, so dreadful that not even a sci-fi writer could have made his ass up. Famous for changing ALL THE NAMES of ALL THE LANDMARKS in the Dominican Republic to honor himself."[29] It is true that Trujillo changed many of the names of landmarks and even cities to honor himself. The use of footnotes clearly depicts a new way to look at history that shows a resistance to the one voice in power and, instead, displays the polyvocality that exists in historical discourse, which this narrative offers. What happens in *Oscar*, though, is an attempt to rewrite history. Even though this text is labeled fiction, it is a different version of history from the perspective of a nonauthoritative voice. With this in mind, Yunior still demands the reader to work and not take his words to be authoritative, especially as he reflects upon Oscar's death: "So which is it? You ask. An accident, a conspiracy, or a fukú? The only answer I can give you is the least satisfying: you'll have to decide for yourself. What is certain is that nothing's certain. I am trawling in silences here. Trujillo and Company didn't leave a paper trail— they didn't share their German contemporaries' lust for documentation."[30] This is a powerful mechanism because it allows readers to reflect about the narrative and make important and grave inferences to the Jewish Holocaust. (Oddly enough, the real Trujillo looked very much like Hitler, choosing to don the toothbrush moustache in a time when it was very recognizable as

Hitler's.) These historical interludes cause readers to choose to believe or not to believe and to be aware of all the facts—those both fictional and nonfictional—that are laid out before them.

So what is the best way to make sense of this work? It is clearly labeled fiction, and those are the rules by which I can *easily* catalogue it. But what about the extensive footnotes that revise the dictatorship of Trujillo? Are the facts of Trujillo's awful dictatorship just now considered true only in the fiction because they were truthfully portrayed within the fiction? I think not, and actually I want to go as far as to say that this type of reading of *Oscar* can prove to be very beneficial as a text that might have a fictional story but one that still accurately shows an outsider's voice within a history of oppression. Certainly many books that are labeled fictional have truths to teach us beyond just the metaphorical and historic.

b. Example: *Fun Home*

Alison Bechdel's *Fun Home: A Family Tragicomic*[31] is another example that shows how genres can be blended and the ways in which the lines between fiction and nonfiction can become blurred. Even its title, "tragicomic," indicates that Bechdel knows full well that she is pushing boundary distinctions from the start. On the back cover it is listed as both memoir and graphic novel, two potentially conflicting styles, especially when it comes to traditional ways of placing and evaluating genres. It has also been called a comic book and a novel, and it has already been made into a very successful Broadway musical. This story is Bechdel's own, about her childhood growing up in the back of a funeral home (that her family referred to as the "fun home"), her coming to grips with her own sexuality as a lesbian, the mystery surrounding her father's death, and the struggles he had with his own sexuality. The structure of *Fun Home* acts as two parallel stories that happen simultaneously, with the graphic image panels telling the stories of the past and the textual narration portraying Bechdel's take on things in the present.

Although *Fun Home* is clearly a nonfictional memoir, there is still a lot of rule-bending that takes place within this text. First of all, the use of graphic images strays far away from the rules and traditions that follow a nonfictional text only being one of words. It is also not organized in an obvious or linear manner, as the reader must jump from the comic strip drawings to the written narration above them. The fact that it is a *graphic* novel is also not to be overlooked. The pictures or panels in the book provide information and insight that the accompanying text does not. The narrative of the book is both nonlinear and repetitive. Themes and events come up multiple times throughout the book, always in light of new information and new perspectives. The book uses the metaphor of architectural structure in the comic panels as well as the story itself. The house is discussed extensively in the story as both shelter and something that needs constant time, attention, and fixing, and it is used as a way for her father to avoid his feelings and his family because he is constantly remaking it. It is clear that he wants to constantly remake himself.

Bechdel's story is also a tangled web of subjects. She tells the story of her father's struggle with his own identity as a homosexual, his presumed suicide (he stepped out in front of a Sunshine bread truck just two weeks after his wife asked him for a divorce), and Bechdel's own struggles coming to grips with her sexual identity. Death is a recurring theme (the family's funeral business sets the scene), as is gender identity. The conflict of the plot is about the relationship between Bechdel and her father. At once a coming-of-age story, it moves seamlessly into Bechdel grappling with her father's life and death. None of these themes in and of themselves make the book particularly genre-blended, but the graphic-pictorial aspect and such a personal memoir is somewhat new. In his *New York Times Sunday Book Review*, Sean Wisley says Bechdel's text is pioneering because it simultaneously pushes "two genres (comics and memoir) in multiple new directions."[32] He also expresses surprise that the book is catalogued as a "graphic novel" since it is no *novel* at all. It is, he says, "a work of meticulous personal reportage."[33] *Fun Home* is an autobiography (but certainly not a chronology), it is a memoir (but graphic because of the meticulously hand-drawn panels), and it is at its core literary, with literary style and multiple (dozens, possibly hundreds) of allusions to other works of literature. Bechdel herself regularly frames her relationship with her father as paralleling Daedalus and Icarus. She simultaneously compares and confuses her childhood home (a Gothic revival home her father kept and repaired meticulously) with the Addams Family house. She includes references to classical literature (*The Great Gatsby*, *Washington Square*, *Portrait of a Lady*, *In Search of Lost Time*, and *The Wind in the Willows*) as well as several classical mythologies (Telemachus, Icarus, and Odysseus). But the story is absolutely, methodically researched, detailed, and accurate. Bechdel writes in the beginning of her book, "I've always been a careful archivist of my own life. . . . I've kept a journal since I was 10. I've been logging my income and expenses since I was 13. . . . All this detritus came in handy as I wrote '*Fun Home*,' as a corrective to the inevitable distortions of memory. I discovered that the actual documentary truth was almost always richer and more surprising than the way I had remembered a particular event. And it was certainly more interesting than any possible way I could have fictionalized it."[34] So the story is accurate, let us say, but the format or framework is one of a comic book. Not something we can take too seriously. Bechdel's book might be one not just of genre bending but one of genre treason.

Part of the interest in this book is because Bechdel is a woman who has been so incredibly successful in the graphic novel genre, which has been traditionally entirely male dominated. Many see this genre merely as glorified comic books, and its authors and readers have been primarily men. Not only was Fun Home a best seller, it was also on many of the best book of 2006 lists and was a finalist for the National Book Critics Circle Award in the memoir/autobiography category. This was a first for a graphic novel. It was given the GLAAD Media Award for outstanding comic book. *Fun Home* was a success in multiple genres.

Part of what makes this book so interesting is the controversy that it has caused, not just because of its mixed genres but because of its themes of homosexuality and identity. Presumably this is because it deals with these in a way that makes that identification acceptable. *Fun Home* was temporarily removed from a public library in Marshall, Missouri, for controversial content. The book was assigned at the College of Charleston in South Carolina in the fall of 2013 for a freshman reading program called College Reads! When the mother of one of the incoming freshmen called to complain, the government decided to take action. The SC state legislature voted to cut $52,000 from College of Charleston's budget, the exact amount needed to fund the reading program. Of course students and alumni protested, but the governor would not veto the budget cut and the school lost funding. People were outraged both by the censorship and the thought that the school might be pushing a "gay agenda" on their incoming freshmen. But part of this controversy was about the fact that this was all coming in such a new format. Why a comic book? Why this kind of nonfiction? They asked. And why do the identity struggles have to be around gay parents and children? South Carolina is a particularly conservative state in the United States, and it is not one that will lightly let these issues be dealt with in publically funded schools. In fact, not only did the money get cut from the college's budget, but according to a subsection in the 2014–2015 budget for South Carolina the College of Charleston had to spend an *additional* $52,000 "for instruction in the provisions and principles of the United States Constitution, the Declaration of Independence, and the Federalist Papers, including the study of and devotion to American institutions and ideals."[35] Presumably this might counteract the literature that lends emotional appeal and maybe even some humor to the author who deals with difficult life circumstances and comes out cheering.

More controversy over this book came when the theatrical version of the book was developed. Broadway has not had huge successes with openly gay themes even though the world of theater and musicals are filled with very happy, well-adjusted, openly gay people. The graphic novel was transformed into a stage production (a musical) by director Sam Gold, who won the Tony Award for best musical for his rendition. Part of the success of the theatrical version was that the play was staged on a round stage or a turntable. Set pieces would pop up from the floor making it resemble, in important ways, the graphic novel from which it came. Tom Greenwald, who was in charge of remarketing the book into a musical said that the main goal for marketing the show was to "make sure that it's never ever associated with the plot or subject matter . . . and make sure that people realize that it's a beautiful, universal, family story or self-identification, reflection, and ultimately, hope."[36] This may have been particularly difficult because Greenwald and his team regularly referred to the play as a "lesbian suicide musical."[37] Bechdel is not only a lesbian but a rather butch lesbian. A woman who herself bends the rules of gender unapologetically. Despite the seeming obstacles, the graphic novel was transformed into a successful, mainstream musical. Perhaps the fact that this is an example of a well-told, compelling story, whatever its format, will help it win readers for a long time.

c. Example: *The Da Vinci Code*

The third example I want to talk about in relation to genre blends is Dan Brown's 2003 novel, *The Da Vinci Code*.[38] It is not a great example of literature (Carroll would classify it as Junk Fiction for sure), but it is a great example of blending in the ways that I am thinking about it. In this book, which uses many historically accurate events woven into its largely fictitious plot, Brown makes some very controversial "claims" about the beginnings of Christianity; specifically that Jesus was not divine, that he was married to Mary Magdelene who is the real "holy grail," and that they had children together whose bloodline still exists in France today. It also suggests that the Catholic Church has spent the better part of its time in the last 2000 years covering up all of these things. But the novel does not claim to be anything but fiction. Brown denies ever trying to convince anyone that any of this is to be believed.

I became intrigued by the controversy about *The Da Vinci Code* while I was killing time in an airport bookstore. *The Da Vinci Code* was prominently displayed alongside of several books attempting to discredit it. Titles claimed to break the code,[39] explore the code,[40] crack the code,[41] and expose the hoax[42] among others. Upon subsequent investigation I have also found countless other books and DVDs explaining the truth and falsity of the "claims" made in the book in addition to documentaries made by both ABC and the History Channel. There are *Da Vinci Code* Bible Study guides, a *Da Vinci Code* diet,[43] *The Da Vinci Fitness Code*,[44] and extensive vacation tour packages where one can travel throughout London, Paris, and Scotland seeing the sights the book discusses and learning art history and decoding techniques along the way. An NBC reality show, *Treasure Hunters*, came out in June of 2006 and was based on the book. Contestants use history and folklore to solve arcane puzzles. *The Da Vinci Code* movie, starring Tom Hanks, was released in May of 2006. *The Da Vinci Code* itself is "the second-biggest selling book in publishing history—[second only to] the Bible"[45] with over 61 million copies sold.[46] It has already been translated into 44 different languages and *Time Magazine* has named Dan Brown one of *The World's 100 Most Influential People* in an article titled "The Novel That Ate the World."[47] Suffice it to say, this novel has made an impact on both popular and religious culture.

So why is it that this *particular* novel has caused such a stir? Has the backlash come about because it presents a religiously controversial thesis? Surely, several other novels have presented misinformation, inaccurate history, and even religious conspiracy theories. In fact, Dan Brown won a lawsuit after being accused of plagiarizing the entire architecture of the plot from a lesser-selling (nonfiction) book from 1983 called *Holy Blood, Holy Grail*.[48] Most people have not even heard of that book, so the issue could not be *just* the particular religious conspiracy theory. Thus

I do not think that it is merely controversial subject matter. Oliver Stone continues to make very successful and widely distributed historically inaccurate films, and there is no cottage industry of publications debunking his "claims." But there is something about *The Da Vinci Code* itself that is threatening to many within the Catholic and Christian communities, which makes this book a different sort of problem than other sorts of novels that suggest things that directly contradict their teachings.

One might argue that it is just a novel, and since we all know novels that are not meant to be taken as factual, we should not be too concerned. In fact, this is the very first thing Brown claims on his website when asked about the veracity of the book. He explains: "*The Da Vinci Code* is a *novel* and therefore a work of fiction."[49] It is not meant to be taken as a scholarly work suggesting any of the events in the plot to be true and he makes no *assertions* or *claims* that what he says in the book is true. Brown does say that although "the book's characters and their actions are obviously not real, the artwork, architecture, documents, and secret rituals depicted in this novel all exist (for example, Leonardo Da Vinci's paintings, the Gnostic Gospels, etc.). These real elements are interpreted and debated by fictional characters."[50] Surely this might be true of much historical fiction to some extent. Potentially, all fiction combines both fictional and nonfictional elements. The fact that *The Da Vinci Code* intertwines the two does not make it unique. Brown adds, "My hope in writing this novel was that the story would serve as a catalyst and a springboard for people to discuss the important topics of faith, religion, and history."[51] Well, clearly it *has* been that kind of catalyst, but with a decisively negative spin that I do not think Brown anticipated. It is too naïve to just dismiss the book as fictional and simply say that we *do know* the difference between fact and fiction. If it were that easy, there would not be as many books attempting to debunk it, it would not be censored in at least one country, and people would not be working actively to get it on the banned book list.

Part of the controversy over the book stems from the "fact page" that appears at the beginning of the book.[52] Brown lists three "facts": The first is about the "Priory of Sion"—that it is a real organization and that several historically famous persons were members (Isaac Newton, Botticelli, Victor Hugo, and da Vinci, in particular). This so-called fact is not based in any historically reliable evidence, however. There is, at least, no historically *available* evidence. The second "fact" is that the Vatican supports a deeply devout sect of the church called "Opus Dei," which "has been the topic of recent controversy due to reports of brain-washing, coercion, and a dangerous practice known as 'corporal mortification'"[53] or self-mutilation. It then gives the address of the newly constructed US headquarters for the building. From all accounts, this appears to be true. Opus Dei is a real organization and they have been in the news recently. To what extent they are supported by the Vatican I am not sure. Of course, I am not sure and cannot be sure *because* of the secrecy that shrouds the Vatican and their practices and even more so by the secrecy of Opus Dei. This secrecy is likely part of the volatile mixture that fuels the controversy over the book, in addition to these "factual" claims. The last "fact" claims that "all descriptions of artwork, architecture, documents, and secret rituals in this novel are accurate."[54] I am not sure what to even make of such a claim. It is one thing to say that it is "accurate" that a painting *exists*, but to say that a particular interpretation (a particular controversial feminist interpretation to be specific) is "accurate" may be a stretch for any *interpretation*. Brown sets his reader up from the very beginning—mixing fact and fiction and presenting it as fact, but still within the context of the fiction.

If we take what is in the novel to be "true in the fiction" and take the fact page (whatever its veracity) to be part of that fiction, it will at least make a consistent whole with which one can make sense of the plot. But this goes beyond my sense of what it means to be "true in the fiction." I take it to be "true in the fiction" that Cinderella had a mean stepmother, but it is harder for me to accept that it is "true in the fiction" that what is true in the fiction is also true outside the fiction, which defeats the purpose of being fictional to start with. And because there is much that is true, that doesn't make it nonfiction. That is, with the fact page at the beginning, what Brown is essentially doing is telling his reader that what is coming is real, and it is a story based on historical fact. This is much stronger than claiming that there will be fictional characters debating real events, or even just that the artworks and documents are real and everything else is made up. The "fact page" allows a reader to understand that what Brown is doing in the book is making real claims about historically real events. Conceptually, this is the first major problem—Brown presents fiction as fact on the first page.

Of course, Brown did not invent the "fact page." Numerous novels have used this sort of set up to get a reader engaged in the story. Umberto Eco uses a similar start in the *Name of the Rose*, where the reader is led to believe that he/she is about to read an historical account by Adso of Melk. Jonathan Swift uses the technique in *Gulliver's Travels*. The opening pages of this novel include a number of letters by the characters. However, the literary devices used by Eco and Swift seem to be somewhat different from what Brown does with his fact page in that he is telling the reader explicitly that significant aspects of the (fictional) plot are not to be taken as fictional. Brown's literary device seems to go beyond the bounds of just engaging readers into the plot.

Critics of *The Da Vinci Code* claim that Brown intentionally presents the *entire* book as fact because of the way it is set up from the beginning. The two main characters are a Harvard professor of religious symbology and art history and a police cryptologist who specializes in code-breaking. Their attempt to solve any kind of mystery would be likely to be interesting to those of us who are not educated about art, history, or decoding. Their conversations are interesting, informative, and accessible, and of course there is sexual tension between them the whole time. One reviewer says, "there is an element of reading [this book, where one is] made to feel like a more interesting person" than one really is.[55] The conversations do, however, revolve around seemingly historically accurate events and tend to allow a reader to believe that he/she understands something that may or may not be accurate historically or religiously. The interpretations of the historical events, artworks, and documents, however, appear to be highly suspect. Again though, the secrecy in which the Vatican shrouds itself does not allow a reader to check the information, as he or she might be able to in other contexts with other subjects. The secrecy of the Vatican makes it next to impossible to check Brown's assertions, so they carry more weight than they might otherwise. This secrecy also limits those who want to disprove Brown. As a professor of the history of Christianity explains, "I knew that the book was fictional, of course, but as I read it I realized that Dan Brown's characters were actually making *historical* claims about Jesus, Mary and the Gospels. In other words, the fiction was being built on a historical foundation that the reader was to accept as factual, not fictitious."[56] Appealing to "but it is just a novel" is not much of a defense at this point, since the story itself does not present itself as such. Admitting that genres blend might be a better way to approach this. Brown, despite his intentions, touched a nerve with this book and made too many claims that felt like real claims. This book was read as nonfiction, even if it was intended to be fiction. The way we read influences the texts we take in, and I think this serves as a prime example.

5. CONCLUSION

These are three examples of how fiction and nonfiction are blended in ways that readers may not have previously thought. A careful reader of mine might have noticed that all of my examples are of fictional works that blend into the nonfictional realm. As it turns out, when nonfiction blends too far into fiction it gets called out as fictional, or worse, fraudulent. An astute reader might also recall the nonfictional work of John D'Agata and his fact-checker Jim Fingal. Fingal wanted the fact-checking accuracy of journalism. D'Agata wanted the effect of a well-written and moving essay. I will talk about fraudulent memoirs in the next chapter, but the examples of nonfiction that blend too far often get sent to the untrustworthy-author file and are largely discounted. Is there a reason why genre-blending *is* important, especially in the realm of blending fiction and nonfiction? I believe this mixing is essential to recognize in order to understand how we process and make sense of these texts. Blending the rules that create an ambiguous dividing line between fiction and nonfiction can be beneficial to a more nuanced understanding of a text. This recognition can facilitate the acknowledgment that understanding genre is part of an active reading process and that we as readers should not assume a simplistic fiction/nonfiction binary. Instead, the blending of genres will cause us, as readers, to make reading a more cognitively engaging activity in which we do more work outside of placing the formula or genre on a text and instead look at the ways in which the genres are blended and acknowledge that we need to actively work to understand what the text does.

I believe that there are a number of implications in my argument that can be effective in heightening the awareness of the ways that we think about the all-important binary between fiction and nonfiction. I believe that people can become better readers by not being so attached to the fiction/nonfiction distinction but rather to the way in which stories are compelling, true to life, and complex, as well as the way that good literature requires a reader to constantly engage with the plot components in order to see connections within the story. This, in turn, makes readers more active in the process of reading itself and can enhance literacy at any level. The danger of the simplistic binary thinking about fiction/nonfiction can potentially do a reader more harm than good. Believing in advance of reading that a text is either fiction or nonfiction changes the way that we process that text. What I advocate is that genre not be something that is assumed or taken for granted but rather something that is recognized as being involved in the active process of reading. I also do not take genre to be something found exclusively in the text itself. Figuring out how genre works for any given text should be something that is involved in the process of comprehending narrative structure. "Did it *really* happen?" should be one of the last questions on our minds as readers if we can learn to read for true engagement, which comes from connecting story lines, imagining characters' actions and decisions, anticipating outcomes of those choices, and enjoying resolutions. The essence of narrative and storytelling is imaginative engagement, indulging in descriptive language, and actively constructing meaning out of disparate parts along with the author. And genre has as much to do with the way in which one approaches the text as it does the text itself. Reading narrative should not be about facts or falsities, and to focus on this one aspect sells short the best things about the pleasure of reading.

NOTES

1. I am thinking in particular of Claude Levi-Strauss' *The Raw and the Cooked*, where he outlines the beginning of our binary thinking.

2. Robert Stam, *Film Theory: An Introduction* (Malden, MA: Blackwell, 2000), 14.

3. See Noël Carroll, *The Philosophy of Horror or Paradoxes of the Heart* (New York: Routledge Press, 1990).

4. See Noël Carroll, "The Paradox of Junk Fiction," *Philosophy and Literature* 18 (1994): 225–241.

5. Carroll, "The Paradox of Junk Fiction," 225.

6. Leona M. Jaglom and Howard Gardner, "Decoding the Worlds of Television," *Studies in Visual Communication* 7 (1981): 33–47.

7. Robert Hodge and Gunther Kress, *Social Semiotics* (Cambridge, MA: Polity, 1988), 7.

8. I do not want to deal explicitly with film, although there are certain numbers of genre categories that cross these boundaries as well. For instance, Docudarams, Mockumentaries, Docufiction.

9. John D'Agata and Jim Fingal, *The Lifespan of a Fact* (New York: W. W. Norton & Company, 2012), 44.

10. D'Agata and Fingal, *Lifespan of a Fact*, 44.

11. D'Agata and Fingal, *Lifespan of a Fact*, 52.

12. D'Agata and Fingal, *Lifespan of a Fact*, 53.

13. Kendall Walton, "Categories of Art," *Philosophical Review* 79 (1970): 338.

14. Walton, "Categories of Art," 338.

15. Walton, "Categories of Art," 339.

16. Worldbuilding is the process of constructing an imaginary world, as with a fictional world. The term comes from science fiction writing but has import with constructed worlds of more generic literature as well.

17. Walton, "Categories of Art," 339.

18. Walton, "Categories of Art," 339.

19. Stacie Friend, "Fiction as a Genre," *Proceedings of the Aristotelian Society* 112, no. 2 (2012): 3.

20. Junot Diaz, *The Brief Wondrous Life of Oscar Wao* (New York: Riverhead Books, 2007).

21. Gregory Currie, *The Nature of Fiction* (New York: Cambridge University Press, 1990).

22. Monica Hanna, "Reassembling the Fragments," *Callaloo* (2010).

23. Gregory Currie, "Narrative and the Psychology of Character," *The Journal of Aesthetics and Art Criticism* 67 (2009): 61–71.

24. Diaz, *The Brief Wondrous Life of Oscar Wao*, 24.

25. Hanna, "Reassembling the Fragments," 511.

26. Hanna, "Reassembling the Fragments," 509.

27. Diaz, *The Brief Wondrous Life of Oscar Wao*, 1.

28. Diaz, *The Brief Wondrous Life of Oscar Wao*, 2.

29. Diaz, *The Brief Wondrous Life of Oscar Wao,* 2.

30. Diaz, *The Brief Wondrous Life of Oscar Wao*, 243.

31. Alison Bechdel, *Fun Home: A Family Tragicomic* (New York: Mariner Books, 2006), 147.

32. Sean Wisley, "The Things They Buried," *New York Times Sunday Book Review,* June 18, 2006, http://www.nytimes.com/2006/06/18/books/review/18wilsey.html?_r=0 (accessed May 26, 2015)

33. Wisley, "The Things They Buried."

34. Wisley, "The Things They Buried."

35. Jenna Lyons, "Two S.C. schools' budgets altered following gay-themed assigned reading controversy," *USA Today College*, July 9, 2014.

36. Kalle Oskari Mattila, "Selling Queerness: The Curious Case of *Fun Home*," *The Atlantic*, (April 25, 2016).

37. Mattila, "Selling Queerness."

38. Dan Brown, *The Da Vinci Code* (New York: Doubleday, 2003).

39. Darrell L. Bock, *Breaking the Da Vinci Code* (Nashville, TN: Nelson Books, 2006).

40. *Exploring the Da Vinci Code*, DVD (The Disinformation Company, 2005).

41. James Garlow and Peter Jones, *Cracking Da Vinci's Code* (Colorado Springs, CO: Cook Communications, 2004).

42. Carl E. Olson and Sandra Miese, *The Da Vinci Hoax* (Ft. Collins, CO: Ignatius Press, 2004 also available on DVD).

43. Stephen Lanzalotta, *The Diet Code: Revolutionary Weight-Loss Secrets from Da Vinci and The Golden Ratio* (Warner Adult Publishers, 2006).

44. Joseph Mullen, *The Da Vinci Fitness Code* (Winter Springs, FL: Fitness Therapy Publishing, 2005).

45. Chris Hastings, "Money, Not Christianity, behind Abbey's Rejection of "Da Vinci Code," Says Sir Ian," *The Telegraph.Co.UK.* February 10, 2005, http://www.telegraph.co.uk/news/main.jhtml?xml=/news/2005/10/02/nvinci02.xml&sSheet=/news/2005/10/02/ixnewstop.html (accessed December 8, 2005)

46. "The Da Vinci Code," *Wikipedia.* http://en.wikipedia.org/wiki/The_Da_Vinci_Code (accessed May 22, 2006)

47. Michelle Orecklin, "The Novel That Ate the World," http://www.danbrown.com/novels/davinci_code/faqs.html (accessed December 5, 2005)

48. Michael Baigent, Richard Leigh, and Henry Lincoln, *Holy Blood, Holy Grail* (New York: Dell Publishers, 1983).

49. Dan Brown, "The Da Vinci Code," http://www.danbrown.com/novels/davinci_code/faqs.html (accessed December 5, 2005)

50. Brown, "The Da Vinci Code."

51. Brown, "The Da Vinci Code."

52. The truth and fiction of novels is a complex issue with lots of recent examples. Most recently, James Frey's novel, *A Million Little Pieces*, has come under scrutiny (most publicly by Oprah) because it was shown that this "memoir" of his life was entirely made up. I think that expectation may be the crux of the issue with these kinds of novels. If they are presented as fact, then we expect them to be fact; if they are presented as fiction, our expectations are less. Brown's book, although it is fiction, is presented as though it is fact.

53. Brown, *The Da Vinci Code*, 1.

54. Brown, *The Da Vinci Code*, 1.

55. Joel Rickett, "The Man behind the Ultimate Conspiracy Novel," *The Times Online,* November 19, 2005, http://www.timesonline.co.uk/article/0,,923-1877099,00.html (accessed December 5, 2005)

56. Bart D. Ehrman, *Truth and Fiction in* The Da Vinci Code (Oxford: Oxford University Press, 2004), vii–viii.

Chapter Four

Memoir

A Case Study

Is memoir fiction or nonfiction? In the last chapter I outlined the differences between those two, but now I am ready to complicate those categories even a bit more. Memoir shares qualities of both fiction (because of its literary style, prose, character development, and plot formations) and nonfiction (because it is all supposed to be true). So the genre itself is already genre-blended in a way. If a memoir is shown not to be true, an author can get into a lot of trouble. But the nature of memoir itself is rife with possibilities for exaggeration, misremembering, and hyperbole, all for the sake of a good story. Although there have been volumes written about the possible truth content of fiction, literature, and narrative, I do not think that the kinds of truth claims made in memoirs have been systematically examined. As I outlined in the last chapter, the boundaries of genre in general are not clear or rigid, but I think that the blurring of the confines of memoir makes that point even more salient. That is, memoir itself tends to use a number of the differing qualities of several genres. For example, memoirs tend to be written as narratives in the first person, but at the same time they are expected to be truthful, accurate, and provide verisimilitude. In this chapter I will show how memoirs can be used to show not only how we construct and understand genre but also how our expectations about the strict nature of truth influence the way we read memoir.

I want to begin not with memoir, but with memoir fraud. I think that memoir fraud is substantially different from mistaking fiction for nonfiction. There is something special about memoir that readers look for beyond merely a *true* story. Memoirs claim to have insights into persons, while mere nonfiction does not necessarily lay claim to these insights. We are in a time in publishing history when most anyone can write and publish a memoir, even at a young age or without substantial life experience, and people publish multiple memoirs. Memoir serves as one of the most powerful forms of testimony to different kinds of beliefs, experiences, and, in particular, traumas. Since memoirs are most generally authors' descriptions of their own personal experiences, it seems that there has not been much need for the fact-checking accuracy that might be expected in other genres like nonfiction or history. If it is the case that memoirs and autobiographies are more akin to the lessons we learned and the insight we have gained from our experiences, rather than a chronicling of event after event, the historical accuracy should perhaps be downplayed to the emotion, the insight, and maybe even a compelling story. It seems, however, that there has been a surprising number of memoirs that have sold well, won literary prizes, and then have been found to be either greatly exaggerated or fabricated entirely. What I wish to do in this chapter is flesh out the issues that seem to be the most bothersome in terms of ethics and epistemology. The reading public has expressed great concern over many of the fraudulent memoirs and might be losing confidence in the publishing industry. So here I want to figure out which issues are important about fabricated memoirs in order to identify what exactly is wrong with a fraudulent memoir and whether our outrage over them is justifiable.

In general, we read memoirs with the expectation that we will be reading true accounts of the experiences of their authors. We often think of memoirs as inspirational in one way or another. Memoirs tend to fall into a few specific categories, including coming of age, addiction/compulsion/recovery, life experience (motherhood, climbing a mountain, a devastating disease, etc.), relationships, trauma, sexuality, experiences in war, brushes with fame or historical significance, and childhood remembrances. Surely there are other categories, but this covers most of them. Memoirs tend to be about one particular theme, time period, or experience, while autobiographies tend to be more of an account of a whole life. One of the things that makes memoir writing so popular and intriguing is that most anyone can write one. In order to do so, one only has to be an expert on one's own experience. In the age of Oprah, we are all experts on our own testimony. First-person testimony seems to be grounds for all kinds of knowledge claims (like the best diet, whether or not vaccines cause autism, whether breastfeeding is in fact superior to formula, etc.). As it is, though, not everyone has the capacity for interesting self-reflection that it takes to write a good memoir, and even fewer people have the storytelling skills to turn interesting life experiences into compelling and interesting stories. (This is why many famous people who are compelled to write memoirs have ghostwriters.) Good storytellers can turn almost any event into an interesting story, but even interesting events, recovery, trauma, and fame do not necessarily automatically make good memoirs.

What is interesting to me about memoir is the special footing it has as its own genre. It really seems to straddle both fiction and nonfiction or at least both nonfiction and narrative. Since we know that the kinds of expectations we have as readers influence the way we read stories, the expectations we have of memoirs are of a very particular kind. We expect memoirs to be interesting, accessible, insightful, relatable, and true. Just like Aristotle's original rules about writing a good tragedy, we do not want to read about a very bad man moving from adversity to prosperity or a virtuous person falling from prosperity to adversity.[1] Neither do these inspire pity or fear (important for Aristotle) nor do they allow us to connect emotionally at all with them. Readers want to feel connected with the writers of memoirs, and they want to connect to their stories. Memoirs have the ability to reveal a lot about their writers in terms of their inner motivations, their ability to deal with a variety of circumstances, and their ability to cope. Memoir, written in the first person, offers an extremely intimate view of a self and because of that offers something in terms of genre that perhaps no other genre does. Something happens, though, when memoir does not live up to the expectations that readers have. Writers can get carried away and take too many liberties with the events, facts, or circumstances. Memoirists sometimes end up looking more like fiction writers than nonfiction writers. And what happens when one crosses that line seems to me to be more than just embellishment. When authors do cross that line, readers' expectations are thwarted, and inspiration can turn into confusion and anger. Writing a good memoir can provide insight and feeling, but what happens when memoirs go too far and stretch the limits of the genre? Memoir fraud informs us even more about genre and our expectations than the genre itself.

1. JAMES FREY AND THE TRUTH
AND ART OF MEMOIR

Oprah has been duped numerous times by the authors of false memoirs. For all her attempts to get America reading, she has been caught up in a recent rash of literary frauds. It all started with the James Frey debacle. Frey's book, *A Million Little Pieces*, was awarded Oprah's Book Club seal of approval, and the sales of the already bestselling book about his addiction and recovery skyrocketed. More importantly, the general public really connected with the book. Readers were able to genuinely see and understand the struggles that their substance-abusing friends and relatives had in getting clean. They connected with their own struggles getting clean. Blogs, bulletin boards, and chat rooms were flooded with praise for Frey's painful rendition of his own experiences. But then someone from *The Smoking Gun* did some fact-checking that Frey's publisher had failed to do. As it turned out, Frey fabricated, embellished, and flat out lied about many of the events that he described in his so-called memoir. As Frey sat on Oprah's stage for a second time to face her allegations, he continued to defend his memoir as merely a small embellishment of the truth. He said in his memoir that he spent 87 days in jail when in fact it was only 3 hours. He was in jail, but that seems more than an exaggeration to make a better story. Frey claimed that he struggled with whether to include some of the descriptions in the book he knew never happened, like his extensive description of a root canal he had with no anaesthetic, which was, for me, one of the most poignant and painful parts of the whole book. He told Oprah that he really struggled with "the idea" of putting it in the book, knowing it had not happened. Oprah retorted back, "No, the *lie* of it. That's a lie. It's not an idea, James. That's a lie."[2]

What is the literary difference between a truth and a lie when telling a story about one's own experience? When I recount an experience, which is more important, the event or the insight? Why is it so important that we know *in advance* whether a story is true or false, based on a true story, not true at all, or something that really happened to someone? For some reason it *is* really important to some readers to know not just whether something *could* happen or whether it really *did* happen. This is related to our desire to know whether what we read is fiction or nonfiction. Part of the reason people were so taken with James Frey's rendition of his experiences is that it really seemed to be something at the extremes of what someone could possibly endure. The first time Frey appeared on Oprah's show, when everyone took it all to be true, an audience member stood up and said, "after reading this book and seeing you come through what you came through, the way you did, and you having the attitude that you did makes me feel that I can do it too."[3] The story was inspirational in part because it seemed not just improbable, but really impossible that someone would have that much bad luck, make that many bad decisions, be that addicted, and live to tell about it from a sober perspective. It would be truly amazing if someone did all of the things that Frey chronicled in his book and lived to tell about it. Frey, at least, *did not* do all of the things that he chronicled in his book, and so the overall effect is not just less inspirational than it might have been. It gives the feeling of a true fraud.

Frey admitted that part of his coping mechanism in dealing with his addictions was sheer self-aggrandizing. He explained, "I developed this sort of image of myself that was greater, probably, that—not probably— that *was* greater than what I actually was. In order to get through the experience of the addiction, I thought of myself as being tougher than I was and badder than I was—and it helped me cope."[4] Oprah asked Frey if he clung to that image because that was really the way he saw himself or if he created that image because he thought it would make a better book. Frey claimed that it was a bit of both. Giving Frey the benefit of the doubt, if he did just imagine himself as this bigger, badder character than he was in reality, perhaps he truly did just imagine himself this way. Perhaps writing this memoir helped him process his experience of being a drug addict, an alcoholic, and a criminal. Certainly those who advocate that telling narratives about ourselves helps to give more coherence to our own view of our personal identity might support Frey in this version of his story. He was giving coherence to his story, and he created a character who was grander than he really was in order to deal with addictions and problems that seemed bigger than he could handle. This might be a reasonable explanation, except for the fact that he was turned down by seventeen different publishers when he tried to sell the manuscript as fiction. This makes me think that he created the bigger and badder character to write (and sell) a better book and not to help him cope with his poor decisions. Recently Frey admitted that "it is OK to write a book and not allow it to be defined by genre or by categorization, to write a book that's not fiction or nonfiction."[5] Frey is also not at all concerned with many literary rules or strict traditions. He works with other writers who develop his ideas, not unlike an artist who has people execute many ideas. He combines reality and fiction all the time and cares not one bit whether it fits into our traditional categories of genres. Recently he released *Endgame*, a novel that also included a YouTube channel, 50 social media accounts, and a real-life puzzle with a $500,000 cash prize.[6] He is hoping that the strict categories that differentiate truth from something else when it comes to story will just go away.

2. FORGERY AND FICTION

Plagiarism is putting your name on someone else's work, forgery is putting someone else's name on your work, and fabricating a memoir is fraud. But this particular kind of fraud seems to be exclusive to the literary arts. While we know that Van Meegren *forged* Vermeer's paintings and John Shmarb forged the work of Brahams,[7] it seems impossible for this kind of memoir-*fraud* to happen in another genre. That is, with fraudulent memoirs there is no *forgery, per se,* because one presents as one's own and *as truth* what is merely fantasy. This is a kind of fraud or deception that is different in kind from forgery. As for Frey, at least his so-called memoir is based on his own experiences. He had been an addict, and he had recovered, and most of what he wrote about in his book was true. In fact, he claims now that only 14 pages of the 448 pages in *A Million Little Pieces* contain inaccuracies—hardly something really worth complaining about in the big picture. But Frey sold us these lies and exaggerations willingly and knowingly, which makes this situation as one that teems with intent. And intentional lies are punished more strictly than lies of mere exaggeration.

Margaret Jones, however, the pen name of the author of *Love and Consequences: A Memoir of Hope and Survival,* concocted an entire story about a young girl being raised in the gang-ridden streets of Los Angeles. The story about Big Mama, who took her in as a foster child and cared for her deeply while life on the streets taught her various kinds of harsh lessons, was heart warming. Inspiration abounds because she paid attention in school, had a loving teacher, and with that teacher's time and support earned a college scholarship. Education got her off the streets and showed her that she had some real value. Margaret Seltzer, the woman who actually wrote the book, grew up in a safe, loving home with both of her parents in suburban Oregon. Her sister was the one who ultimately ratted her out to the press, but she knew nothing of the project until she saw the book on the shelves of the bookstore.[8] Seltzer was able to fabricate this entire story about a girl with no home and no security without ever having experienced it. She also sold the story to a publisher without ever meeting the publisher in person and the publisher did no fact-checking at all.

We frequently read *fictional* accounts of characters who do all kinds of things that authors could not possibly experience. William Styron, for instance, was a white male novelist. He did not know (although he could imagine and describe in very moving detail) what it was like to be a slave like Nat Turner, whose "autobiography" he wrote. He also did not know what it was like to be a mother who experienced the Holocaust as he describes in *Sophie's Choice*. But when he sells his work *as fiction*, it does not seem to cause as much of a stir as when an author sells her work as memoir and it turns out to be fiction. William Styron's works generated great controversy when he wrote from such perspectives, but it only caused a stir once it became widely known that he was white. When the reading public thought the author of *The Confessions of Nat Turner* was black, the book was widely acclaimed. Margaret Seltzer's books, on the other hand, were pulled off of the bookseller's shelves immediately. After a class-action lawsuit, refunds were given to James Frey's readers who bought his books thinking they were buying a true story. In other cases, literary awards were revoked. Memoir fraud seems to me a different kind of controversy than Styron writing from perspectives that are not his own.

One of the ways I might be able to pinpoint what the important issue is with the fraudulent memoirs is to examine what the essential difference is between a memoir and a work of fiction or a memoir and a historical novel. A memoir is most generally a narrative of personal reminiscence of an author, often dealing with one's own outward experiences with other people in his/her life. Some suggest that memoirs differ from autobiographies in that memoirs focus more on the feelings and subjective experiences of the author rather than an autobiography's focus on the chronicling of events. Outside of the academy, memoir and autobiography (literally from the Latin self-life-writing) are generally interchangeable. Novels, on the other hand, even though they may contain elements of truth or references to real persons or events make no explicit claim to truth or reality. Truth is incidental with fiction but central, at least epistemologically, when it comes to memoir. Further, contemporary memoir uses the literary conventions of the novel: figurative language, interior monologue, metaphor, symbol, dialogue, plot and character development, first person narration, and well-developed narrative arcs. The novelistic style, however, also uses a creative style of organization. It is not a merely a temporal or chronological list of events. Novelistic style imposes a structure (primarily causal but not exclusively) on events and requires creation and careful consideration about what to leave in, what to leave out, and how to make significant emphases. Memoirists must pick and choose from real experiences (or their own memories that may or may not vary from the actual event) in a way that novelists have full liberty to create. Successful memoirs read more like novels than do the old-style autobiographies that are life-span-extended chronologies. And one of the most important similarities is that both novels and memoirs tend to be about human insights and experience.

The difference between memoirs and fiction rests on an epistemological distinction, not one that is merely moral or literary. That is, we have certain kinds of beliefs that accompany us as we read memoirs. Part of *understanding* memoirs is *believing* memoirs. In many cases, if you did not know whether a book was a novel or a memoir, you would not be able to tell the difference just based on literary style or narrative construction, assuming the novel was written in the first person. It seems to me, however, that since the literary or narrative style is what the two genres have in common, it is also the source of the blurring of lines between memoir and fiction. That is, the often-cited mistaking truth for fiction or fiction for truth is an epistemological problem that leads also to moral problems. As John Paul Eakin explains, when memoirists "fail to tell the truth, then, they do more than violate a literary convention governing nonfiction as a genre; they disobey a moral imperative."[9] Fraudulent memoirs, then, lead people to have certain kinds of beliefs about persons and events that are in fact false. Personal experience, first-hand experience, and testimony generally all function as a version of base-level facts that authors tend to use to make larger, often moral, arguments. Functionally, we divide fact and fiction very easily, with personal experience falling on the side of fact. When it seems that an author has purposefully taken advantage of that division, readers become legitimately incensed. It is not just a matter of a simple mistake, it is fraud. Epistemologically we have been fooled, but those beliefs often lead us to have certain emotions and to gain insights into our own selves. Learning that it was not just an honest mistake, but that someone had purposely perpetuated a fraud, leads to legitimate upset on the part of the reader.

Philippe Lejeune suggests that there is a kind of "autobiographical pact" that the author and reader of memoir agree to.[10] This is a kind of pact that the author makes with his/her reader, one that suggests good faith on the part of the "author" as presenting his/her life experiences as transparently as possible, and the reader understands how to interpret this sort of text. Lejeune explains that "for the reader, who does not know the real [author], all the while believing in his existence, the author is defined as the person capable of producing this discourse, and so [the reader] imagines what [the author] is like from what [the author] produces."[11] The "author" is a literary creation of his/her text as Foucault's "author function" might indicate, which is at the same time identical with his/her real identity associated with his/her proper name. At the beginning of a memoir, an author enters into an autobiographical pact with the reader by making clear that the "I" of the text refers to him/herself and only to him/herself, and it is made clear to the reader that the author, the narrator, and the protagonist are identical. According to Lejeune, this pact is not quite this explicit but resembles something like the following: "I swear to tell the truth, the whole truth, and nothing but the truth, as much as it is possible, making allowances for lapses of memory, errors, involuntary distortions, etc."[12] Memoirs, autobiographies, and biographies, unlike fiction, are *referential* texts that are like "scientific or historical discourse which claim to provide information about a 'reality', exterior to the text, and so submit to a test of verification."[13] Memoir is not identified as a relationship between the extra-textual reality and the text, nor is it an internal analysis of the textual structure. What makes a memoir is "the implicit or explicit contract proposed by the *author* to the *reader*, a contract which determines the mode of reading of the text and engenders the effects which, attributed to the text, seem to us to define it as memoir.[14] Thus, memoir is different from both fiction and history because of the autobiographical pact offered by the author even though it retains important elements from fiction (a good narrative) and history (extra-textual, factual accuracy).

The autobiographical pact is challenged with the case of Rigoberta Menchú, who wrote a memoir called *I, Rigoberta Menchú: An Indian Woman in Guatemala*, which outlined her experiences in the Guatemalan

Civil War. Menchú received the Nobel Peace Prize in 1992 for her work promoting rights for indigenous Guatemalans, and this book was a significant part of those efforts. The work is really one of *testimonio,* though, a form of narration that involves testimony often combined with the experiences of others, as well as historical fiction. It is always told from the first person. *Testimonio* is a standard literary genre in South America. Menchú readily admits at the beginning of her work, "I didn't learn it from a book, and I didn't learn it alone. I'd like to stress that it is not only my life, it's also the testimony of my people."[15] The descriptions are horrific, detailing in graphic prose the slave labor conditions of the coffee farms on which many of the indigenous peoples were forced to work and the torture and murder of countless indigenous men and women by a brutal military. She describes witnessing the murder of her own brother, which has since been shown to be descriptively accurate, but she herself did not actually witness it.[16] She describes witnessing the murder of her mother, which does seem to be factually true. The narrative is incredibly gripping and quite graphic. The stories are powerful and well told, but the events that she describes did not all happen to her, and we would be hard-pressed to call this work an autobiography or a memoir. We certainly cannot call it history. It might be historical fiction, or, more accurately *testimonio.*

But we (Westerners) do not think of *testimonio* as a legitimate genre, primarily because it blends narration, memoir, history, first-person testimony, and autobiography in ways that we just do not know how to make sense of. Since this is not a standard genre in the West, Menchú has been subjected to much criticism of her book. Part of the concern was that it became an increasingly popular college textbook after it was first published in 1984. It was taught in history classes as a primary source documenting the Guatemalan war. It was taught in anthropology classes as first-person ethnography, and it was taught in literature classes as an example of *testimonio* and genre studies. But as it was being taught in the university, many conservative critics suggested that Menchú only used her experiences to further her academic career and to bolster her status as a human rights activist. The notorious conservative critic Dinesh D'Souza even went so far as to say that "undergraduates do not read about Rigoberta because she has written a great and immortal book, or performed a great deed, or invented something useful. She simply happened to be in the right place and the right time."[17] Commentator David Horowitz has actively tried to discredit Menchú, calling her a "Marxist terrorist," and has suggested that her book and human rights work constitutes "one of the greatest hoaxes of the 20th century."[18] But the issue of her being a human rights activist fighting against injustices in Guatemala seems to be a very different issue from the so-called truth content of her testimony. This seems to be the case of a genre-blended work (of a standard genre that exists elsewhere that we just do not acknowledge) that we simply do not know how to make sense of. First-person testimony offers an extremely powerful form of knowledge for us that is one of the most reliable, if it is trustworthy. When memoirs are offered up as moving, heart-wrenching, and inspirational in the ways that *I, Rigoberta Menchú* is, finding out that it is anything other than direct testimony changes the way that we think about the genre. And it might change the way that we think about memoir in general.

Another possible violation of the autobiographical pact is Forrest Carter, the author of *The Education of Little Tree*. The book is about a boy who is orphaned in the 1920s and is sent, at five years of age, to live with his Cherokee Indian grandparents. They teach young Forrest, whom they dub Little Tree, about the way of the land, respect for nature, love, farming, society, and education. The lessons are gentle and loving, accepting and generous. The book was used in the American public school system for many years as a memoir that taught environmentalism, self-reflection, and pacifism. Eventually it was discovered that the book been written by Asa Earl Carter, a white segregationist from Alabama and a member of the Ku Klux Klan (KKK). Asa Carter was a speechwriter for George Wallace, the segregationist governor of Alabama in the late 1960s and early 1970s. One of the things Wallace is most remembered for is blocking the steps to the University of Alabama, stopping black students from enrolling at the university. In his 1963 inaugural address as the governor of Alabama, Wallace declared, "In the name of the greatest people that ever trod this earth, I draw the line in the dust and toss the gauntlet before the feet of tyranny. And I say: segregation now, segregation tomorrow, segregation forever." Those were the powerful words written for him by Asa Carter.

In the early 1970s, Carter seemed to fall off the map. He had gone to reinvent himself as a writer. He moved to Abilene, Texas, and started over. He renamed himself Forrest, after Nathan Bedford Forrest, who was the first Grand Wizard of the Ku Klux Klan. He first published two novels, *The Rebel Outlaw: Josey Wales* (1972) and *The Vengeance Trails of Josey Wales* (1976), which were cowboy novels that did relatively well and even led to a Clint Eastwood–directed movie, *The Outlaw Josey Wales*, in 1976. *The Education of Little Tree* was also published in 1976 and celebrated relative success. Forrest Carter worked hard to deny that he was Asa Carter. He denied it specifically in an interview in *The New York Times* in 1976, saying he was "no politician but both a cowboy and an Indian."[19] Evidence indicates, however, that they were one and the same man. Knowing this, it is hard to take seriously the lessons of environmentalism, generosity, and gentleness that are espoused by the narrator of *Little Tree*. Asa Carter despised people of color and Jews in particular. Carter commentator Joe Richman said that Asa Carter "reserved special hatred for the Jews, who he felt were really to blame for the corrupting power of popular culture. [Carter] once said, 'The Negro is the virus, but it's the Jew that inserts it in the veins of America.'"[20] Forrest Carter, on the other hand, taught of tolerance and acceptance. *Little Tree* even had a loving Jewish character, Mr. Wine, a peddler who befriends Little Tree and tells him that "if you learn to place a value on being honest and thrifty, on doing your best, and on caring for folks, this was more important than anything."[21] It seems impossible that the man who penned the words "segregation now, segregation tomorrow, segregation forever" could also write of such kindness and respect. But the same person did write all of those words. The movement from memoir to fiction was swift once Carter was found out, and it did not take Oprah all that long to remove *The Education of Little Tree* from her recommended reading list.

It might be helpful here to determine whether memoirs are closer in kind to history or to fiction in terms not just of definition but also in the way we assess them for quality. Which is more important to a successful memoir, historical accuracy or a compelling story? It seems to be both, except when one fails miserably, and then it is *that* criteria which matters. Boring or badly told memoirs certainly do not cause us much concern. They are just ignored. Fraudulent memoirs, on the other hand, do seem to trump boring ones as problematic. Although my sense is that the telling of the narrative is what we are looking for in memoir alongside inspiration gleaned from personal insight through individual journeys, it is the historical accuracy that is more easily critiqued. *The Smoking Gun* initially suspected James Frey's *A Million Little Pieces* because of a lack of police records in Ohio, not because his story seemed utterly implausible.

With fraudulent memoirs, it seems that there are at least two significant issues at play. The first is that the author presents a view of the self as being transparent and honest, when in fact it is not. The "accuracy" of the self and possible access to that self is of course endlessly complicated. There seems to be some sort of cultural myth that asserts that there is a singular "I" that can write a narrative, story, or description of events that get neatly translated onto the page, and that singular story can be directly given to a reader and the reader can make it out to be "true" in some meaningful sense.[22] The fact remains, however, that the construction of personal identity is never that tidy. Personal identity is neither straightforward nor directly translatable, and it is something that continues to evolve, especially, I would think, during the process of writing about one's lived experiences.

Of course, one might legitimately have a confused sense of self that might lend itself to an inaccurate memoir. This seems to be the defense of Misha Defonseca's memoir *Misha: A Mémoire of the Holocaust Years*. Misha's parents were taken away from her Belgian home in the early part of the Second World War. Her father was a war criminal who gave up state secrets. She concocted the story as a child that her parents were sent to Auschwitz, and she ran away from the care of her grandfather to find them. Along the way she was adopted by a pack of wolves who took her in as their cub. The acceptance of the usually vicious animals was demonstrated in stark contrast to the inhumanity of the Nazis. As she repeated the story over and over through her adult years, the story became very real to her. Eventually, after years of living in the States, her friends convinced her to publish her very moving story. After initial praise for fearlessness and great humanity, fact-checkers provided the publishers with evidence that her father was taken by the government as a war collaborator. Misha was not a child of the Holocaust. She later explained that "the book is a story, it's my story. It's not the true reality, but it is *my reality*. There are times when I find it difficult to differentiate between reality and my inner world."[23] This story, about her searching for her (incidentally, non-Jewish) parents, was truly a coping mechanism that she used to help her deal with a tragedy that happened to her in her youth. She told the story repeatedly, and it became more and more real to her. In this case, then, it is not as clear that she was intentionally trying to deceive, but she was trying to create an identity that was more palatable than the one her real circumstances provided her. I would argue that our sense of self or personal identity is largely constructed or at least greatly influenced by the kinds of stories we tell about ourselves, especially the ones we tell repeatedly and the ones we tell ourselves and others about the

ways in which we have come to be who we are. We tell stories about
who we are by telling stories about what we have done and what we
have experienced, and the mere repeated telling of those stories shapes
the way we think about ourselves and radically shapes our memory of
who we are. Although there is no singular answer to the question of how
the self is constructed or how we gain the clearest insight into the self,
it seems abundantly clear that the stories we tell convince others about
who we are but are even more convincing to us about the roles we play
in our lives and the kind of persons we are. The stories we tell shape
the way that we think of ourselves, and it is evident with both Frey and
Defonseca they needed inaccurate (false) stories to be able to deal with
different but terrible circumstances in their lives. I am not sure any one
is really immune from using false stories about themselves to be able to
cope more effectively with life circumstances.

3. TRANSPARENCY

I think that the notion of transparency, as discussed in relation to photography, can help to frame some of the issues with the transparency of
self. It is transparency of the self that I think we desire to have when
reading memoirs. Kendall Walton explains that one of the things that
appeals to us about photographs is their realism, but what is really special about photographs is that they are always of something that really
exists.[24] Portraits (paintings) can be life-like, but their relationship to
their subjects is necessarily different from a photograph's relationship
to its subject. Walton claims that photography is like an aid that can
help us with our vision. Photographs can help us "see into the past," he
says.[25] His notion of photographic transparency allows us to literally
see our dead relatives, to see the events of the past, and to see ourselves
as younger than we are now. Paintings, portraits specifically, are not
transparent, and Walton says that there is a difference not just of degree
but of kind between photographs and portraits. Ultimately, Walton
argues that there is a certain kind of *contact* that is achieved through
photographs that is unlike any other kind of perception.[26] He says that
photography produces this kind of contact with its subject in a way that
portraiture can never achieve.

Although I know that Walton's argument is specifically about photographs and visual perception, I wonder how some of the most important

concepts might apply to my issue with the false memoirs. It seems to me that the perception of memoirs is something akin to our perception of what photography can offer us: transparency, accuracy, and realism. This is related to the standard distinction between fiction and nonfiction, but I think that the memoir issue goes deeper than that. The fiction/nonfiction distinction refers to some relationship between the events of the narrative text and some external states of affairs. The memoir/non-memoir distinction appeals to the same relationship, but with memoir the events are assumed to be true and accurate, and the experiences and insights an author offers are assumed to be his/her own. So memoir might be like photography in that it is ideally transparent, for it presents a view of the author's experience that is accurate, realistic, and true. Perhaps we can literally see the experiences of the author. It seems to me that there is an *expectation* of something akin to photographic transparency that readers have when reading memoirs. When someone fakes a memoir, it would be like staging a photo or digitally altering a picture so that it still looks realistic and the viewer does not know. Thus, fraudulent memoirs offer us the illusion of transparency of self when, in fact, the realism, accuracy, and ultimately the truth of the experience have been falsified. Readers who think they are getting a transparent view into another's experiences and later find out those were faked feel justifiably duped. The contact the reader felt with the author is thrown into question, and no matter how good the plot and the prose, readers do not know how to process what they initially took to be truth. Presumably, readers need to reassess and adopt a different stance toward the work, but in reality this seems to be somewhat difficult for readers to do.

But just as Walton's view on the transparency of photography has been called into question because of the complicated subtleties of some of his claims, the application to memoir also needs to get called into question. Cynthia Freeland questions Walton's claims that we literally see our dead relatives and that there is real transparency. She questions whether the contact that we feel is fictional—the photographic prop still functions as a prop in a game of make-believe. People often confuse what Walton claims as epistemological transparency with what Freeland calls "manifestation."[27] That is, what Freeland calls the manifestation of an image is what supplies "a viewer with a sense of contact or presence with the represented subject."[28] Simply, there is literal, direct transparency. (I do literally see my dead ancestors.) But there is a different kind of psychological contact that can be provided through that image. We carry images of our loved ones not so that we can see them but so that we can feel connected to them. We look at loved ones who have died so that we can remember the feelings that they evoke and remember more clearly. Just as we might mistake our literal view of a photograph with the fictional view in which it is part of our game of make-believe, we might also mistake what we think memoirs are. We may understand them as being a literal "seeing through" to a particular life, with the psychological contact or manifestation that we feel when we imagine a life as described through words. Well-written memoirs, indeed well-written stories, evoke wonderful emotions, but it is not the same as having direct access to a life. With truthful memoirs we tend to think that we carry away accurate representations of the author's experiences and feelings. Likely this is what we also desire from nonfiction. With fraudulent memoirs we often end up questioning the whole genre. Had we never learned that a particular memoir was not faithful, we might heap praise and awards for such moving stories. It is only after the fact, when we learn that we thought something was true that was not, that we feel genuinely taken advantage of.

The second important issue that I think is at play in the case of fraudulent memoirs is that the author presents a particular state of affairs as having happened, as having historical accuracy, when such events did not happen. Sometimes there is more at stake with this issue than at other times. When I was a child, my (older) sister shoved a pea up her nose so far that we had to go to the doctor to get it removed. I remember this clearly, and should I ever write a memoir I will be sure to include this story. It was really important to me that the doctor told my mother that she would have expected *me* to do something like that, but not my older sister. This made me feel like a very mature four-year-old. It is one of my earliest clear memories. Of course my sister remembers that *I* was the one who shoved the pea up my nose, and she was the one who felt superior for not doing such a silly thing. Should I write a memoir, perhaps I will need to get my medical records from my pediatrician's office to verify. But I know the pediatrician has passed away. My mother has passed away, and my father does not remember the incident at all. My sister, who remembers it clearly, insists that I was the one who shoved the pea up my nose. So perhaps I should not write about this in my memoir? Or perhaps it does not matter which one of us did it. In my memoir, my *feeling* would be of more significance than the event.

Or perhaps it is just a silly thing that does not matter at all. I could appeal to Lejeune's autobiographical pact and claim that it is just how I remember it. Historical accuracy of this kind of event seems amusing but utterly insignificant. Which events *are* important enough to require historical accuracy if not my own childhood? The exact number of days someone spent in jail?[29] Perhaps events in which many people were affected would be more important than individual remembrances, or events that have documentation would be more important to get right, like the records of a foster child in Los Angeles. Events that involve historical significance seem to me to trump those of individual memory. So Frey's truthful lapse is not that important to me. People were outraged by him because his story was so compelling. Addicts used him as an inspiration and felt duped. But I think that with issues of historical memory there might be other issues at play. Misrepresentation of genocide or the Holocaust, for instance, seems to me a different category. In terms of the issue of historical accuracy, I will divide this into two further components: memory and history. I will with deal with each in turn.

4. MEMORY

Memory is not something to which we have easy, clear access. Psychologists often argue against what might be called the "video tape recorder view of memory."[30] This view suggests that we have a detailed record of our experiences that are faithfully recorded in the hinterlands of our minds, and although we might need to go to great lengths to retrieve some of those memories, like through hypnosis, the memories are in there, they are retrievable, and they are accurate. Psychologists argue that this simply is not true. Instead, the consensus emerging from the psychological literature is that memories are anything but clear or literal representations of events. Memories are interpreted and reinterpreted through time, our retelling of events, the occurrence of new events, the need for consistency in our own beliefs, and of our own basic need for narrative construction. Further, in terms of simple descriptive memory, there is an important distinction to be made between semantic and episodic memory. Semantic memories are small, individual packets of memories that can be verified, agreed on, and even validated. Semantic memories are things like the name of my elementary school, the date of my husband's birthday, and the number of inches in a foot. Episodic memories are series of events that are strung together at least in a chronological order if not also in a causal sequence. These are the kinds of memories that are susceptible to revision of all sorts and the kind of memories out of which we create stories. That is, they are revised by subsequent experience, other memories, other people's renditions of the events, coherence or consistency making, and even our own conscious or unconscious revision to make the events or ourselves more likable or appealing to others. My memory of my sister pushing the pea up her nose is episodic. Thus, where we long for the videotape ideal and we may even claim to have it ourselves when we insist we are right about the way we remember certain events, this kind of transparency is not available, either. Semantic memories are often easily fact-checked, and these are the ones that trip people up when writing memoir, but it seems as if the episodic memories are the ones that are memoir-worthy: sequences, the connected feelings, and eventually the insights. It is these episodic memories that build the backbone of a memoir.

But what am I to do with my fragile and fractured memory? Alison Bechdel said that she kept a meticulous journal as early as she could remember and used it carefully when writing *Fun Home*. But most of us do not keep meticulous notes on our childhood or even our adulthood. I have to dig deep into the computer to figure out what classes I have taught every time I fill out a self-evaluation for two years prior. This information (my teaching schedule) is easily retrievable, but not actually very interesting. It is certainly not memoir-worthy. What is memoir-worthy, formative experiences and the insights that follow, is not reliable. But the episodic memories that we construct through dialogue and description that we fill memoir with have to be close to accurate or at least the documentable parts need to be right. The accuracy of memory is one of the things that makes the genre of memoir itself so complicated. It asks us for nonfiction accuracy, narrative prose, and personal experience and insight. These might not be possible in one account.

5. HISTORICAL ACCURACY

Stephen Ambrose, author of *Band of Brothers* and *Undaunted Courage*; Michael Bellesiles, author of *Arming America: The Origins of a*

National Gun Culture; Joseph Ellis, author of *Founding Brothers: The Revolutionary Generation*; and Doris Kearns Goodwin all wrote very popular history books. These books were awarded Pulitzer Prizes, Bancroft Awards, and were on the all-time bestsellers lists. All of the authors were found guilty of fraud. Ambrose and Goodwin were accused of plagiarism, Bellesiles was accused of "misrepresenting and perhaps even falsifying his research findings," and Ellis was accused of fabricating episodes in his own life, like having fought in Vietnam when he had not.[31] Prizes were revoked and academic jobs were lost. It seems that it is important that academic and popular *history* be historically accurate. At the same time, we want history to be interesting and engaging, and these historians were part of a new wave of popular history that gave better stories and was written with a more compelling prose than a typical history textbook. On the other hand, although we need to hold history to some strict standards, it is questionable whether we need to hold memoirs to the same historical standards. The historical events those historians wrote about, although they are of course subject to some interpretation, contain certain facts (whether or not one actually served in Vietnam, say) of the events that play essential roles in one's credibility as an interpreter of those events. In some cases, the argument could be made that historical accuracy is more important than in others. One example where I take it to be particularly important that memoirs are as historically accurate as possible are Holocaust memoirs.

In 1995 Binjamin Wilkomirski published a memoir called *Fragments: Memories of a Wartime Childhood 1939–1948* about his experience as a child survivor of the Holocaust. Wilkomirski was born in Riga, Latvia. The Nazis killed his father in front of him when he was a toddler. He was moved to Poland to hide with other family members, but before long he was taken to two different concentration camps. At the second camp he was reunited with his mother not long before her untimely death. After the liberation of the camps, Wilkomirski was sent to an orphanage in Krakow and then eventually to Switzerland, where he was adopted by a loving Swiss couple. His mere survival is nothing short of a miracle and certainly worthy of an important memoir. His very moving memoir won numerous awards, including the National Jewish Book Award for autobiography, the Prix Memoire de la Shoah in France, and the Jewish Quarterly Literary Prize in Britain. He has been asked to speak at Holocaust child survivor conferences all over the world. Binjamin Wilkomirski, however, does not exist and never did. Bruno

Grosjean (now Bruno Dössekker), who was born in 1941 in Switzerland and adopted in 1946 in Switzerland, wrote a fictional memoir. Adoption records from Switzerland along with DNA tests eventually verified that Bruno was given up by his mother (with whom his DNA matched), spent some time in a foster home, and was adopted around the age of six by a childless couple. Wilkomirski fabricated, or invented, or imagined the events he included in his very moving and disturbing memoir. All of the literary awards were revoked. Wilkomirski/Dossekker, despite all evidence to the contrary, still claims to this day that it was he who endured the experiences detailed in his memoir.

Herman Rosenblat, who *was* in fact a child survivor of the Holocaust, had his memoir pulled from the press in December 2008 before it was ever released at all. Rosenblat had become famous for an unlikely romance that began while he was held captive in Buchenwald. A Christian farm girl likely saved his life by throwing apples over the fence to him on a regular basis. Twelve years later, the two met on a blind date at Coney Island and eventually celebrated over 50 years of marriage. Rosenblat concocted the story for a "best love story" contest and won. His prize was to be a guest on the *Oprah* show. While Rosenblat later confessed that he fabricated the story, he claims that he did it because he felt he needed to bring something inspirational out of his Holocaust experience. He explained, "I wanted to bring happiness to people, to remind them not to hate, but to love and tolerate all people and I brought hope to many. My motivation was to make good in this world."[32] When he appeared on Oprah's show, she told the Rosenblats that theirs was "the single greatest love story" she had encountered in her 22 years on the show. I am sure she was outraged to hear that she had been duped again.

Why is it the case then, as I would suggest, that faked Holocaust memoirs are a more egregious moral fraud than Frey's exaggerated drug experience? This is not just any old historical accuracy we are talking about, but what is taken to be one of the most severe examples of systematic, long-term evil in human history. In addition to this, there is a cottage industry of Holocaust deniers who use as fodder the examples of fabricated, falsified, or even exaggerated Holocaust accounts. This can lend doubt to the severity of the entire event. Holocaust survivors, family members, and historians have fought for decades against people who deny the severity and even the existence of the event at all. The Holocaust has been given a sacred space of sorts of by historians as something that is only ever taken very seriously, partly because there is that group of people who want to deny its existence and severity. Much of what we now know about the Holocaust is based on oral history—memoirs and memories. In the not-too-distant future, when all of the first-hand testimony is gone, all that will be left are the memoirs of the *experience* of what it was like. A historian at the Holocaust Memorial Museum in Washington, DC, who does many of the interviews with Holocaust survivors, explains that "Most people in an oral history don't tell you facts. They tell you what it felt like . . . sometimes survivors make mistakes when, in hindsight, they interpolate historical data into their own lived experience."[33] They also misremember, exaggerate, fill in, and edit out. Historical documents cannot describe the *hunger* or the *fear* that a child felt in the way that a memoir can. It seems to me to be essential that the Holocaust memoirs that claim truth really are true, *especially* about the Holocaust. This is not to say that there might be wonderful and moving fictions about experiences of the Holocaust, but they seem to have a different power over the imagination than true stories do. However, it is naive to assume that a memoir can function as a one-to-one correspondence between a lived experience of an event and the event itself. It is never that tidy. Rather, it seems more accurate to say that an appeal to lived experience allows for one particular interpretation of reality rather than a singular one or even an "accurate" one. Thus Holocaust memoirs need to be as accurate as possible, keeping in mind that they remain narratives and not documentations or chronicles.

One further issue concerns the reliability or unreliability of human memory along with so-called "recovered memory" or "false memory syndrome." Memories recovered while hypnotized are what Wilkomirski claims allowed him to recall the detail that he outlined in his memoir—details of his experiences in a concentration camp before the age of four. He continues to claim its reliability even in the face of historical documentation, photographs, and even DNA evidence, which are in direct contradiction of his clear memories. There was a large wave of people, beginning in the 1980s, who claimed to have recovered repressed memories from their childhoods of some sort of childhood trauma, most often of sexual abuse, their involvement in satanic rituals, or alien abductions. Without going into too much depth here, to say the least, these claims are most often (but not always) very unreliable. Recovered memories are most often made available through hypnosis and suggestion. When people are hypnotized they lose their inhibitions and are more open to suggestion, and they can "remember" things that didn't happen.[34] Physical evidence is rarely found or is no longer available in many of the cases. Forensic scientist Terence Campbell claims that "the accumulated data related to long-term memory indicate that people rarely remember much that occurred before the age of four, and moreover, memories from between the ages of four and eight tend to be quite unreliable" as well.[35] Thus, in the case of Wilkomirski at least, the reliability of his memories of being a child of the Holocaust might be severely called into question.

6. CONCLUSION

To my own conclusions, I may have uncovered more questions than I have revealed answers. What I have done is tried to identify where memoir lies between the realms of history and fiction or between documentation and fancy. I think it also might be clear that not all of the examples of fraudulent memoir are equally condemnable. Of the examples I cited it seems that there is a continuum of moral blame. On one end of malicious intent is Margaret Seltzer's entirely fabricated story. At the other end of the continuum is Herman Rosenblat, who told a largely true story but who embellished it to put a more positive spin on his Holocaust experience. James Frey, Misha Defonseca, and Binjamin Wilkomirski all remain in between in the murky waters of ill-intent and self-delusion. All of these examples, had they been published as fiction or even as "based on a true story," would not have encountered the moral and legal problems that they did, but I am not sure the most important issue is only one of labeling and marketing.

The second conclusion I might draw from all of this is that well-told narratives still hold great power over us. If the authors in my examples had written less compelling prose, many of them would not have gained the attention that they did. Oprah would not have put Frey's book on her Book Club list had it at least not been very personally compelling. Wilkomirski wrote a very compelling story of the kinds of things that happened to children in the Holocaust. One Holocaust psychologist says that "only a few books about the Holocaust will still be in wide circulation fifty years from now . . . and even though publishers have withdrawn [Wilkomirski's book], she hopes that [it] will be one of those few. The main thing, she says, is that the story is well told."[36] There is an element in all of my examples of prose that is convincing, convincing enough for a reader to feel as though he/she has *contact* with the author. When we find out the contact is based on a lie, whether big or small, we lose confidence in our autobiographical pact, and rather than focusing on the compelling narrative, we slip more easily into our legalistic mode, demanding refunds and initiating law suits. As readers, I hope we can gain more than only what might be documented from stories, whether they are true or fictional.

NOTES

1. Aristotle, *Poetics,* Section 2, part XIII.

2. "Oprah's Questions for James," http://www.oprah.com/oprahshow/Oprahs-Questions-for-James, (accessed March 11, 2016)

3. "Oprah's Questions for James."

4. "Oprah's Questions for James."

5. Alexandra Wolfe, "James Frey Hasn't Given Up on Writing," *The Wall Street Journal,* September 25, 2014.

6. Wolfe, "James Frey Hasn't Given Up on Writing."

7. This is a fake example, but written up in *The Journal of Aesthetics and Art Criticism* by Stephen Cahn, in "The Strange of John Shmarb; An Aesthetic Puzzle," 1975.

8. Mokoto Rich, "Gang Memoir, Turning Page, Is Pure Fiction," *The New York Times,* March 4, 2008, http://www.nytimes.com/2008/03/04/books/04fake.html? (accessed July 5, 2016)

9. John Paul Eakin, "Introduction: Mapping the Ethics of Life Writing," in *The Ethics of Life Writing* (Ithaca, NY and London: Cornell University Press, 2004), 2–3.

10. Philippe Lejeune, *On Autobiography*, trans. Katherine Leary (Minneapolis: University of Minnesota Press, 1989), 3–30.

11. Lejeune, *On Autobiography*, 11.

12. Lejeune, *On Autobiography*, 22.

13. Lejeune, *On Autobiography*, 22.

14. Lejeune, *On Autobiography*, 27.

15. Rigoberta Menchu. *I, Rigoberta Menchu: An Indian Woman in Guatemala* (Brooklyn, NY: Verso, 1984), 1.

16. Greg Grandin, "It Was Heaven They Burned," *The Nation,* September 8, 2010, http://www.thenation.com/article/it-was-heaven-they-burned/ (accessed June 12, 2016)

17. Grandin, "It Was Heaven They Burned."

18. Grandin, "It Was Heaven They Burned."

19. "Is Forrest Carter Really Asa Carter? Only Josey Wales May Know for Sure," *New York Times*, August 26, 1976, http://www.nytimes.com/1976/08/26/archives/is-forrest-carter-really-asa-carter-only-josey-wales-may-know-for.html (accessed July 5, 2016)

20. Alex Blumberg, "180 Degrees," *This American Life,* Originally Aired June 14, 2014.

21. Blumberg, "180 Degrees."

22. This point might be augmented by the suggestion that we live in a much more voyeuristic time than ever before. Over the past three decades we have seen the Oprahization of the confession and trauma story, the increased usage of Facebook (500 million users as of this writing), reality TV, personal blogs, YouTube, and call-in radio shows, all of which allow our personal/anecdotal experiences to stand in for the singular I. We live in a time where the whole notion of privacy is rapidly declining and our own public recounting of our personal lives has become common practice.

23. Rachel Shields, "Adopted by Wolves? Bestselling Memoir Was a Pack of Lies," *The Independent World,* March 1, 2008, http://www.independent.co.uk/news/world/europe/adopted-by-wolves-bestselling-memoir-was-a-pack-of-lies-790000.html (accessed January 29, 2015)

24. Kendall Walton, "Transparent Pictures: On the Nature of Photographic Realism," *Critical Inquiry* 11 (1984), 250.

25. Walton, "Transparent Pictures," 251.

26. Walton, "Transparent Pictures," 269.

27. Cynthia Freeland, "Photographs and Icons," In *Photography and Philosophy: Essays on the Pencil of Nature*, ed. Scott Walden (Malden, MA: Wiley-Blackwell, 2008), 59.

28. Freeland, "Photographs and Icons," 52.

29. James Frey said in *A Million Little Pieces* that he spent 87 days in jail, when it was, in fact, 3 hours.

30. Gil Einstein and Mark McDaniel, *Memory Fitness: A Guide for Successful Aging* (New Haven, CT: Yale University Press, 2004), 34.

31. Peter Charles Hoffer, *Past Imperfect: Facts, Fictions, Fraud—American History from Bancroft, and Parkman to Ambrose, Bellesiles, Ellis, and Goodwin* (New York: Public Affairs, 2004), viii.

32. Motoko Rich and Joseph Berger, "False Memoir of Holocaust Is Canceled," *The New York Times*, December 28, 2008, http://www.nytimes.com/2008/12/29/books/29hoax.html?_r=2. (accessed March 11, 2016)

33. Blake Eskin, *A Life in Pieces: The Making and Unmaking of Binjamin Wilkomirski,* (New York: W. W. Norton & Co, 2002), 158.

34. See Einstein and McDaniel, *Memory Fitness*, especially Chapter 3, sections on "a real world example of false memory: repressed childhood sexual abuse" and "the compelling nature of false memories" (47–52).

35. Terrence Campbell, "Repressed Memories and Statutes of Limitations: Examining the Data and Weighing the Consequences in Intersections of Psychology, Psychiatry and Law: Readings in Forensic Science," *American Journal of Forensic Psychiatry* 16 (1995), 29.

36. Eskin, *A Life in Pieces*, 219.

Chapter Five

Narrative Knowledge

People love to tell stories. When something scary, or funny, or out of the ordinary happens, we cannot wait to tell others about it. If it was *really* funny (or scary or out of the ordinary) we tell the story repeatedly, embellishing as we see fit, shortening or lengthening as the circumstances prescribe. When people are bad storytellers we tend not to pay close attention to their stories; our minds drift, and we hope for a swift conclusion. We tend not to remember those stories as well as the ones that were carefully constructed and skillfully delivered. Storytelling is one of our primary forms of communication with other people. Narrativity is the principle way that human beings order their experience in time. It is also one of the primary ways that humans make coherent sense out of seemingly unrelated sequences of events. In this chapter I will explain how ordering and making sense of the events in the stories that we hear and tell are, in themselves, a form of knowledge. It is a form of knowledge that is often overlooked or minimized, and so the stories and the skill of telling stories are also often overlooked and minimized. What I will argue here is that reading, telling, and hearing well-constructed narratives are not just idle pastimes that we have created for entertainment purposes or even as a mere means of communication. Rather, there are real epistemological benefits to reading, hearing, and telling well-constructed narratives. That is, understanding narrative is a form of knowledge that is different from knowing what or knowing how. It is a form of knowledge that helps us to understand *what it is like*: what it is like to be a different gender, in a different age, in a different historical period, or just what it is like to be anyone but me. It helps us understand what it is like to be someone else, and this understanding helps create empathy. By practicing what I call narrative reasoning, we develop this skill. In a similar way, by practicing discursive reasoning, we develop discursive reasoning skills. In turn, we develop an enhanced reasoning ability that arises from narrative reasoning and narrative meaning construction. Ultimately, those who are able to develop the capacity to reason narratively are able to have a more comprehensive understanding of the human experience because they can make better sense of their own experiences and the experiences of others. People who can reason narratively are able to get more out of reading narratives and have a better sense of how human action is likely to get integrated into new coherent stories. Narrative understanding provides insight into the ways in which we understand ourselves and others and can help us develop a more comprehensive sense of empathy.

Connect to Ch 1 ! !

1. DEFINING NARRATIVE

To begin, I want to go into some detail about what I mean when I talk about narratives, since the reasoning skills that emerge from engaging with narratives are related to the way that we come to understand and make sense of them. Also, narratives are significantly different from both fiction and genre, both of which I have talked about already. Since I do not intend to suggest a *theory* of narrative, I will talk about what constitutes narrativity and what sort of features contribute to increasing the narrativity of a story. Narrative is generally the representation of an event or sequence of events. It is related to description, but it also goes beyond just description. "My cat has fleas" is a description of a situation or state of affairs. "My cat was bitten by a flea" is a narrative about my cat (not a very good one though) that includes a description of something that happened. Some theorists (Barthes and Rimmon-Kenan, for example) argue that there need to be more than one event or state of affairs in a text or work in order for it to minimally be considered a narrative. For my purposes, the change in states of affairs from one to another is essential for understanding the cognitive aspects that can be gained from engaging with narrative. Although I do not advocate a minimal requirement for something to be considered a narrative, at least two, if not multiple, states of affairs increase narrativity significantly.

Narratives also have a unified subject and some relatively easily understood temporal structure. Although many narratives do not order all of their events sequentially, good narratives will have a temporal order that can be gleaned from its reader.[1]

An annal might be something that is temporally ordered and will likely have more than two events or states of affairs, and for this reason it might be put into a category of "story form," but, for my purposes, it does not count as a narrative proper. The primary principle of organization of an annal is, however, that it is *merely* a temporal list of events. It cannot count as a full-fledged narrative, since it may be a temporal list of events that have no unified subject. For example, "The Space Shuttle *Challenger* explodes in 1988, the Berlin Wall comes down in 1989, and there was a massacre at Srebrenica, Bosnia in 1995." This is a temporally ordered list of events and counts as an annal. However, viewed in isolation, the event "The Space Shuttle *Columbia* blows up upon reentry to Earth; the Space Shuttle *Challenger* explodes upon takeoff" has some characteristics of a story form, namely a seemingly unified subject and some possible connection between the events, but it contains none of the elements of a recognizable narrative except for a unified subject (space shuttle disasters). The connection between them has only to do with subject matter but does not have any sort of timeline that is obvious just from what is said.

A chronicle might also fall in the category of story form. A chronicle includes more than one event and/or state of affairs and has a temporal order and a unified subject (a subject being either a topic or a character). A chronicle is a list-like description of at least two events that temporally, but noncausally, connects a unified subject. To develop the former example into a chronicle, we could add some dates or times and say something like this: "the Space Shuttle *Challenger* blew up upon takeoff in 1986; the Space Shuttle *Columbia* blew up upon reentry in 2003." This has a unified subject (space shuttle disasters) and a retrievable temporal order, but it is not a full-fledged narrative because it does not display a connection between events other than a temporal ordering of the events that it recounts.

Causation is often said to be the essential element that makes a narrative a narrative. Readers want to know how not only *that* one event followed another but also *how* the events are related and in what way one event may have caused the other to come about. It is often assumed that one event always causes another, but in most circumstances it tends to be a bit more complicated than that. It is not a simplistic view of direct or necessary causation that is the link needed to do this work, however. Noël Carroll explains that causation is "too strong a relation to hypothesize as the relevant connection operative in all narrative linkages."[2] If causation were the singular necessary relation that unifies narrative structure, then earlier events in narratives would always necessarily causally entail later events. Since this is not the case in all narratives (and perhaps not even most narratives), this cannot be the one thing that makes these groups of events or states of affairs narratives, no matter how unified the subject or temporally sequenced the events are. The connection between the two events may be at least *causally relevant* if not *causally necessary*. That is, the connection between events may not be strictly logically necessary but is related in such a way that a reader can infer causation. Carroll explains that most "narratives are not strings of causal entailments; instead, the earlier events in a sequence of events *underdetermine* later events."[3] What seems to be the case is that an earlier event can be the cause that is necessary to a sufficient condition but is not necessary itself. These conditions are what J. L. Mackie calls INUS conditions: *I*nsufficient, but *N*ecessary parts of a condition that is itself *U*nnecessary but is *S*ufficient for an effect of an event.[4] That is, an earlier event in a narrative is at least a causally relevant (but not causally necessary) condition or component for bringing about later events. In a more strictly causally necessary model, earlier events in a narrative would necessitate the latter events. Carroll explains, "on the causal input model, the earlier event plus some causal input necessitates the succeeding event . . . [but] the narrative relation is often weaker than that of necessitation or causal entailment."[5] Thus INUS conditions can function as the linchpin that holds the narrative connection together, but those conditions are much less causally strict than the directly necessary causal relations. Carroll illustrates INUS conditions in the following example: "The thief enters the bank to rob it, but subsequently, as he exits, he is apprehended by the police."[6] In this narrative, the first event does not causally *necessitate* the second event. Although robbing the bank is causally *relevant* to being apprehended by the police, it is not *entailed* by it. Robbing the bank is, however, a necessary part of the sufficient cause of the police apprehension, but it is not necessary in and of itself. More simply, that there is a thief who enters the bank to rob it *explains* the fact that the police later apprehended him. Further, many of the earlier events may not even be causally relevant but may only be *contributions* to a causally necessary condition. For definitional purposes here, the necessary, direct, causal connection needs to be bracketed, qualified, and minimized potentially only to explanatory features.

Philosopher Arthur Danto argues that causation does not dictate narrativity at all. Rather, he argues that it is an explanation that is the key to narrative. He explains that "the events in question are connected end points of a temporally extended change—as the beginning and end of a temporal whole—and it is the change thus indicated for which a cause is sought."[7] Thus Danto focuses on the explanatory change that happens rather than the causal necessity between two events. To provide the cause is to explain the relationship between events. With the bank robbing example, if we look at just the two events (the thief enters the bank and the thief is apprehended by the police) then we do not necessarily know what the connection is. With narratives that have good causation built in we are either told or we can easily infer what the cause is of one event to the second event. The cause could be a number of different explanations. It could be that the thief wanted to be caught and so tipped the police off, which is why the police were there and were prepared to apprehend the thief. Being able to reason through and make sense of narratives require one to be able to fill in this explanatory gap using information provided or by inferring from other clues. Understanding that there could be multiple explanations is part of understanding how to reason through, ideally, finding the best possible explanation. For my purposes, I will focus on this kind of inference-making that we use to fill the explanatory gap as being the key to narrativity. In order to make good narrative inferences we have to be given good explanatory cues within the text, so that we can make the right inferences. Making the right inferences is an integral part of understanding the text in a more global way.

Narrative inference-making is a form of abductive reasoning. There are three basic kinds of reasoning or inference-making. Inductive reasoning derives general conclusions from specific observations. Deductive reasoning derives specific conclusions from general observations in order to that follow logical arguments. Abductive reasoning finds the inference to the "best explanation" and fills it in between premises and, in the case of narratives, between events. This is what we do when we reason through narratives or stories. We make narrative inferences, we insert causation, and we make connections between events that are not explicitly spelled out for us.

If the elements in a narrative bear no sort of causal relation to each other, then they can seem to be more of an order of coincidence than of a narrative. E. M. Forster provides an example of an incredibly short narrative. "The king died and then the queen died."[8] This is merely a chronicle since there is no necessary causal or identifiable underlying cause or explanation between the first event and the second event. It is not clear to a reader, nor can it really be discerned, what the relationship is between the two events although they seem to have a unified subject and there is an implied temporal order. But it is not clear whether the queen's death is related to the king's death. The following alteration changes this from a chronicle to a narrative: "the king died and then the queen died, of grief."[9] This is a narrative because the relationship between the two events is made clear. There is no explanatory gap that needs to be filled. The reader does not have to guess why the queen died. One might *guess* or *infer* from the first story that the two events are related because of their unified subjects, but from so little information it would be pure speculation. In the latter example however, not only do we have a directly causal explanation, we can also fit it into the following schema:

1. The king died
2. The queen was overcome with grief over her husband's death
3. The queen died

Moving from the first state to the second, the explanatory gap gets filled with the simple explanation that she died of grief. This could not be done in the earlier example.

Narrative *explanation* does not focus only on how one event is produced or affected by another but also on the more subtle transition from beginning to end in terms of explanation and plot construction. The explanation involved in narrative is not merely a series of events that happen to a unified subject. What makes narrative distinctive are the clues that help readers to account for the change that happens between the beginning and the end to make the explanatory gap into a coherent story. Narrativity is the ability to account for the change that happens between the beginning and the end to make the explanatory gap into a coherent whole.

To this point, I have been dealing with extremely short narratives so that I might explain what the component parts are in terms of definitions. But real narratives, from the stories that people tell to the long novels that we read, are much longer, much more complex, and require much more from us as readers to combine together what is going on in a story to connect all the pieces. In more complex narratives than I have been dealing with so far, plot is the structure through which events are connected to a narrative. A narrative is constructed of events only to the extent to which the plot crafts events into a narrative. Events are gathered together and it is the plot that makes the events stand out beyond what they would be in an annal or chronicle. Plot also combines two important aspects: chronological and nonchronological. The chronological aspect of plot characterizes the events of the narrative and shows the reader how the events follow a particular timeline. The non-chronological aspect of the plot connects the events together in such a way that no matter how temporally diverse the events actually are, they can be seen to form a coherent whole. Plot structures how and in what order the reader becomes aware of what happens in the story. Although the same set of events can be told in a different order or with a different plot, there must be some consistently identifiable transformations that can serve as a basis for the narrative so that it can be handled in different meaning-preserving sequences.

The other part of the nonchronological dimension of plot is that of the human motivations found developed through the story. One of the main reasons we read narratives, or perhaps one of the main motivations to continue once we are into the story, is to see how human motivations are played out within the context of the story. Although this is not going to fit neatly into anything that even resembles necessary and sufficient conditions of what a narrative might look like, it does seem to be one of the main incentives we have for reading.

2. HOW WE UNDERSTAND STORIES

Narrative structure is the key underlying feature of both literary fiction and nonfiction. Narrative prose is usually connected to a narrator, a story line, or plot. It is presented in a sequence (usually words or pictures or some combination of the two), and there is often a discernable beginning, middle, and end. Aristotle gets the credit for pointing out the vast importance of the beginning, middle, and end to good narrative construction. When I use the term *narrative,* I intend it to refer to the structure of the prose. When I say fiction here I mean either fiction as a literary genre (most associated with novels and short stories) or as an abstract philosophical category having to do with an intentional stance a reader takes toward a given work. I want to address here what it means to understand a basic narrative, whether it be fictional or nonfictional. Narrative is most generally what we mean when we say story. Narrative is a particular form of communication that conveys description, cause, sequence, insight, and character development most generally. Narrative is to be distinguished from argument, poetry, and scientific writing among others, which are often referred to as discursive texts. Following a narrative is not always linear or temporal. That is, we rarely read stories that say this happened, and this happened next, and then this other thing happened after that. Those stories are really boring. The narrative structure itself involves the need for inference-making as part of the story. Since causation and temporality are not always given at the outset, linearity is also not a given. That is, a linear sequence would tell the reader what happened and then what happened next or what happened and what caused it. This might be more like a chronicle. But many (even most) narratives tend not to just list events in chronological order but are written so that the reader has to do some of the work to pay attention to connections, feelings, seemingly irrelevant pieces of information that in fact are relevant, and the way in which events impact other events. Unlike reading through an argument, however, where a sequence of statements logically leads its reader to a reasoned conclusion, narrative structure instead requires its reader to follow a sequence of statements or happenings as it unfolds. Often, one is not sure where the story leads until the reader reaches the conclusion. The reader must make a conscious effort to figure out what is going on in the narrative and must work to understand how what he/she is reading can form into a coherent whole. W. B. Gallie explains that "in following a story we must always keep our minds open and receptive to new possibilities of development, new hints, clues and leads, up to the very last line: besides exercising our intelligence in making predictions or seeing complicated but definite lines of continuity, we must be ready constantly to reassemble and reassess different possible relevancies, links, and dependencies, [and] still unexplained juxtapositions."[10] However, we must be *trained* to follow stories, especially ones that are not direct and linear. As I said above, learning to understand narrative is a skill one develops over a long period of time, understanding many stories, telling many stories, and reading many books. This skill allows us to get more and more from narratives as we develop our ability to make inferences, predict better outcomes, and imagine more deeply.

In her book *Narrative Comprehension*, Catherine Emmott claims that the reader must know, at the very least (1) which characters are present in the physical environment, (2) where the action is located, and (3) what the approximate time of the action is.[11] These three things are required because the actions of one character will affect other characters in a particular context and "whether or not precise details of the time and location are necessary to read a particular story, the reader needs enough information to make orientational judgments such as 'is the action occurring in the main narrative "present time" or a flashback "past time"?'"[12] Each sentence of a narrative adds information about these three story markers and helps the reader to do what Donald Braid calls a "repeated reframing" of the events understood by the reader.[13] Repeated reframing helps the reader to "predict the narrative course and grasp the coherence that informs the narrative and gives it meaning."[14] The organizing principle may seem atemporal, but the coherence-making required on the part of the reader happens spatially and temporally as each sentence adds more and more information for the reader. Simultaneously, as we comprehend story structures and repeatedly reframe contextual clues as we read, we also assess the plausibility of the events of the story. This assessment is the beginning of the active construction of genre that happens in the reader.

Beyond the "who, where, and when" categories, coherence-making is the other essential part of understanding narrative. Coherence-making is essential partly because coherence is not explicit in the world outside of narrative. Coherence is always constructed by the observer, but it never exists in the "real" world. It provides the sense that the beginning, middle, and end all work together to form a whole coherent story. Experiences are never coherent in this way until they are explicitly narrated. For instance, I can tell you a story about something that happened to me this morning that makes causal sense, but the actual events of this morning, until they are carefully chosen (I always leave the most boring parts out of my narrations) and constructed into a story form, are not coherent in this way ("After I had my coffee, I was much better prepared to take on what was about to happen."). Making sense of a narrative should be a conceptually less difficult task than making sense of a real, un-narrated event because I am giving a setup and telling you, directly or indirectly, what the important parts are of my experience. Although the narrative should provide a basic structure, readers must be able to take in the combination of information and put it together into a coherent whole. What is significant here is the relationship between the text and the reader, in the way that the narrative is structured in such a way as to facilitate a certain kind of understanding generated by the reader. The narrative itself stands separately from the narrative understanding or comprehension that the reader has. The way that the narrative is constructed has a direct impact on the way that its reader will be able to understand and construct the story.

Many of the pleasures that we can get from reading narrative come from the outcomes of this kind of comprehension. I make inferences and predictions, and when they turn out to be correct I feel satisfied. These inferences or guesses or predictions are one of the things that make narrative prose different from other kinds of prose. With a chronicle, for example, or a scientific paper, the kind of inference-making one gets to do is minimized in comparison to what we do with narrative prose. Noël Carroll calls this kind of satisfaction a "transactional value" of reading, as the "value we derive by, among other things, exercising our powers of inference and interpretation in the course of reading."[15] Presumably, the notion of the transaction comes from Louise Rosenblatt, who emphasized the organic relationship between the reader and the text. Theories of reading have varied widely over the years. Formalism, for example, emphasizes the text itself as the primary locus of meaning. Reader-response criticism focuses on the experience of the reader. Intentionalism claims that the meaning of the text comes from what the author intended. But Rosenblatt argues that the meaning is created by the *interaction* between the reader and the text. Neither one creates meaning on its own. She argues that each transaction or encounter between the reader and the text constitutes a unique experience. Since every reader brings different knowledge, beliefs, and background assumptions to a text, no text could ever have the same exact meaning to every reader. Readers regularly make predictions about what might happen, they make inferences about why certain characters did various things, and they make (moral) judgments about whether or not the characters behaved as they should have. But these predictions are not just about typical genre structures. These predictions are also filtered by one's beliefs and experiences, as well as how much experience one has reading. More sophisticated readers will often have better comprehension, and comprehension is an active process on the part of the reader, so then the genre of the text cannot be exclusively within the text itself.

Rosenblatt not only argued that multiple interpretations of a text were legitimate but also that some interpretations were superior to others given some set of criteria. She argues, however, that "a full understanding of literature requires both a consciousness of the reader's own 'angle of refraction' and any information that can illuminate the assumptions implicit in the text."[16] Narrative comprehension then involves both making sense of the formal structures within the text and simultaneously working the sense of the story into one's own schemas of how the world works, what is possible and what is probable, how empirical experience fits with what is being narrated, and how wish satisfaction and fulfillment are fleshed out as the reader makes sense of the narrative. So if one reads and believes wholeheartedly (and unreflectively) that the text is fictional, then the kinds of possible and probable world-generating beliefs are not challenged. But if one does *not know* if the book is "true" or not, then one must actively work to make sense of the text in ways that one does not have to work if those assumptions are made in advance.

So many of the pleasures of reading come from narrative comprehension and making the kinds of inferences and predictions that we tend to make when we read narrative. Genre helps us to make particular kinds of predictions about what is going to happen as well as inferences about why various events might have happened already in the plot. Reading a comedy or a romance or a thriller or a Western will vary in terms of the kinds of predictions and inferences one might make in reading. Genre is critical in helping a reader to get these sorts of predictions right since the satisfaction of these is a large part of the pleasure we derive from reading. Knowing the genre then, fiction or nonfiction, romance, science fiction, or comedy, can help us to make better *predictions* (because we know the kind of things that are likely to happen) and more accurate *inferences* (so we understand better *why* various things happen in the text), and genre can help us to better frame our sense of causation. Understood within the framework of the transactional theory, genre is not *in* the text but is generated out of the text in an interaction between the text and the reader. Genre may be less important here than even understanding that narrative comprehension is a special kind of assessment that we learn to do with narrative. And the kind of knowledge that we can glean from this is distinctive from other kinds of knowledge, specifically knowing that and knowing how.

With what I have laid out thus far I want to be clear that I am neither suggesting a theory of narrative nor am I dictating a set of necessary and sufficient conditions for something to qualify as a narrative. What I do want to do is gesture toward what seem to be some of the overarching components that constitute narrativity. I do not take causation to be the necessary or sufficient condition that makes something a narrative, even though it may play a large part in providing the explanatory gap in some narratives. I also want to make clear that the kinds of narratives I am attempting to include here vary from the traditional to the nonlinear and the oral storytelling traditions that come from long ago. It seems important to me to start with the very basic to show how narratives work before moving to exceptions or exceptionally complicated narratives and certainly before literature can be accounted for in any meaningful way.

To reiterate, narratives are representations of at least two events with a unified subject and a retrievable temporal order that generally have an explanatory gap that needs to be filled in by the reader. Good narratives will allow enough information for that gap to be meaningfully filled, and I think that it is that gap that makes us wonder about what will happen and why. It will be important in what follows to understand the aspects of the narrative as being different from the abilities that readers need to have in order to develop the cognitive skill of narrative reasoning. Narrative knowledge has to do with both a reader's ability to make sense of the parts of the narrative and with how much a reader can potentially make accurate inferences, connect together disparate pieces of plots, and interpret the text in ways that are appropriate to the reader's own life situation.

3. NARRATIVE REASONING

There are two general models from which most of our reasoning is generated: discursive and narrative.[17] Discursive reasoning relies on logical, direct arguments, while narrative reasoning depends on the narrative aspects of a story to order a certain experience. Discursive reasoning moves from premises to conclusions and moves forward by using reasoning or argument as opposed to story. It is here meant to include deductive reasoning, possibly inductive, but not abductive (the inference to the best explanation). Discursive reasoning is the ideal of a *formal* system of description and/or explanation. It is not *merely* linear, syllogistic reasoning systems, but not much is required to reach a valid conclusion. Discursive prose is often the way we instruct, direct, or bullet-point information. It is what we desire when we ask people to get to the point. Narrative psychologist Jerome Bruner explains his version of this kind of reasoning as one that "employs categorization or conceptualization and the operations by which categories are established, instantiated, idealized, and related one to the other to form a system."[18] When we have clear categories, we know where to put certain kinds of information or how to categorize particular (or new) experiences. The imaginative application of discursive reasoning, Bruner says, leads to "the ability to see possible formal connections before one is able to prove them in any formal way" while the imaginative application of the narrative "leads instead to good stories, gripping drama, [and] believable (though not necessarily 'true') historical accounts."[19] Discursive reasoning helps us to categorize, connect, and theorize. It helps us make abstract arguments and universal claims by helping us to make connections between the particular and the universal.

Discursive reasoning is exemplified by the ubiquitous logical argument: "Socrates is a man, all men are mortal, therefore, Socrates is mortal." Although there could be *stories* told about Socrates' mortality (there are, in fact, many) this classic syllogism has no real narrative structure. A narrative about Socrates would look something more like this: "There was a man called Socrates, who, because of his suggestion that people needed to question the folkways of knowledge in ways they had never done before, was tried as a heretic, condemned as guilty, and made to drink hemlock." There is an identifiable line of argument in the syllogism about Socrates that the second story lacks. There is, however, in the story an identifiable narrative structure that allows the reader to follow the events in the narrative and to understand how the conclusion (that Socrates is put to death) logically follows and even sufficiently entails what came before. There is no logical conclusion in the story that can be *proven* from what comes before, but there is an identifiable narrative structure that can be pointed to. Although making the suggestion that people question the folkways of knowledge does not necessarily entail death by hemlock, it is easily discernible in this short narrative that this is the sufficient cause of the outcome of the story.

Discursive and narrative reasoning have different operating principles, but both have their own criteria for success. They differ fundamentally, however, in the ways in which they go about verification. Bruner goes so far as to assert that "a good story and a well-formed argument are different natural kinds" even though both are used as ways of communicating information and of convincing others.[20] Although I think he means by "natural kinds" something different than philosophers generally mean, this is a strong category distinction that fully divides the kind of working through that is possible with each. He explains that the discursive "verifies by eventual appeal to procedures for establishing formal and empirical truth" while the narrative "establishes not truth but verisimilitude" and lifelikeness.[21] Both can be used as a means to convince others, but what they convince us of is fundamentally different. Arguments convince us of their conclusions and possibly their truth, while narrative convinces us of its lifelikeness and believability. Truth often comes in as a distant second, however, to well-constructed and well-executed stories. Narrative lines of reasoning do not generally prove anything, but they do show how something might have come to be the case. There are certain causal or underdetermined causal linkages within a narrative that readers should be able to discern that are not as easily identifiable or linear as what is found in discursive reasoning. We regularly utilize both narrative and discursive reasoning in order to organize and make sense of our experiences and how to fit those into a larger structure of understanding. We explain our lived experiences in terms of plot, and more often than not, those plot structures produce the most sensible statements and explanations of our experience and beliefs. Both are legitimate and rational ways of understanding and ordering our experience of the world, but both produce cognition and understanding by different means that correspond with the inherent structure of their own logic.

The way that causation is construed in the way narratives are defined and/or identified is extremely important because this is one of the factors that differentiates narrative structure and discursive structure. If narrative structure were merely based on direct causation, then narrative reasoning and narrative meaning construction would look a lot more like discursive reasoning than it in fact does. Thus it is important to note the differences between the ways that causation could be construed in the different kinds of reasonings.

Although these two modes of understanding are complementary, it is important to note that they are neither *reducible* nor *translatable* to one another. It seems dubious, and maybe even worse, futile, to attempt to either reduce or translate from one to the other since they are, at base, fundamentally different kinds of reasoning. This is not to say, moreover, that stories cannot exemplify both the narrative and discursive structures.

Further, it is clear that we get better at discursive reasoning with practice. This would seem to be the underlying assumption of much of the philosophy taught, especially of critical thinking and logic courses. The explicit expectation in these classes is for students to learn to identify various valid and invalid logical inferences. Students are taught these inferences with the hope and expectation that they will be able to identify the same inferences in their own reasoning and the reasoning of others, whether it be in a philosophical treatise, arguments of their own making, or late night conversations over wine. In teaching students even basic logical rules like Aristotle's Barbara syllogism (all men are mortal, Socrates is a man, Socrates is mortal), modus tollens (if P then Q, not Q, then not P, or, if I am in Greenville, then I am in South Carolina, I am not in South Carolina, therefore I am not in Greenville), and modus ponens (if P, then Q. P, therefore Q. If I am in Greenville then I am in South Carolina. I am in Greenville. Then I must be in South Carolina), students are often able to apply these logical inferences to their own, and their friends', reasoning processes. The most fun I have with these is using them to analyze the opinions section of the newspaper. Local papers provide the best examples. The formalization of logical structure, formal reasoning, and the identification of logical fallacies are an essential part of the development of reasoning capabilities. It is clear that we get better at discursive reasoning with practice as we value and teach math, scientific reasoning, and data analysis among others. It is now up to me to show two things. First, how it is that narrative reasoning is substantially different from discursive reasoning and, second, that we are able to get better at narrative reasoning with practice. Only once I have done these two things will I really be able to begin to make any further arguments about what the epistemic and cognitive benefits are of reading narrative and, in particular, well-constructed narrative.

4. NUSSBAUM ON NARRATIVE

Martha Nussbaum makes the argument that reading literature can help us to expand our study of ethics because we can practice expanding our moral imaginations by engaging in narratives. She argues that with literature, the conjunction of the form and the content together allows a particular style to emerge that can prompt us to reflect on our own moral situations in a significantly different way than we can with philosophical ethical treatises. She explains that "certain truths about human life can only be fittingly and accurately stated in the language and forms characteristic of the narrative artist."[22] Her suggestion is that, by adding good literature to the study of ethics, we should be able to produce a more comprehensive and meaningful understanding of ethical life. Although many would quibble over whether or not Harry Potter counts as "good literature," as Nussbaum advocates we should read, Lauren Binnendyk has several studies about the ways in which that cultural iconic narrative is able to serve to help develop moral reasoning for preadolescent children.[23] Think good and evil, the importance of family and friends, and self-identity. Either way, practice with narrative can provide something that we cannot get with discursive teachings.

Part of the basis of Nussbaum's claim is that the *style* of narrative is uniquely qualified to present what she calls a view of life. She explains that the "telling itself—the selection of genre, formal structures, sentences, vocabulary of the whole manner of addressing the reader's sense of life—all of this expresses a sense of life and value, a sense of what matters and what does not, of what learning and communicating are, or life's relations and connections."[24] All of this, in addition to the notion that events are never experienced except through a human perspective (although there may *ideally* be omniscient narrators, we can never experience narratives except through a particular perspective), adds to the fact that reading literature, according to Nussbaum, helps us to experience the world more fully. Life is never presented straightforwardly but always through the lens of a speaker, whose lens(es) may be or are likely to be very different from ours. Nussbaum also suggests that "literature is an extension of life not only horizontally, bringing the reader into contact with events or locations or persons or problems he or she has not otherwise met, but also, so to speak, vertically, giving the reader experience that is deeper, sharper, and more precise than much of what takes place in life."[25] Reading good literature then can make us more moral, her argument goes, since we can experience the world in ways that we cannot on our own through our own experience. For Nussbaum, narrative and literary imagining are not opposed to rational argument or discursive reasoning, but they can provide benefits that discursive reasoning on its own cannot provide.[26]

Nussbaum makes an additional argument in her book *Poetic Justice* that reading good literature can help one to become a better citizen. By using the imagination in the ways that literature requires of us, we can imagine, practice imagining, and get better at imagining the position of others. Unlike more social scientific or historical texts, literary narratives typically invite their readers to centrally imagine characters' experiences—experiences that are often very different from their own. In the way that the text invites the reader to participate, it gives the sense of a number of different kinds of possibilities between the characters and the reader. Novels present themselves in ways that are necessarily from a particular perspective, either from an omniscient narrator or from one or more of the characters. But it is not just that literary narratives present themselves this way. It is more to the point that literary narratives ask the reader to see a given state of affairs in a particular way over other, alternative ways. Nussbaum writes that "the novel presents itself as a metaphor. See the world in this way, and not in that, it suggests. Look at things as if they were like this story, and not in other ways recommended by social science."[27] By practicing doing this, we can learn how better to be "judicious spectators"[28]—and in turn better citizens. The emotion of a judicious spectator must be, importantly, the emotion of a *spectator* and not a *participant*. It must be that of an observer and not an insider. Nussbaum explains, "this means not only that we must perform a reflective assessment of the situation to figure out whether the participants have understood it correctly and reacted reasonably; it means, as well, that we must omit that portion that derives from our own personal interest in our own well-being."[29] We imagine the lives of others that are presented through narrative form. By expanding the moral imagination we are better able to empathize with others, and we can become better at public thinking. Nussbaum argues that this can make one a better juror, citizen, and public thinker.

The underlying assumption that Nussbaum uses here, which is the explicit notion that I want to defend, is that through engaging with well-constructed narratives (what Nussbaum focuses on specifically is "good literature" and my scope of narrative is purposefully much *adding to Nussbaum*

broader than that) our own way of reasoning is changed through the moral imagination; our reason is heightened and thereby influenced through the *structure* of what we read. Although it is not true that we automatically or even quickly begin to pick up the thinking patterns of the kinds of narratives we read, it is true that in certain ways our reasoning abilities are influenced by the reasoning structures with which we engage. What Nussbaum focuses on is the form or the structure of literature, in addition to its inherently subjunctive, or what-if, nature. This structure is what she argues to be so different from the philosophical or discursive structure of other ethical treatises that might cover similar ground. Similarly, bad literature, says Nussbaum, can cause one to become morally corrupt. With the shift of focus that I want to provide, morally bad content will not be the corrupting influence cognitively (although it might be with another focus) as much as poorly told and poorly delivered stories. So while there is a long history of philosophical criticism about the potential moral corruption caused by literature, the corruption I might worry about is less dependent on the *content* of the story as much as it is on the form and the delivery. Thus, while my distinction between discursive and narrative reasoning is played out in Nussbaum's work (which argues that narrative can make us more moral, within specific constraints) it does the same work for my argument that suggests that narratives can help us to be better able to reason.

5. IMAGINATION AND UNDERSTANDING

It is clear now, that there are (at least) two different kinds of reasoning skills that we use regularly and can develop with practice. Without going into great detail about what the imagination can do in conjunction with this, I will say that the imagination plays a very important role in narrative reasoning and narrative meaning construction. Narrative reasoning and the capacity to imagine are mutually dependent, and both should begin to develop at an early age. Imagination can help to facilitate causal judgments about how things might have turned out differently. Historians use this kind of speculation, as do philosophers with our thought experiments. In a much more mundane sense, we do this in our everyday lives. This is, in fact, how we can learn from our mistakes; we identify what went wrong and then imagine alternate ways things could have turned out and what we could have done or said differently to make those alternatives happen.

Utilizing our imaginations requires more than just discursive reasoning. Psychologist Paul Harris explains, "there is a great deal of work showing that when adults listen to a narrative they build in their mind's eye, so to speak, a mental image or a model of the situation that is being described and of the events that unfold. And it is that mental model that they retain over a long period of time rather than the particular words."[30] We tend to keep the gist of the story[31] in what Daniel Dennett might call the Cartesian Theater,[32] as opposed to any particular sentences that might constitute the story. Thus when called to tell the story, we can adapt as the circumstances prescribe. Badly told or badly constructed stories, on the other hand, are more difficult to build in imagination than well-constructed stories. Badly told stories are ones that do not make even implicit causal connections and are difficult to follow. They go on too long before getting to a point or a punch line, have irrelevant details, or do not develop the motivations of the characters. Thus well-constructed stories facilitate a better use of the imaginative faculties. Harris argues that these mental models, constructed in the imagination, develop out of the early childhood engagement with narrative and pretend play. The capacity that children have to engage in make-believe early on is not something that they lose as adults. Rather, adults, although we unfortunately engage in much less *physical* pretend play than do children, use this capacity to imagine and narrate various kinds of possible situations and outcomes.

Harris cites an example that is helpful to understanding the development of the schema of discursive and narrative reasoning. He describes a study conducted by Sylvia Scribner that showed that, in the absence of formal education, children and adults alike adopt an "empirical orientation" toward reasoning.[33] That is, they use their own experience to "supplement, to distort or even to reject the premises supplied by the interviewer; they reason instead on the basis of their empirical experience."[34] After two or three years of formal education they are able to adopt what might be called a "theoretical" or "syllogistic" approach to reasoning. With the discursive capacity to reason better developed, subjects were able to "focus on the claims encapsulated in the premise of the problem, even when those premises do not fit into their everyday experience and they confine their reasoning to what follows from these premises."[35] Although Harris ultimately argues that the discursive capacity is not something unusual or unnatural that can only be developed through formal schooling, it is important to note that this capacity to reason is significantly different from the more literal empirical stance.

According to Harris, encouraging a make-believe attitude helps to engage the analytic stance. For example, Harris conducted an experiment with four- and six-year-olds where he began by telling the children something contradictory to what they knew, like "all fishes live in trees." Then the children were given a second, minor, premise: "Tot is a fish." The question thus posed to the children was, "Does Tot live in the water?" An empirical approach to this question should prompt a "yes" answer, but an analytic approach, if the child accepts the initial premise that is counter to what they know, the logically correct answer is "no." These hypotheticals were presented to each group of children in two different ways, as matter of fact or with a make-believe prompt like, "let's pretend I'm on another planet," and the experimenter continued the hypothetical in a dramatic, story-telling voice. Within both age groups, the make-believe presentation prompted more logical replies than the matter-of-fact presentation. Harris' conclusion to all of this is that counter to the common suggestion that narrative, fiction, and/or make-believe scenarios generally constrict, rather than enhance epistemological performance, he has shown how setting up theoretical analytic scenarios—even when asked to imagine that fish live in trees, that there is a wardrobe with no back on it that leads to a magical world, or that there is a magical ring that can make one disappear—allows analytic reasoning to continue and to develop. Harris explains that even with a wide variety of make-believe cues given to the children, they all seem to converge in producing a similar psychological stance. Harris explains that this stance prompts "children to treat the problems as descriptions of an imaginary world; this imaginary world contains creatures and events that violate their everyday knowledge."[36] Thus unlike many theories that argue that make-believe (fiction or narrative) works counter to healthy reasoning because it enlists fanciful premises, Harris shows how it is, in fact, the case that these reasoning structures continue to function well in an epistemologically significant way.

I would like to take Harris' argument one step further and suggest that not only do discursive reasoning processes remain intact, and can even be enhanced by engaging in narrative, but that the narrative ability to reason is engaged, and thereby enhanced, to an even greater degree by reading, hearing, and telling well-constructed narratives. Parallel to what Harris points out about the development of discursive reasoning from an analytic education, the development of the narrative-reasoning ability emerges in a similar way. When we begin to learn to reason, it is not entirely discursive or empirical. *We learn through the structure of stories*. That is, we learn to reason through the reasoning provided to us through hearing and telling stories. We learn to reason through narrative. By engaging with narratives, we practice using our narrative reason. The structure found within narratives helps us to imagine more broadly than we are called to with discursive thinking. Narrative comprehension or understanding is enhanced from engagement with narrative structure in the same way that discursive understanding is enhanced from engagement and practice with discursive structure. This is significant because it tells us about our engagement with narrative generally, fiction more specifically, and gives us insight into the role that the imagination plays in the world as we construct it. The way we construct our narratives (fictional and nonfictional) is importantly tied to the way we understand, order, and construct our own reality and our own personal identity. Whatever information might be available from a given sequence of events *as a story* must be *turned into* a story. Thus even the creation of a narrative from a sequence of events requires the narrative capacity to reason. The more developed one's ability to narratively reason, the more one can get out of stories. The better one is at constructing stories, the more intelligent one should be able to become—assuming intelligence is related to the ability to retrieve information readily and to find coherence where it does not obviously exist.

Thus engaging with well-constructed narratives helps us to be better reasoners in a general way, more general than the way Nussbaum argues but for similar reasons. Reading fiction in particular can help with this skill perhaps even more readily than not engaging with it, as good stories from early on can help us to develop this capacity. Reading narrative fiction and experiencing life both involve people's performing actions in pursuit of goals and having various emotional reactions to events. Thus understanding how our different inferencing mechanisms work might help us to be able to develop these capacities further. The inferencing mechanisms that are used to make sense of the everyday world are the same ones utilized during the comprehension of narratives. There is no real justification to believe that readers (or moviegoers or game players, etc.) would turn these inferencing mechanisms off while engaging with fictional narratives as the concern might go with some Platonists.

6. TELLING STORIES

What actually goes on around us often approximates pure chaos for our senses. Sounds, smells, feels, familiar and new, bombard us all day every day. We naturally focus on some and push others to the background. What we bring consciously to the foreground, what we pay attention to most, is the material that we actively make meaning of. The most important events we tell to other people. But we rarely, if ever, just report events unconnected to the way we interpret how they fit into the bigger picture of what is important to us. Storytellers organize stories in two primary ways—through space and time. That is, storytellers like to spatially orient their listeners to where they were when the action of the story happened. They want listeners to be able to imagine the relevant landmarks of their stories so they can get a more accurate mental representation of what happened. Storytellers also want to convey a sequence of events but not always in a temporal list. Good stories reveal the sequence of events but, importantly, emphasize what caused various things to happen. This insertion of causality is often where the story-crafting or story-altering comes in. In one study about the extent to which we alter the stories we tell about ourselves, Barbara Tversky had a group of undergraduates keep track of stories they told over the period of several weeks. Each student kept track of the gist of each story told, the intended audience, their purpose in telling the story, and the intensity of the story relayed as well as their feeling about the event, whether it was positive or negative. The students then recorded whether they had distorted the story by either adding or leaving out information or exaggerating or minimizing relevant details. They were also asked to report whether or not they had misrepresented any of the events in their story. Tversky's findings seem to be about what one would expect. Students told stories about common themes, more often than not painting themselves in a positive light. What was surprising to Tversky was the amount that students, by their own admission, altered their stories. Tversky reports that "students added, omitted, exaggerated, or minimized information in at least 61 percent of the stories the retold, sometimes altering a story in more than one way."[37] According to Tversky, "distorting seems to be the norm, not an aberration."[38] It does seem to be the case that storytellers tend to distort more by leaving out important information (36 percent of stories) than by adding parts or inventing portions of the story that did not happen at all (13 percent). None of this is particularly surprising. We tell stories to others not only to convey information but also to present a certain image of ourselves to others and to retell and refine our own beliefs about ourselves and others. One of the other noteworthy findings from this study, and influential in the ways we tell stories to each other, is that storytellers amended their stories based on their perceived audience. Importantly, listeners know how to interpret stories and often do not make all literal assumptions about what others tell. Hearers can be very good at understanding the gist of a story and not insisting that all of the facts must be true. Even though we might not always be truthful or accurate storytellers, as listeners we also have interpretive skills. Both telling and listening are part of the meaning-making or sense-constructing that we do to sort out the barrage of things that happen around us every day. And every day we tell stories for the benefit of both ourselves and others to actively construct meaning out of our own interpretation of the events we experience.

If it is legitimate to assume that there are (at least) two different kinds of reasoning methods (discursive and narrative) and that we can clearly be trained to think in the discursive mode, it can be legitimately argued that we can be and are trained to think in the narrative mode as well. It would seem also that it is just as important that we foster our narrative reasoning skills, since it is such a widespread and important form of communication. But I think that narrative reasoning is downplayed greatly. As I discussed earlier in the chapter about school curriculum and whether or not we can "learn" from fiction, I showed clearly that since we do not have a sense that we learn content from reading narrative we do not learn anything at all. But narrative reasoning is what we get from reading narrative. Not from a single reading, and not from the content, but from being able to make sense of stories, knowing how to skillfully relate experiences, and how to relay information through good narratives (which is often what makes good teachers really memorable—not that they give good Powerpoint presentations but that they tell good stories). More often than not, cultural knowledge is captured best by oral stories. Think of healing practices, cooking knowledge, and town histories. These are conveyed through story and not lists of instructions.

What I really want get to is that the kind of reasoning skills that one can acquire from reading narratives could make one a better thinker, not just morally in the way that Nussbaum might argue but more broadly. It could be argued that the epistemological benefits of reading literature are significantly different from the epistemological benefits of engaging with other kinds of nonnarrative art, like looking at a painting or listening to music. Although they may also have their benefits, narrative literature provides something distinctive and unique that really nothing else can teach. The epistemological benefits of reading literature may in fact be greater than with other kinds of arts. That is, when we ask the question "Can we learn from art?" or, more particularly, "*What* can we learn from art?" philosophers have had trouble answering this because whatever it is that we seem to gain from art or literary narrative is non-propositional. We might be better prepared to answer this question now by saying that we gain narrative reasoning skills from reading literature. In turn, these reasoning skills add not to our storehouse of propositional knowledge, necessarily, but to our storehouse of skills that make us more interesting and more empathetic human beings—the kinds of human beings who need narrative arts and good conversation, who are interested in other human beings, and who have knowledge that is more than just propositional.

NOTES

1. I rely here on Noël Carroll's article "On the Narrative Connection," in *New Perspectives on Narrative Perspective*, ed. Willie Van Peer and Seymour Chatman (Albany, NY: SUNY Press, 2001), 21–41, for my description of narrative elements although I elaborate beyond Carroll's initial descriptions.

2. Carroll, "On the Narrative Connection," 26.

3. Carroll, "On the Narrative Connection," 26. My italics.

4. J. L. Mackie, "Causes and Conditions," *The Nature of Causation*, ed. Myles Brand (Urbana, IL: University of Illinois Press, 1976), 307–44.

5. Carroll, "On the Narrative Connection," 29.

6. Carroll, "On the Narrative Connection," 27.

7. Arthur Danto, *Narration and Knowledge* (New York: Columbia University Press, 1985), 235.

8. E. M. Forster, *Aspects of the Novel* (Orlando, FL: Harcourt, Inc., 1927), 86.

9. Forster, *Aspects of the Novel*, 86.

10. Walter Brice Gallie, *Philosophy and the Historical Understanding* (New York: Schocken Books, 1964), 43–44.

11. Catherine Emmott, *Narrative Comprehension: A Discourse Perspective* (New York: Oxford University Press, 1997), 103.

12. Emmott, *Narrative Comprehension*, 104.

13. Donald Braid, "Personal Narrative and Experiential Meaning," *The Journal of American Folklore* 109 (Winter 1996): 9.

14. Braid, "Personal Narrative and Experiential Meaning," 9.

15. Noël Carroll, "The Paradox of Junk Fiction," *Philosophy and Literature* 18 (1994): 234.

16. Louise Rosenblatt, *Literature as Exploration* (New York: Appleton-Century, 1938), 115.

17. Psychologists Donald Polkinghorne (*Narrative Knowing and the Human Sciences*. Albany, NY: SUNY Press, 1988) and Jerome Bruner (*Actual Minds, Possible Worlds*. Cambridge, MA: Harvard University Press, 1986) both use the term "paradigmatic" (and Polkinghorne uses "logico-scientific" in addition) for what I will prefer to call discursive reasoning. Discursive captures the logical, direct aspect of reasoning more accurately, I think, than paradigmatic or logico-scientific, which for philosophical purposes does not capture the directness of the brand of reasoning in which I am interested.

18. Bruner, *Actual Minds, Possible Worlds*, 12.

19. Bruner, *Actual Minds, Possible Worlds*, 13.

20. Bruner, *Actual Minds, Possible Worlds*, 11.

21. Bruner, *Actual Minds, Possible Worlds*, 11.

22. Martha Nussbaum, *Love's Knowledge* (Oxford: Oxford University Press, 1990), 5.

23. Lauren Binnendyk and Kimberly Schonert-Reichl, "Harry Potter and Moral Development in Pre-adolescent Children," *Journal of Moral Education* 31, No. 2 (2002): 195–201.

24. Nussbaum, *Love's Knowledge*, 5.

25. Nussbaum, *Love's Knowledge*, 48.

26. Historically there is a concern about the moral implications of engaging emotionally with fiction (falsehoods) beginning with Plato. Martha Nussbaum expresses this concern in *Love's Knowledge*. She explains that "according to one version of the objection, emotions are unreliable and distracting because they have nothing to do with cognition at all. According to the second objection, they have a great deal to do with cognition, but they embody a view that is in fact false" (40). What I am suggesting here, however, is that by engaging

emotionally with fiction, our cognitive skills will not be compromised so much as different reasoning skills (the narrative ones) will be enhanced.

27. Martha Nussbaum, *Poetic Justice* (Boston: Beacon Press, 1995), 43.

28. Nussbaum appeals to Adam Smith's notion of the judicious spectator to show how emotive identification with someone on trial (if you are a member of a jury) or a fictional character (if you are a reader) is a superior position to take over an emotionally detached observer. She explains, "Sympathetic emotion that is tethered to the evidence, institutionally constrained in appropriate ways, and free from reference to one's own situation appears to be not only acceptable but actually essential to public judgment. But it is this sort of emotion, the emotion of the judicious spectator, that literary works construct in their own readers, who learn what it is to have emotion not for a 'faceless undifferentiated man' but for the 'uniquely individual human being'" (78).

29. Nussbaum, *Poetic Justice*, 48

30. "Who Needs Imagination? An Interview with Professor Paul Harris," *Harvard Graduate School of Education,* March 1, 2002.

31. See Roger Schank, *Tell Me a Story: Narrative and Intelligence* (Evanston, IL: Northwestern University Press, 1990) for more on story gists and story skeletons.

32. See Daniel Dennett, *Consciousness Explained* (Boston: Little, Brown and Co., 1991). Although Dennett actually argues against a Cartesian theater, the metaphor is a useful one.

33. Sylvia Scribner, "Modes of Thinking and Ways of Speaking: Culture and Logic Reconsidered," in *Thinking: Readings in Cognitive Science*, ed. P. N. Johnson-Laird and P. C. Wason (New York: Cambridge University Press, 1997), 483–500.

34. Paul Harris, *The Work of the Imagination* (Malden: Blackwell Publisher, 2000), 98.

35. Harris, *Work of the Imagination*, 99.

36. Harris, *Work of the Imagination*, 105.

37. Barbara Tversky, "Narratives of Space, Time, and Life," *Mind & Language* 19 (2004): 386.

38. Tversky, "Narratives of Space, Time, and Life," 386.

Chapter Six

Belief and the Mind

It seems like every time I look in the news there is another story about how "science" has proven something or other. "Science" can tell me what the best diet is, and "science" has proven today that Girl Scouts really do make the world a better place.[1] According to *Good Housekeeping* magazine, scientists have proven that unicorns are real and that we have fossils to prove it (but they looked more like rhinoceros' than the pretty mythical creatures we think of).[2] We give a lot of credit these days to scientists and the claims that they make. In some ways we mindlessly honor the advice of "science," like when we take medicine, and in some ways we reject it all together. Lots of people worldwide do not believe that climate change is caused by human action despite what science says about it. So what can science give me in my quest to understand how reading influences our understanding of the world around us?

Well, to this point in the book, I have primarily used philosophical arguments to explain the ways that we interact with narratives. Now I want to shift gears a bit and use some of the relevant neuroscience in reference to the ways in which our beliefs about what we read is either fiction or nonfiction literally changes the cognitive processes of reading itself. So, I am going to appeal to science here only in one particular way, to see how whether or not we believe something to be true can influence the way we think about it. Although there has not been a huge amount of scientific research on this specific difference (it is a bit cumbersome to get participants to read novels and newspapers while they are in fMRI machines), the research that has been done is quite informative. This research allows us to understand better how we process narrative and discursive prose differently. I will appeal to these scientific findings only when I believe that they are reasonable tests that actually measure things I take to be relevant to my argument. I argued in the previous chapter that we make sense of them differently, but now I want to show how we actually processes them differently at the level of the brain.

1. BELIEVING WHAT YOU READ

Even though we may not even realize it, as readers, we want to know in advance of reading whether or not what we are reading is true or fictional. This is one of the first distinctions that schoolchildren are taught when they begin to read for content (generally about the third grade). What genre is it and how do you make sense of that particular genre? Expecting fiction is a totally different mindset than expecting nonfiction. Presumably, knowing this helps us make sense of what we are reading. Some readers skip the category of fiction entirely, choosing instead books they know to be true, believing that somehow the veracity will make the story more informative, more emotional, and perhaps more significant. Many readers have told me that they find true crime, in particular, much more compelling than fictional crime. Others think that fiction's essential role is to present us with experiences and situations that fall outside of the scope of our own lives or our own possibilities.

But when we read narratives, novels in particular, it seems to be of the utmost importance for us to know in advance whether the events and experiences described *really did happen or not*. This not only provides a sense of epistemic stability, but more pragmatically, it keeps our categories clean and the information quickly accessible for inference-making processes. And yet stories affect our *emotions* whether they are true or fictional, so neither category can lay claim to being more emotionally affective. Even so, we still want to know. If, for example, after reading something we believe to be true, we later find that it was fiction (even if it is only in small part inaccurate, exaggerated, or fabricated), we do not just shrug our shoulders and say it does not matter. Instead, the experience leaves us in a state of irritation and cognitive dissonance, especially if the story seemed to correspond with things that we already believe about the world. It seems to me that there are some interesting complexities behind this kind of dissonance. I think that the key to understanding this dissonance is understanding how belief works. Belief is the linchpin, since our mental attitudes about a text really do prescribe the ways in which we respond to the text. The kind of beliefs we have about a text dictate expectation. And in reading, expectations are everything.

2. THE PARADOX OF BELIEF

I want to return to the paradox of fiction, which is foundational in philosophical work on fiction and centers entirely on the particular role that belief plays in our emotional responses to fiction. The paradox relies first on the assumption that emotional responses occur only with events that are believed to be true. Second, the paradox says that despite the first obvious claim, we respond with all kinds of emotions to stories we believe are fictional on a regular basis. Hence the paradox: Why do I have emotional responses to things I do not believe happened? Philosophers, aestheticians in particular, have developed a small cottage industry, or perhaps even a large industrial complex, of responses to this puzzle. In the last generation of aesthetics, since 1975 when Colin Radford published the first article naming and outlining the paradox, it is not an exaggeration to say that it has been one of the most popular topics for dissertations and conference papers in aesthetics (including my own dissertation). Most resolutions to the paradox generally attempt to show that our emotional responses to fictional stories are not inherently inconsistent, incoherent, and irrational, as Radford claimed that they were.[3] They do this either by showing that the emotions that result from engaging with fiction are not the *same* as the emotions that result from real events or by showing that we do not have to *believe* what we are reading in order to be affected. Either way, the emotions we have in response to events we do not believe are true are defended as being rational and normal. But note that the paradox is framed in terms of belief and nonbelief, not narrative and nonnarrative or storied and linear. Recall Derek Matravers' claim about the so-called consensus view (which he thinks is totally misguided) that fiction is always associated with imagination and nonfiction is always associated with belief. If the paradox of fiction is framed only in these terms and not in terms of narrative/nonnarrative, the possibilities for resolution are extremely limited. I want to look at the belief part, however, before changing the terms of the debate.

I believe that there might be some insight to be had by going beyond the scope of these typical responses by employing the insights that neuroscientists have developed about belief, coherence, and narrative comprehension. While the paradox of fiction provides a starting point, my real goal is to explore the different ways in which we approach narratives (as opposed to discursive, nonnarrative texts) and especially how preconceptions about a narrative's truth or falsity influence the way it is processed in the brain. After examining some empirical evidence, I will argue that what someone believes in advance of reading a story—whether they believe it to be fiction or nonfiction—greatly influences the way the brain itself processes the narrative. This exposes the highly integrated, contingent, and constructive relationship the reader has to a narrative that differs fundamentally from the more detached and less personal relationship suggested by the premises that lead us to the paradox of fiction. The paradox of fiction assumes from the outset that we either straightforwardly believe or do not believe the content of the story we take in. It also assumes that *fiction* is fundamentally the same as *narrative* and so confuses the impact of what we read. Fiction has to do with truth status, while narrative has to do with the kind of storied prose that structures the events we read about.

In addition to explanations about the ways we know and understand narrative, I will also use models of narratives in my attempt to explain how our comprehension works. I will talk about situational models that describe the mental representations in which readers immerse themselves into a story world. But I will contrast these models with the memory-based models that emphasize automatic memory processes that support narrative comprehension rather than the big-picture processing that is necessary for creating mental representations. By integrating these two different frameworks together and adding an explanatory layer of the ways in which brain processing is thought to work to facilitate narrative comprehension, I will describe a conceptual map of how we mentally organize individual linguistic pieces in order to construct a comprehensive, narrative blueprint. If I can do this, I will then be in a better position to address the paradoxical nature of the fiction/nonfiction problem by explaining the ways in which we process and understand both genres in different ways.

3. NARRATIVE COMPREHENSION

I have suggested that it matters whether we believe in advance whether something we read is true or fiction. Now I want to look at whether or not believing something to be true or not changes the way we actually process stories cognitively. Several studies show that belief about whether or not a narrative is true influences behavioral factors such as memory, speed of reading, and how it is processed, encoded, and understood.[4] Several neuroscientists have shown with neuroimaging that there are specific areas and neural circuits involved in narrative processing, and several of these studies suggest significant differences between brain states in cases of belief and disbelief. I suggested earlier that coherence is the truth condition that trumps correspondence in the case of narrative comprehension. If coherence is largely what expresses the nature of truth and comprehension when we read narratives (as opposed to discursive texts), then it depends on neural and cognitive processes that can vary depending on a reader's belief state. In that case, how a reader interprets and understands narratives changes based on her belief about truth. But how we apply the information we get from narratives seems to be less impacted by one's initial belief state. Moreover, the beliefs we have about what we read act as a structured framework for the way in which we relate the information to preexisting knowledge. That is, whether or not we believe a story to be true also dictates how the brain processes the pieces of the story.

Even the possibility of having narrative comprehension calls upon a battalion of cognitive processes. As a reader, we imagine characters' goals and emotions, make moral judgments about characters' situations, make logical inferences about relationships between events and causes, and evaluate and verify narrative truths based on our own knowledge and experience. When we read narratives, however, we do not just take in sentences predigested. Rather, we engage in an active process of internalizing both specific information such as a character's current predicament and the global story structure. We must do a lot of work in order to make sense of all the different elements of a narrative. Numerous explanatory frameworks have been suggested to describe how readers construct and move through a representation of what a narrative depicts or describes, but of course we cannot expect exhaustive explanations from these frameworks alone.[5] Raymond Mar explains several of the most prominent frameworks, including both situational and memory-based models.[6] He suggests that narrative comprehension depends on three broad categories. First, memory encoding and retrieval; second, integration; and third, elaboration or simulation.[7] Each of these tasks uses particular brain regions, but most notably the prefrontal cortex, temporoparietal region, anterior temporal and temporal poles, and the posterior cingulate cortex. In terms of these three categories, I will show how the construction of narrative comprehension works and provides the available neuroimaging data that support each explanation.

Memory is the most important underlying, necessary condition that allows us to understand and tell stories at all. Without memory we would have no material with which to create new stories, to reevaluate what we have read in the past to what we now understand, or even to grasp our own stories or experiences. Without memory we would have no narrative self and no sense of personal continuity. The same goes for the construction of our mental representations of narratives or the way we imagine from the inside how stories unfold. Without a continuous flow of memories, narratives lose their comprehensibility, their emotional effectiveness, and their coherence. Raymond Mar discusses one useful memory-based model of narrative comprehension. It pinpoints four specific activities that are carried out by specific brain regions in the frontal cortex that are relevant for narrative comprehension.[8] With this model, the retrieval, monitoring, manipulation, and encoding of the content of working memory first occur on a kind of sketchpad that is directly accessible to consciousness and involves the mid-dorsolateral frontal cortex, an area implicated in the processing of time, ordering, and integration of sequential information.

Second, long-term memory is important for the maintenance of cues for memory encoding and retrieval. This happens in the ventrolateral frontal cortex. These brain areas also show activation during the processing of inconsistent or unexpected information and when decisions are made based on recent memory.[9] Information retrieved from memory is either rejected or accepted before being integrated into the developing representation. With widespread connections to the limbic system (which controls the emotions) and the basal ganglia (which helps us with movement and spatial orientation), the ventromedial prefrontal cortex links together the things that we believed to be true with emotional associations. These also contribute to our decision-making processes that have to do with both fact and emotion, as it turns out.[10] Additionally, the prefrontal cortex (connected with personality, planning, complex cognitive behavior, and decision-making) is connected with the *rejection* of products of memory retrieval that are irrelevant to the narrative under evaluation. The anterior prefrontal cortex, however, is involved in the *acceptance* of information retrieved from memory that will be integrated into the reader's growing narrative representation.

The third part of Mar's memory-based model of narrative comprehension points to the integration of new incoming information with prior knowledge and knowledge about previous events. The stories that are held in memory connect to areas associated with the new stories and begin to order the new information in terms of causes, effects, location, and time. Neuroimaging data indicate that working memory functions primarily in the prefrontal cortex. The frontal regions also contribute to filtering out of irrelevant information.

Fourth, the posterior cingulate cortex is one of the areas that work to further integrate new information with prior knowledge.[11] Additionally, this area also contributes to visual and spatial imagery processing, episode retrieval, and the emotional variation of memory. These integrative activities combine old pieces of information from memory and put together a compatible but different set out of the stories that they form. To put it very simply, we use memory to understand the way the world is and then, as we take in each new story, it either changes our representation of the world or it does not. Readers who read with great regularity are able to construct a rich and progressively more recognizable story structure within their minds. The two sets together interact in ways that are determined both by previous world knowledge and the information that comes along with new stories. New stories then connect with our real-world experience.

Finally, simulation is possible when the reader approaches the narrative as a big system rather than focusing only on its individual parts (like we tend to do when we analyze it). The parts, such as sentence processing, diction, rhythm, or scenery descriptions, disappear from consideration and are absorbed into the representation of the narrative with which the reader consciously engages. This highly integrative process requires brain areas that the reader uses to understand both narrative and real-world situations such as anticipating the emotions of others. It is at the level of simulation and comprehension that we can begin to map the brain areas used in both everyday functioning and narrative processing and to see how the overall comprehension differs.

4. NARRATIVE IN THE BRAIN

At this point, it is important to expand my focus to include the reader and his/her own individual environment and personal history, since the imagined narrative world and the concrete external world tend to overlap and sometimes integrate. For example, when we read about Sherlock Holmes at 221B Baker Street, we do not just think about the real residence that exists there, but we imagine what London looked like during the time he was writing, how streets work, how buildings work, and how Holmes' way of thinking really was well adapted to solving mysteries. Narrative comprehension requires the visualization of scenes presented in the written text, a task facilitated by the angular gyrus (which is largely responsible for language processing and spatial orientation) and the posterior cingulate cortex (involved in a number of processes but here relevant to episodic memory retrieval).[12] When we read, we simulate characters' goals, actions, and emotions, and these activities call on areas such as the temporoparietal junction, medial prefrontal cortex, and temporal poles, which are all vital to help us to create theory of mind or what it is like to imagine another time, place, or person. Importantly, this kind of simulation processing happens in narratives and our daily social interactions.[13] In addition to the simulation of emotion, readers also simulate actions described in stories with the same brain regions that play a role in actual movement.

One study conducted by Véronique Boulenger and her team presented participants with sentences describing either arm- or leg-related sentences (e.g., "He kicked the habit") or literal sentences (e.g., "He kicked the ball") and found that both the premotor and motor cortices were active.[14] What that means is that the movement differed with the arm- and leg-related sentences. Leg-related sentences activated the dorsal motor cortex where leg movement is processed, and arm-related sentences activated the lateral motor cortex where normal arm movement is processed. These researchers were able to show the connection between the movement of the body and the meaning of words and how the brain processes them in different ways. So, literally, the body physiologically experiences action words in a way it does not experience other nonphysical words, whether we read them or merely speak about the actions to which they refer. Now, this is not to say that we need to act out what we read or even that we twitch as we read descriptions of action scenes. What it does show is that the way that we understand the written word is relevantly similar in terms of brain processing to the way we experience physical motion. Think of this in sexual terms and it makes perfect sense. Reading sexually explicit material has a tendency to make readers feel certain things physically. In terms of brain activity, when we read we experience the action in a significant way.

To further explain the nature of story comprehension from the textual elements of a narrative (i.e., words, sentences, and plot), I want to look into the way a reader's comprehension process or strategy might change when the structural elements vary. Jiang Xu and his colleagues found unique activation patterns at the word, sentence, and narrative level when participants read Aesop's Fables in one of three different ways: word lists, unconnected sentences, or coherent narratives.[15] Most relevant for the relationship between the reader and the development of narrative comprehension was the differential activation *within* the narrative condition. That is, at the beginning of the narrative, the left hemisphere was in high demand while the reader collected fine-grained, linguistic, and descriptive information about the narrative (i.e., detail about characters, objects, geography, or time). Toward the end of the narrative, however, the right hemisphere showed greater brain activity. This provides further support for an argument that the right brain is involved in the integration of information into a whole, coherent narrative representation.[16] Mar also points to a number of lesion studies that support the thesis that patients with right brain damage tend to confabulate, have difficulty drawing inferences in stories, and often recall or justify bizarre information inserted into narratives by researchers just as they would normal or relevant information.[17]

Narrative comprehension is a dynamic, interactive system built from the swarm of information bits that materialize and subsequently evaporate within the mind in the midst of both reading and hearing stories. It engages key brain areas in the attempt to build a working, conceptual narrative structure and can hopefully thereby produce narrative comprehension and narrative understanding. This comprehensive structure depends largely on a coherence-based model of understanding. With some stable and some replaceable bits of information, the connecting pieces in this explanatory narrative structure are predominantly relational. That is, the connections between informational bits (holding information such as who the protagonist is, setting, and emotional valence) are related to each other and interact with each other based on relationships established by information from personal memory, cultural expectations, and the information's placement in the story grammar or progression.

5. BELIEF AND THE NARRATIVE

Now that I have explained how narrative comprehension might work cognitively in terms of a few brain areas, I want to outline what role belief in the accuracy of stories might play before considering the relationship between truth, belief, narrative processing, understanding, and its application. An assessment of belief asks us not only to differentiate between the types of beliefs we hold but also to keep in mind how these different beliefs, whether dispositional (beliefs that we hold all the time) or occurrent (beliefs that we have, well, currently), are structured in such a way that they might change our interaction with the same information. If they do, then they could also change our disposition or attitude toward a particular narrative. According to neuroscientist Sam Harris and his team, when readers consider the truth or falsity of a proposition, the prefrontal cortex—which, among several functions, links factual knowledge with relevant emotional associations and participates in reality monitoring—shows increased activity when we believe a proposition is true.[18] A simple example of a proposition I would believe to be true is "eagles fly." When I think about that proposition, I use my prefrontal cortex. Brain activity changes, however, when I *do not believe* a proposition to be true, such as "eagles swim." Neuroimaging data taken when participants are presented with propositions they do not believe show activation in areas that are also associated with pain perception and the judgment of the pleasantness of tastes and odors. This area is active when individuals evaluate the self-relevance of words[19] as well as in error detection, reward-based decision-making,[20] and in the change of behavior based on predictions about future circumstances.[21]

Harris compared the activity of individuals' evaluations of mathematical and ethical category truth statements and found a similar pattern of increased activation in the prefrontal cortex between the two conditions.[22] This suggests that the neurological state of belief and disbelief differ from a proposition's content or claim and emotional associations that we have with it. Harris later provides further support for this in a neuroimaging study examining religious belief.[23] Though it is rather uncomplicated from a coherence perspective to see how a

Christian might respond to the statement "The Biblical God exists" with a "Yes, I believe that to be true" and a nonbeliever with a "No, I do not believe that to be true," the neurological activity behind these different responses makes the distinction much more tangible. This is consistent with the findings of his previous study about belief and disbelief, in which Harris found that participants who believed a statement was true, regardless of whether it was religious or nonreligious, showed prefrontal cortex activation, whereas those who believed it to be false did not show the same activation pattern.

6. BELIEF AND FICTION

Given what I have shown about narrative comprehension and belief I can now ask how the belief that a story is fictional or nonfictional changes how the reader processes and thereby understands it and integrates it into other experiences he or she has. To figure this out, I will look at whether the neural context of narrative comprehension changes with the cognitive context. That is, the kind of information processing demanded by the narrative at particular points might change because of certain kinds of beliefs one holds, like whether it is believed or not. If I approach the question by looking at behavioral studies, I can look to the kinds of information that readers pay attention to the most during narrative comprehension as an indication of the effect of belief. According to Rolf Zwaan, using models of discourse processing, we generally sort information into three comprehension levels:

1. Surface structure: the exact form of the text, including diction and syntax
2. Textbase: the network of propositions that represent the text's meaning
3. Situation model: the representation or mental simulation of the state of affairs the text represents.[24]

Using these levels as a guide and measuring reading time and memory, Zwaan found that individuals who read short narratives that they *believed* were fictional paid more attention to surface structure and textbase information. Those who believe they were reading fiction also read more slowly compared those who read the same set of narratives when they were presented as news stories. The readers who believed they were reading news stories paid more attention to situational information (i.e., they recognized plausible inferences based on the text and did not associate implausible inferences as coming from the text) and read more quickly. The time one takes to read a story is significant, since it is considered a clear external manifestation of cognitive processing. Reading time usually increases when readers focus on information at the textbase level in order to facilitate coherence, as opposed to a focus on situational information only.[25]

Zwaan conducted another psychological study on the effect of genre *expectations* and reading comprehension. He wanted to investigate how genre labeling, like with fiction or nonfiction, dictates the way the brain processes information. For instance, when reading what I believe is nonfiction, my brain processes everything as currently happening, whereas in a fictional work the brain uses a "wait-and-see strategy" before committing to what is true within the text.[26] So the preconceived beliefs a reader has about a text are influential, but the way that one actively constructs beliefs within and about the text matter, as well. The beliefs that we build as we follow a story dictate the way in which we think about what genre the work should fit into, and this in turn impacts the way in which we evaluate the text itself.

There have been a number of studies that show when study participants read narrative (as opposed to expository text) they have both superior recall memory and better overall comprehension. There have not been any studies to date that outline the variation in either the degree or the depth of recall memory after reading specifically fictional or nonfictional narrative texts, however.[27] Deborah Henderson and Herb Clark have been able to show that readers do recall a larger quantity and more in-depth information from a narrative that is labeled fiction than one labeled nonfiction.[28] This ability to remember fictional narratives better than nonfictional ones may be the result of the different kinds of selection and integration of information. That is, when a reader anticipates reading a fictional narrative, she might use a cognitive strategy that requires less integration than she would need with real-world information. When reading fiction, the existing situation model or mental representation would be kept active longer than when reading the news or nonfiction. In this case, information inconsistent with the mental model would be quickly discarded and not updated into the working narrative model (as with the coherence model when beliefs that are inconsistent are dismissed, as well). But the expectations that readers have about fictional narratives are not as tightly constrained by the real world, as they are the fictional worlds that are limited by their fictional truths and need for internal coherence. Our expectations about nonfictional narrative accounts *are* limited because they are supposed to correspond accurately with the real world. It is possible that a wider, more diverse start during fiction reading would permit more connections to a diversity of information. Thus when reading fiction, one might pick up on more potential cues for both information retrieval and more elaborate memory for the details absorbed from the narrative.

So far, I have identified four significant themes that emerge from this neuroscientific work:

1. Memory and understanding of information gleaned from a narrative depend on beliefs about the narrative's truth status prior to the reading of the text.
2. Readers pay attention to surface structure and textbase information when reading fictional narratives.
3. Readers pay attention to situational information when reading nonfictional narratives.
4. Comprehension strategies (i.e., the type of information readers pay attention to in order to construct a narrative representation) depend on the reader's genre expectations.

If, as Zwaan and the previous discussion suggests, "text comprehension is guided by a control system that comprises pragmatic information about the reading goals associated with a given text genre,"[29] then I am justified in supposing that beliefs are deeply connected to the way that we understand narratives and play an important role in the way that we understand them. We already know that in both narrative comprehension and belief construction there is strong activation in the emotional-processing centers of the brain, such as the prefrontal cortex and amygdaloid complex (the part of the brain responsible for memory and emotion)[30] as well as areas that are used for the creation of a unified self and a theory of mind.

Even before a reader delves into a narrative, his/her emotional state or mood may also direct his/her choice of what to read depending on anticipated emotional consequences as well as cognitive goals (i.e., whether he/she is reading for information or for entertainment). Other neuroscientific studies have also confirmed that "the reader's current emotional state affects the processing of verbal statements that imply emotional reactions."[31] Several psychological studies also illustrate how our expectations or beliefs about a situation influence what and how quickly we "see" or identify the identity of objects[32] and how we judge other people based on expectations (suggested by others) about their personality. Based on this evidence, it seems clear that narratives are not exempt from the influence of emotions and belief states because they impact the neural circuits that are activated and consequently direct our attention to particular information that we later use to build a coherent, narrative representation.

7. BELIEF AND EXPECTATION

Now that I have explained how prior belief influences how we process and understand narratives by focusing our attention on different aspects of textual analysis, it seems clear that I need to show what the implications of this are for my larger project. More importantly, how might knowing that we actually process what we believe to be fiction and what we believe to be nonfiction in different ways change our inter-action with narratives and narrative worlds? Should we ban fictional narratives because they might change our beliefs about the real world? Plato would be thrilled! Various governments throughout history have banned fictional works for as long as they have been published. Fiction can be very dangerous in this way, and for people who cannot tell the difference, fiction can change the way people feel about the world. But this is not all that surprising of a finding, and philosophers (at least) have been considering the ways in which fiction influences us for centuries. This might give credibility to some of the Christian critics of the Harry Potter series, for example, for suggesting that magic exists or that good and evil might be so easily personified. The ways in which belief influences the way we process narrative is not necessarily always a drawback for fictional narratives either. Psychologists James Pennebaker and Janel Seagal suggest that there are even health benefits[33] to reading fiction (Aristotle would have suggested that a good old-fashioned cry is always a good thing!) and that we can learn quite a lot about social situations that we might not have the opportunity to experience ourselves.[34] Several philosophers (Martha Nussbaum and

Lionel Trilling, for example) have also claimed epistemic and moral benefits that accompany reading fictional narratives.[35] Often, however, readers cannot easily detect false information in narratives even when they are warned it is there and they integrate it just as they would factual information.[36] This makes sense given the breadth and diversity of brain regions used in narrative processing and the overlap of these areas in processing similar information in the real world. Melanie Green and John Donahue found that individuals who read an article about a young boy addicted to heroin (that they believed was factual but were later informed was fictional) showed critical feelings toward the *author* but had difficulty changing their beliefs about the content of the actual narrative they read.[37] Consequently, the information was already integrated into their worldview and accepted as true. The label *fictional*, however, does not preclude the integration of information into the reader's worldview as we know from numerous studies—both formal and personal— on the persuasiveness of fiction.

8. IMPLICATIONS OF NARRATIVES BEYOND THE MIND

What I have shown here might shed some light on why some cultural stories can be so compelling, persuasive, and possibly even injurious if the information is false or fabricated. Even if readers believe a story is fictional, a demoralizing depiction of a *real* subculture will influence how readers view members of the group afterwards. Fictionalized stereotypes can do real damage. It is important, therefore, to take care to recognize when narratively informed beliefs should be evaluated in terms of either correspondence or coherence. Despite our susceptibility to false information and the strong input that belief has over narrative processing and understanding, narratives are a prime source of both communication and enjoyment and should not (and potentially *cannot*) be eradicated from our communicative system. They reflect our cognitive architecture in a way, ordering information based on contextual, emotional, and causal-temporal relevance.

One of the more interesting implications of understanding the ways in which we process narratives is our large cultural affront when we find out books we read, which were sold to us a "true," turn out to be, in part or whole, fictional. Many of the cases I talked about in the memoir chapter help us to understand the ways in which we get upset when we read a text thinking it is one thing and it turns out to be something completely different. People feel really duped and get really upset. But it seems that what might also be going on is that since we literally process belief narratives and nonbelief narratives in different ways, we actually just have a hard time reorganizing the information we took in the first time. I think it is clear that not only do we make sense of fictional narratives differently from nonfictional narratives but that we also have a tendency to get invested in our own beliefs about a particular story. We have emotional residue that impacts the way we think of the story that cannot be cleared away easily.

9. CONCLUSION

These examples also lead us back to two things I discussed earlier in the book: our conflation of correspondence and coherence models of truth, and the paradox of fiction. As for the correspondence/ coherence confusion, it seems clear that in these cases of being told that a story is true when it turns out not to be, readers enjoy reading narratives both because they are well-told and also because they are (correspondence) true, and thereby potentially more inspiring. But when we are disappointed that what we thought was true turns out not to be, we experience cognitive dissonance. I do not merely shift from thinking it is fact to thinking it is fiction, but I have to reconceptualize the ways in which I understood the narrative in the first place. Just looking at the overlap of prefrontal cortex activation during belief and narrative comprehension, we can see the difficulty in distinguishing emotional connections with the information from our perception of its reliability. The emotional connections as well as the information the reader has contributed to the construction of narrative comprehension are not reversible once the narrative reaches a certain level of comprehension, especially given the differential encoding of information as either situational, for nonfiction narratives such as news stories, or at a surface level for literary narratives. This emotional dissonance disrupts our *understanding* of the story in total; it calls into question the coherence I have seemingly already established. Cognitively, then, I just do not have the mechanism to entirely reconceptualize the ways in which I understood the story.

Further, largely what we enjoy about reading narratives is what is gained through the coherence of the story, not the mere correspondence of the events to reality. When I criticize memoirs for not having correspondence truth, I miss out on the coherence aspect of the ways in which the story is told. I also miss out on working the imagination at all. In terms of the paradox of fiction, I can see now that it is initiated by a correspondence model of truth. Our emotional responses to fiction *are* irrational if I only hold to that kind of correspondence relation about events in the world and those narrated through story. But narrative does not appeal merely to a correspondence model, it appeals also to a coherence model, since that is much more closely tied to the way that I actually process and comprehend narratives. Thus the truth or fiction of a narrative should be played down significantly with this recognition, and the literary features that make up the narrative should be highlighted. This plays on the earlier chapter having to do with narrative knowledge. Content, or propositional knowledge, is not all there is. The capacity to understand narrative structure influences greatly how well we can take in and integrate new information. Whether a narrative is well-told or not should take precedence over whether or not it is true, and this seems to be supported by the ways in which we actually process stories. What should take first priority is the narrative coherence that stories have, above and beyond anything else, and as readers we should appreciate the ways in which coherence allows us narrative comprehension.

NOTES

1. Karen Kaplan, "Science Proves It: Girl Scouts Really Do Make the World a Better Place," *Los Angeles Times*, July 12, 2016.

2. Kayla Keegan, "Yes, Unicorns Were Real—and Now We Have the Fossils to Prove It," *Good Housekeeping,* March 29, 2016.

3. Colin Radford is famous for making the claim that our emotional responses to fiction are "inconsistent, incoherent and irrational" in his article "How Can I Be Moved by the Fate of Anna Karenina?" *Proceedings of the Aristotelian Society* 49 (1975): 67–80.

4. Rolf Zwaan, "Effect of Genre Expectations on Text Comprehension," *Journal of Experimental Psychology: Learning, Memory, and Cognition* 20, no. 4 (1994): 920–33.

5. See especially Walter Kintsch, "The Role of Knowledge in Discourse Comprehension: A Construction-Integration Model," *Psychological Review*

95 (1988): 163–82; Morton A. Gernsbacher, "Two Decades of Structure Building," *Discourse Processes* 23 (1997): 265–304; Rolf A. Zwaan, Mark C. Langston, and Arthur C. Graesser, "The Construction of Situation Models in Narrative Comprehension: An Event-Indexing Model," *Psychological Science* 6, no. 5 (1995): 292–97; Mark J. Beeman, Edward M. Bowden, and Morton A. Gernsbacher, "Right and Left Hemisphere Cooperation for Drawing Predictive and Coherence Inferences during Normal Story Comprehension," *Brain and Language* 71 (2000): 310–36.

6. Raymond Mar, "The Neuropsychology of Narrative: Story Comprehension, Story Production and Their Interrelation," *Neuropsychologia* 42 (2004):1414–34.

7. Mar, "The Neuropsychology of Narrative," 1417.

8. This is the Moscovitch and Winocour's "Working with Memory Model" as cited by Mar, "The Neuropsychology of Narrative," 1417.

9. Evelyn Ferstl, Mike Rinck, and D. Yves von Cramon, "Emotional and Temporal Aspects of Situation Model Processing during Text Comprehension: An Event-Related fMRI Study," *Journal of Cognitive Neuroscience* 17, no. 5 (2005): 724–39.

10. The prefrontal cortex, along with a host of other brain areas, is necessary in decision-making; Antoine Bechara, Hanna Damasio, and Antonio R. Damasio, "Emotion, Decision Making and the Orbitofrontal Cortex," *Cerebral Cortex* 10 (2000): 295–307, quoted in Harris, Sheth, and Cohen, "Functional Neuroimaging," 141–47.

11. Robert Mason and Marcel Adam Just, "Neuroimaging Contributions to the Understanding of Discourse Processes," in *Handbook of Psycholinguistics*, ed. Matthew J. Traxler and Morton A. Gernsbacher (Amsterdam: Elsevier, 2006), 765–79.

12. E. Mellet, S. Bricogne, F. Crivello, B. Mazoyer, M. Denis, and N. Tzourio-Mazoyer, "Neural Basis of Mental Scanning of a Topographic Representation Built from a Text," *Cerebral Cortex* 12 (2002): 1322–30, quoted in Mason and Just, "Neuroimaging Contributions to the Understanding of Discourse Processes," 8.

13. Mar, "The Neuropsychology of Narrative," 1429.

14. Véronique Boulenger, Olaf Hauk, and Friedmann Pulvermüller, "Grasping Ideas with the Motor System: Semantic Somatotopy in Idiom Comprehension," *Cerebral Cortex* 19 (2009): 1905–14.

15. Jiang Xu, Stefan Kemeny, Grace Park, Carol Frattali, and Allen Braun, "Language in Context: Emergent Features of Word, Sentence and Narrative Comprehension," *Neuroimage* 25 (2005): 1002–15.

16. Beeman's right hemisphere network as described by Mar in "The Neuropsychology of Narrative," 1418, suggests that the right hemisphere appears suited for coarse, distal coding of loose associations, while the left

hemisphere deals with the more specific coding of immediate and obvious connections as it selects and integrates the inferences activated by the right hemisphere into the discourse structure.

17. Mar, "The Neuropsychology of Narrative," 1421.

18. Harris, Sheth, and Cohen, "Functional Neuroimaging," 141–47.

19. Harris, Sheth, and Cohen, "Functional Neuroimaging," 141–47.

20. George Bush, Brent A. Vogt, Jennifer Holmes, Anders M. Dale, Douglas Greve, Michael A. Jenike, and Bruce R. Rosen, "Dorsal Anterior Cingulate Cortex: A Role in Reward-Based Decision Making," *Proceedings of the National Academy of Sciences* 99, no. 1 (2002): 523–28.

21. This study indicates that individual neurons in the dACC encode current and recent cognitive load that allows for faster reactions to incoming information that is similar in difficulty to previous information, and slower reactions to information of a different difficulty. This adapts inferences and decision-making to the problem, providing an advantage in changing environments. Sameer A. Sheth, Matthew K. Mian, Shaun R. Patel, Wael F. Asaad, Ziv M. Williams, Darin D. Dougherty, George Bush, and Emad N. Eskandar, "Human Dorsal Anterior Cingulate Cortex Neurons Mediate Ongoing Behavioural Adaptation," *Nature* 488 (2012): 218–22.

22. Harris, Sheth, and Cohen, "Functional Neuroimaging," 141–47.

23. Sam Harris, Jonas Kaplan, Ashley Curiel, Susan Bookheimer, Marco Iacoboni, and Mark Cohen, "The Neural Correlates of Religious and Nonreligious Belief," *PLoS ONE 4,* no. 10 (2009): 1–9.

24. Zwaan, "Effect of Genre Expectations," 930.

25. Randolph Cirilo, "Referential Coherence and Text Structure in Story Comprehension," *Journal of Verbal Learning and Verbal Behavior* 20 (1981): 358–67.

26. Zwaan, "Effect of Genre Expectations," 930.

27. Allan Eng, "Learning and Processing Nonfiction Expository and Narrative Genre" (PhD dissertation, University of Toronto, 2002).

28. Deborah Henderson and Herb Clark, "Retelling Narratives," paper presented at The Cognitive Science Society Annual Conference, Nashville, Tennessee, 2007.

29. Zwaan, "Effect of Genre Expectations," 930.

30. See especially Keith Oatley, "Why Fiction May Be Twice as True as Fact: Fiction as Cognitive and Emotional Simulation," *Review of General Psychology* 3 (1999): 101–17; Ferstl, Rinck, and von Cramon, "Emotional and Temporal Aspects of Situation," 732–33; Raymond A. Mar, "The Neural Bases of Social Cognition and Story Comprehension," *Annual Review of Psychology* 62 (2011): 103–34; Harris, Sheth, and Cohen, "Functional Neuroimaging," 145.

31. Ferstl, Rinck, and von Cramon, "Emotional and Temporal Aspects of Situation," 732.

32. Esterman and Yantis found anticipatory visual cortex activation in category-specific regions (i.e., facial anticipation showed activation in facial recognition areas such as the fusiform gyrus and superior temporal sulcus, and house expectation showed increased activity in the parahippocampal gyrus) when observers expected to see each of these items. Additionally, observers more quickly categorized the objects when they matched their expectations. Michael Esterman and Steven Yantis, "Perceptual Expectation Evokes Category-Selective Cortical Activity," *Cerebral Cortex* 20 (2010): 1245–53.

33. James Pennebaker and Janel Seagal, "Forming A Story: The Health Benefits of Narrative," *Journal of Clinical Psychology* 55, no. 10 (1999): 1243–54.

34. See especially Oatley, "Why Fiction May be Twice as True as Fact," http://www.newenglishreview.org/Keith_Oatley/Why_Fiction_May_Be_ Twice_as_True_as_Fact/ (Last Accessed, January 2, 2017); Raymond Mar and Keith Oatley, "The Function of Fiction Is the Abstraction and Simulation of Social Experience," *Perspectives on Psychological Science* 3, no. 3 (2008): 173–81.

35. Martha Nussbaum is famous for her views on how moral development can be enlarged by reading literature. See especially *Poetic Justice: The Literary Imagination and Public Life* (Boston, MA: Beacon Press, 1995).

36. Elizabeth Marsh and Lisa Fazio, "Learning Errors from Fiction: Difficulties in Reducing Reliance on Fictional Stories," *Memory & Cognition* 34, no. 5 (2006): 1140–49.

37. Melanie Green and John Donahue, "Persistence of Belief Change in the Face of Deception: The Effect of Factual Stories Revealed to be False," *Media Psychology* 14 (2011): 312–31.

Chapter Seven

Evidence or No Evidence?

✗ audience
Moh

Philosophers are known to question how it is that we know things. The technical term for this is epistemology, but that is really just a fancy word for how it is that we know and how reliable our knowledge is. So I want to ask the question here: How do we *know* that reading is good for us? What evidence is good enough to prove it or to have reason to believe that we should spend our valuable time reading, reemphasizing reading fiction in the schools, or fund prison reading programs feeling confident that it will make a difference for the inmates? Well, at least one person has doubted that there is sufficient evidence to know whether or not reading can benefit us. He asks an epistemological question: How can we *know* that reading is beneficial? There is no doubt much pleasure to be found in reading fiction, but I think there is more to it than that, as well.

1. CURRIE'S WORRIES

Greg Currie questions the kind of evidence that is even possible about the value of reading. Before going too far, I want to note that Currie is one of the most cited experts on narrative and narrative theory in the world. He has written dozens of influential articles and books about fiction, narrative, and literature. Although Currie's claims are specifically about the lack of moral improvement readers can get from literature, his concerns about the lack of evidence are more generally indicative of the

173

skeptic's position. He says that we should just accept the fact that we derive pleasure from fictional literature, but he does not see the need to justify our pleasure by making up reasons that it is good for us either cognitively or morally. He says that academics like to justify their own pleasure in reading with endless explanations of the ways in which reading benefits us—without the luxury of any actual data. Fictional literature, according to Currie, should be put in its place with other modern hedonistic indulgences. Although Currie is only one opinion on the matter, I take seriously his concerns. I believe them to be a rather well-articulated version of some of the larger, more general concerns. As I have noted, we have minimized fiction reading in the schools. It is something thought to be a great luxury for our time, and when we cannot measure its effects we tend to think it must not have any value. Although I heartily disagree with most of what Currie says, I will out-line some of his objections against literature so that I can clarify what seems to be at stake with the larger issue. The question about whether literature can really benefit us is an old one, but it seems to be getting new exposure in many different venues.

Currie has published articles in the *New York Times Opinionator*[1] and in the *Times Literary Supplement*[2] in which he questions the nature of the evidence used to support claims that there are positive effects of engaging with literary fiction. He says that although people all seem to *believe* that reading literature is morally beneficial, there is, in fact, *no empirical evidence* that this belief is true. He suggests that the kinds of claims that people make about the benefits of reading literature have mostly to do with the moral insights that we are supposed to gain from grappling with the complexities that attend to reading extended narra-tives. He mentions the work of Martha Nussbaum and Lionel Trilling specifically, although there are plenty of others who make these kinds of claims. He suggests that if reading makes us better at moral thinking, then if we read enough, we would become "moral experts."[3] Presumably, the logical extension of the argument is that English professors would be the most moral among us, but since there is no evidence of that, it seems unlikely that reading literature can really make us more moral.

Currie also questions whether moral expertise exists at all since it is virtually impossible to know what moral expertise is. Currie cites psychologist Paul Meehl as demonstrating that "study after study has shown that following simple rules—rules that take account of many fewer factors than an expert would bother to consider—does at least as well and generally better than relying on an expert's judgment."[4] These experiments tend to deal mostly with predictions and explanations of both moral and immoral behaviors. For Currie, since the possibility of moral expertise is thrown into question, it is thereby also doubtful that literature can train us to become moral experts or even to be better at anything, whether it be moral, cognitive, or practical. He also provides the too easy counterexample of those who were known to be quite literate, like many of the highest ranking officers in Hitler's army, who seemed to have no qualms about carrying out some of the most horrific crimes against humanity the world has ever seen. Obviously, the literature read by the SS officers failed to develop moral expertise or even a minimal sense of empathy. With one counterexample, he doubts even the possibility that there could be circumstances—probably lots of exceptions, even—to the rule that reading might benefit us morally. I do not want to defend an extreme claim like "all reading necessarily makes everyone who reads better off morally." Instead, I would want to defend a much more moderate claim along the lines that "often, literacy has a tendency to develop important capacities that can help us to become better humans in a number of ways." Specifically, my claim has to do with the way we develop a capacity for empathy, the way we construct cognition, the way we improve our social interactions, and the way we make sense of the experiences of others. I might also point out that the Nazis systematically burned books because they knew full well the potential that books had to positively influence a culture, strengthen a community, and maintain cultural history and memory.

Some psychologists maintain that reading is supposed to bring moral clarity through simulation, psychological insight, and introspection. Unfortunately, however, both insight and introspection are unreliable and unattainable, according to Currie. This, he says, is easily shown with numerous examples throughout philosophy and psychology. He even goes so far as to suggest that more than 50 percent of authors of serious literature are mentally unstable.[5] He asks, "what does this suggest about the credentials of creative writers when it comes to insight into the mind?"[6] He answers his own question by saying that "literary creation depends heavily on the use of imagination, and this, it turns out, is pretty unreliable when it comes to projecting emotional states."[7] Authors tend to be unstable; therefore, their writings cannot reflect accurate or stable projections of other minds, empathy, or any other kind of meaningful human insight. Literature then, according to Currie, is an unreliable source of explanations about the way the world really is. It provides a distorted view of human relationships and reflects the inner worlds of unstable persons. This is another straw man argument, which I take to be an exceptional dismissal of "high" literature. I cannot presume to defend the mental clarity or stability of creative fiction writers, but I can explain the ways in which narrative structure can help to increase a healthy theory of mind for readers.

Although Currie doubts the reliability of insight and introspection I think it is well documented that literary fiction actually does help to develop theory of mind through regular reading practice. I am also skeptical about whether it is the job of narrative fiction to provide us an *accurate* representation of the world and social relationships within it. This seems an exceptionally odd ideal for *fiction*, because so much genre fiction focuses on fantasy, romance, science fiction, and imaginary worlds. Readers do not go to these kinds of books to get realistic accounts of the world, even though they may provide realistic accounts of human nature and history. It also seems to me that the effect of much good art is to highlight a perspective, a particular way of viewing the world, and not a transparent or accurate one that everyone agrees with.

2. EVIDENCE PLEASE

Currie also exhibits an extreme skepticism about the kind of evidence that might give us a reliable indication that we can learn anything from engaging with literature or that we might be benefitted by it in some other way. He says that there is no psychological evidence that would reliably show that reading literature is good for us. He concedes that this might just be the current state and it is possible that experiments could be developed, but he maintains that even that is doubtful. Currie's seemingly most damning argument against the contention that reading literature might benefit us in some way is about this lack of evidence. In my understanding of his argument, he does not seem to think that there *can* be evidence of such a benefit. He wants statistical proof that reading literature makes us better persons—specifically, morally better persons. He says that "we measure the effectiveness of drugs and other medical interventions by thin margins of success that would not be visible without sophisticated statistical techniques; why assume literature's effectiveness should be any different?"[8] He wants the kind of statistical data that show measured outcomes that are a result of moral expertise, or even moral knowledge that might be constituted by an ability to identify why we make various choices, an indication that we can predict what we would do in a certain situation, or to understand why others make the kinds of choices that they do. Currie says, however, "we don't really know, very often, what sorts of people we are. We regularly attribute our own failures to circumstance and the failures of others to bad character."[9] I will put aside the possibility that Currie does not believe that we can have *any* moral knowledge and focus on the argument that there just cannot be real evidence that reading literature provides moral knowledge or develops moral expertise. I will also more fully examine the kinds of possible evidence and address some of the underlying assumptions that this question demands. That is, I take Currie to suggest that psychological tests could or should be performed on individual readers. Statistical data should then indicate whether or not the reader has gained some sort of moral insight from the characters, or the plot, or the structure of the narrative, which will benefit that reader in some way having to do with moral outcomes.

Currie claims that there is no direct causal evidence that reading literature benefits us, despite our general cultural tendency to believe it does. I want to be exceptionally careful about the way in which I talk about causation, since this is a very loaded term. Currie says that there is no evidence that reading a work of literature, *War and Peace*, he suggests, *causes* one to behave better or *causes* one to have better insight into morality that would lend itself to a kind of moral expertise or moral understanding. I do not doubt that this would be nearly impossible to demonstrate via reliable statistical methods. That kind of causation likely does not exist when reading literature, and I am not sure how we would ever really gain evidence or proof of it.

Anne Eaton demonstrates this point about causation nicely in an example I will borrow. Eaton claims that direct and immediate causation is extremely rare in discussions of this sort. She offers the example of the ways in which smoking causes cancer, among other things. She explains that "even in cases of extreme smoking, lung cancer affects only a small fraction while the disease regularly strikes in the absence of any smoking at all. Smoking is neither necessary nor sufficient for contracting the disease, yet there is nevertheless widespread agreement both among experts and lay people that smoking causes cancer."[10] I take the question of what the benefits of reading are to be similar to the link between smoking and cancer. Currie says that because there are no necessary and sufficient conditions about which to identify and create statistical data, there can be no causation and no evidence. I think this is a shortsighted way of approaching the link between the two. Chain smoking for 10 hours straight does not *cause* cancer, but smoking regularly for years on end significantly increases the statistical probability that one will develop cancer. This *is* a form of causation, *not* mere correlation, despite the fact that smoking is neither necessary nor sufficient. Literacy works in comparable ways. That is, the higher one's skill level, the better the possibility that one can be influenced by what one reads. I do not just mean that readers are influenced by the stories themselves but rather that readers develop the capacity to make inferences, understand characters' motivations, and to develop an enhanced understanding of the kinds of reasons people have for making the decisions that they do. The more a reader engages in good narrative, the more he is likely to reflect on one's own beliefs and behaviors and to practice making the kinds of inferences that narratives encourage us to make.

Currie argues that we should approach literature with the attitude that takes literature for what it is and nothing more; a grownup's game of pretend. What does reading do for us? Currie says it produces "pretend learning,"[11] and "aesthetic rewards,"[12] but never real knowledge. He says that we should "give up the idea that what is going on in literature-land is true learning, and make do with the pleasures of pretend learning."[13] He describes literature as "cognitive pornography,"[14] which is pleasurable but not productive and can do us real harm if we continually mistake the image for the real thing.

3. UNDERSTANDING SIMULATION

One of the first ways I want to defend the way we learn from narrative fiction is to show how it is a useful tool to help us understand the world around us. Whereas the standard arguments center around what kind of thing fiction *is* (and mostly in what sense it may or may not be true), I want to question how we are capable of learning from the world around us generally and how fiction might serve as a model for the ways in which we understand our surroundings. Part of this goes back to ancient Greece and the beginnings of the way that our philosophical ancestors talked about art, making, skill, craft, creating, and the ways in which art (both visual and literary) represents the physical world. Most commonly, the Greek word *mimesis* is translated as representation, imitation, or copy. We generally understand the notion of *mimesis* as a relatively unthinking, or slavish, rendition of the real world. Mimetic representations are mirror images, photographs, and representational paintings. Plato certainly contributes to this account when he describes the divided line as well as in the Allegory of the Cave (*Republic* books VI and VII). Here he describes one metaphysical reality as a pale imitation of the next, but the less imitative they are, the more real they are. The less imitative they are, the closer they are to the Forms. This way of understanding *mimesis* has had a powerful history. Art, because of this interpretation, is often seen as only a mirror image of that which is real, and this view of art has allowed for many dismissals of it throughout history.

But this is not the only way of understanding *mimesis*. As Keith Oatley describes it, there is a secondary set of meanings for *mimesis* that have to do with the way we dream, construct, build worlds, build models, and imagine. Oatley says *mimesis* is about "recognizing what goes on beneath the surface."[15] In relatively simple terms, *mimesis* understood as copy leads to a correspondence theory of truth, but *mimesis* as world-building leads to a coherence theory. Correspondence is dependent upon a certain kind of match between reality and that which is depicted. Paintings and photographs are good examples of this kind of correspondence. They depict their realities accurately and realistically. But coherence requires something different. As Oatley explains, fictional narrative "depends more on coherence among its elements than on correspondences between different specific elements of the model and elements of the ordinary world."[16] What is key here is not the correspondence part but the relational part. It is not a mere photograph or exact representational copy but a constructed world put together based on the ways in which *relationships* work in the real world. This account of *mimesis* is the one that Aristotle advocates, and it is central to his work in his classic instruction manual on how to write a good tragedy (or a good play more generally), the *Poetics*.

If we think of fictional literature as world-building or world-creating, the effect is vastly different than just that of a copy. Good fictional literature is very much a constructed world, with relationships, descriptions, and conflicts and resolutions that often very much resemble what goes on in the real world. But it is not a mere copy of the real world. If *mimesis* can be thought of as world-creating or world-constructing and not just a copy, then we must think carefully about the ways in which we make sense of our own world and the ways in which we make sense of the fictional worlds we read about. As it turns out, the work of the imagination is the linchpin we need to understand our own real worlds and the real people who surround us day to day. Narrative fiction is just one other use that we have of the imagination and its applications.

One of the ways we build models of our own worlds is to simulate other people's thoughts, beliefs, and feelings. Literary or narrative fiction serves a role for helping us to enter into or simulate the lives of others, both real and fictional. Simulation theory, as advanced in philosophy, psychology, and cognitive science, advocates the position that we understand the mental and emotional lives of others by simulating their mental states, beliefs, and desires by imagining what it might be like to hold those mental states ourselves. Most people learn to do this at an early age without any particular training through normal development. This is also a strong basis for empathy, which describes our ability to identify with another and thereby actively imagine their mental states and beliefs as well as predict their emotional states and decisions. Most normal people are relatively good at both simulating the feelings of others and predicting the behavior of others whom they simulate.

But simulation is not mere imagining. It is something much more specific. Simulation theory is the explicit account that suggests that we have particular ways in which we imagine, or simulate, the beliefs, desires, and feelings of other people. We need to simulate these mental states so that we can better predict other people's behaviors. Simulation theory is often contrasted with theory, which suggests that we know what other people are going through because we develop very general theories, or folk psychologies, about the way people behave and believe and about how causation works. As people take in more and more information, theories can be revised. Notably, theory theory is different from simulation theory because simulation theory allows not just general rules about behavior to be applied to understanding the lives of others but suggests that the more you know about someone, the better able you are to simulate, or imagine from the inside, what it is that they are experiencing. Although some take these two approaches to be inconsistent, I do not believe that they are. Theory theory likely accounts for general knowledge that we have, but simulation theory accounts for the more specific uses of the imagination that cover cases where we know people intimately or have experience with someone who we have seen behave in consistent ways in the past.[17]

What is important about this for my purposes is that simulation theory accounts for the ways in which we understand character. Literary fiction is just one possible vehicle that happens to describe character. But understanding a literary character involves feeling like you know what is going on inside a character's head, why he/she does certain things, and how he/she will feel when things happen in the plot. Simulating fictional characters is then another application of the way we simulate real people. But the simulating we do of real others is often much more contrived and difficult than it is with fictional characters, because our friends and loved ones never allow us intimate access or clear, reliable introspection into their thoughts and motivations in the same way that fictional characters do.

Not only is simulation one of the primary ways in which we understand other people, it is also a key part of the way we generate empathy, and it allows us to imagine the ways in which we might behave ourselves given some future circumstances. ("What *would* I do if I won the lottery?") But simulation is not only about imagining the inner lives and inner motivations of other people. According to Oatley, simulating others serves two primary purposes. First, he says simulations "provide information by offering a model when access cannot be direct."[18] Analogously, we use models of the solar system because we cannot perceive the solar system in any meaningful way. We also love the models that come on our smart phones. Models of the weather, time, and maps are all generated out of a small handheld device that helps us to interpret the world around us in countless ways. Oatley suggests that people form models of the ways in which other people think—because since we cannot ever have real or direct access. Oatley even goes so far as to say that "the very function of the human mind is to make mental models. It is by making models that we understand how things work, including how things work when they are not in one's immediate sight."[19] If simulation is something we do regularly with real others, fictional literature provides an excellent *model* of the way in which we understand other people—characters, if you will. Further, he says, "mental models of fiction enable us to think about selves in the social world."[20] The fact that fiction is not (correspondence) true is completely irrelevant if what we are really doing is world-building and imagining why others do the things they do.

One of Currie's concerns was that we could not *learn* anything from reading fiction. It is pleasurable, he says, but not productive or useful. But it is clear that although we do not learn facts from reading narrative fiction, what we can do is learn to simulate and imagine, and those are particular skills that we develop over time and with practice. I also might emphasize here that we should be very careful about the books and characters that we choose to simulate. Just as the real-life people we simulate and empathize with influence where our sympathies lie, the characters in our books can likewise influence us as well. Wayne Booth suggests that the books we read are like good friends.[21] We should choose our friends wisely, as they can exert great influence over the way we see the world and the way we behave in it. Likewise, the books we choose, the characters we most deeply sympathize with, empathize with, and identify with can all influence the way that we make sense of our own realities.

4. EMPIRICAL EVIDENCE

As it turns out, there is some empirical evidence about the ways in which fiction impacts us, and there are a variety of different kinds of evidence. Fiction and reading are both studied extensively outside of English and philosophy departments. In fact, there is a whole sub-discipline of psychology that studies fiction and its effects on the brain and behavior. Psychologists also study empathy, the imagination, and the way we use and understand metaphors, and because psychology is a field that inherently employs lots of empirical evidence, psychologists have been able to develop a variety of methods that can give us an idea about what reading, and specifically reading fictional literature, can do for us.

Within the field of psychology, a variety of methods exist to collect data about a topic. In studies focused on the effects of fiction, the two main methods employed for data collection are the correlational study and experimentation. Each method differs from the other, having its own benefits and ideal uses. The most prominent difference between the two methods of data collection is the type of conclusions that can be drawn from each. A correlational study involves no manipulation of variables but analyzes the relationship between two or more things. Since nothing is manipulated, no causal conclusions can be drawn from correlational studies. The data from a correlational study may show that a relationship exists and the strength of that relationship. Experiments, on the other hand, allow different kinds of information to be gathered about the relationship between two or more things because the requirements for an experiment are very strict. For something to qualify as an experiment, it must meet the following four requirements: There must be at least one manipulated independent variable, at least one dependent variable, there must be random assignment, and there must be a control group. When the experimenter manipulates the independent variable, he/she should be able to observe the measured dependent variable, which leads to the ability to draw causal conclusions. Random assignment and control help to rule out extraneous variables that could possibly account for the relationship between the independent variables and the dependent variables.

5. EMPATHY

So how is it that psychologists test or measure empathy? First, we have to agree about what empathy is so we know exactly what to measure. Most generally, empathy is understood to be the capacity to feel what another person is feeling *from their perspective*. Empathy is *not* about what I would feel if *I* were going through what someone else is going through. It requires work of the imagination to understand how to adopt as much information about what the other person believes, thinks, and feels to be able to imagine how *he/she* is feeling as he/she experiences various situations. So, empathy is what I would feel if I were in someone else's shoes. Narratologist Suzanne Keen says that empathy is "a vicarious, spontaneous sharing of affect, can be provoked by witnessing another's emotional state, by hearing about another's condition, or even by reading."[22] When we experience empathy "we feel what we believe to be the emotions of others."[23] Since it includes both feeling and believing, it incorporates both affective and cognitive aspects.

Sympathy is often mistaken for empathy because it is closely related. Sympathy is perhaps the first step to empathy, but it is really only an expression of feeling *for* someone else's emotional state, usually one of sadness, hardship, frustration, or grief. With sympathy, we do not feel the emotions ourselves, we just recognize that others are feeling something. I sympathize with a friend whose husband has died or with her frustration trying to lose weight, but I do not feel the grief or frustration myself. Keen also emphasizes the importance of *personal distress* as a construct that is related to both empathy and sympathy, but it is different. Personal distress, she says, is "an aversive emotional response also characterized by apprehension of another's emotion, differs from empathy in that it focuses on the self and leads not to sympathy but to avoidance."[24] Empathy, sympathy, and personal distress all differ, then, depending upon whom the emotion is focused: the self or the other.

Amy Coplan, however, questions how broad the definition of empathy should be. She defines empathy as "a complex imaginative process through which an observer simulates another person's situated psychological states while maintaining clear self–other differentiation."[25] According to Coplan, empathy has three essential features: affective matching, other-oriented perspective taking, and clear self–other differentiation.[26] These three requirements are necessary and sufficient for an emotion to count as empathy. I will use each of these in what follows to help clarify how empathy can be measured and how it might be shown to result from our interaction with fiction. Coplan also suggests that there are different brain regions that are involved in two different kinds of empathy: cognitive and emotional. She describes a low-level system that involves "emotional matching or mirroring" that produces what she calls emotional empathy. The more advanced system, cognitive empathy, involves "perspective taking and the cognitive understanding of others' mental states."[27] This indicates that there are (at least) two ways of experiencing empathy and accounts for both the affective and the cognitive varieties. Cognitive empathy also requires the ability to simulate, which I talked about earlier.

There is one other way that scientists attempt to explain the nature of empathy. A recent discovery in the world of neuroscience is a special type of cell called the mirror neuron. First discovered in the brains of Macaque monkeys, these specific neurons were observed to be firing when the monkeys watched other monkeys perform an action they had just performed. Based on this observation, neuroscientists believed this specific type of neuron could possibly help to explain how humans relate to one another, specifically how they feel empathy. Due to practical and ethical limitations of not being able to insert electrodes into human's brains, pinpointing a single neuron, as had been done with monkeys, proved to be a difficult task. With humans, instead of pinpointing an individual neuron at work when watching others perform an action and performing that same action themselves, researchers isolated a small area of active neurons. Even that small area contains millions of neurons, making it impossible to pinpoint just one or even a small group. Although there is evidence that mirror neurons exist in the human brain, further research is needed to isolate an identical individual mirror neuron as found in the monkeys. The discovery of the mirror neuron system in the typical human brain suggests that humans are wired to feel empathy and see others as similar to them rather than different.[28] While mirror neurons still fall into the "black box" of the brain, we are able to readily find and measure evidence that we do regularly and easily mirror the actions of others (like yawning) and that we do so unconsciously. We can see and measure the effects of mirror neurons much more easily than we can measure the neurons themselves. These mirror neurons are likely the basis of the low-level emotional empathy that Coplan talks about. Mirror neurons function reflexively, without involving cognition.

6. HOW DO WE TEST AND MEASURE EMPATHY?

There are a variety of ways that psychologists test for empathy. Many were developed initially to test for autistic tendencies but are now commonly used outside of this particular field. Many of the tests are easily applied to empathy-related research in general in addition to the ways in which empathy might be generated by fictional prompts. One of the most common tests is called the Mind in the Eyes (MIE) test.[29] Originally called the "Reading the Mind in the Eyes" test, participants would look at 25 pictures of the eye region of actors' and actresses' faces and were asked to choose one of two words provided that best described what the person in the picture was thinking or feeling. Simon Baron-Cohen found that this test was successful in measuring social sensitivity in adults who had high-functioning autism and Asperger syndrome but who score lower than the general population. Although this first test did fulfill its original purpose in identifying social sensitivity in adults, other problems with the test remained. For each question, participants had to choose one of only two options. Even if a participant did not know the answer to a question, there was a 50 percent chance of getting the item right just from guessing. The test was also not subtle enough to differentiate between individuals with social sensitivity, those with autism and Asperger syndrome, and other individuals who simply scored in the lower range of the test. Based on the test scores, people who did not have Asperger syndrome or autism but who had an autistic child were identified as having low social sensitivity. Aware of these problems, Baron-Cohen revised the test to create a version to counteract these specific issues.

The current version of the test involves participants looking at black and white pictures of only the eye region of actors' and actresses' faces and then choosing one of *four* possible mental states that they feel is the best descriptor for the emotion reflected in the actors' eyes. Baron-Cohen included more images in this version of the test, in hopes of making the test more sensitive to individual differences. He also increased the word choices from two to four for each image and added more complex emotional words in hopes of making the test more difficult and making guessing the correct emotion less likely. The test is still scored in the same way with high scores indicating greater sensitivity to nonverbal interpersonal cues and lower scores indicating problems with social sensitivity.[30]

Another popular measure used for empathy is the Interpersonal Reactivity Index (IRI).[31] This measure consists of four, seven-item subscales. Each of these subscales focuses on a different aspect of empathy. The first subscale is perspective-taking, which measures one's tendency to take the view of others in daily life, such as imagining what a situation looks like from a friend's perspective. The second subscale measures empathic concern, which is the tendency to have feelings of sympathy and compassion for others. An example of empathic concern is feeling badly for people when you see them begging on the street. The third subscale measures personal distress, the tendency to feel distress in response to the distress of others. This could include feeling distress in a situation that is emotionally stressful for another person. The fourth subscale is called the Fantasy Scale, which measures one's tendency to imagine oneself in fictional situations. Imagining oneself in fictional situations includes activities such as daydreaming and imagining what it is like to be in a novel one is reading. While the IRI does measure multiple facets of empathy, it is not designed to measure overall empathy. Instead, each subscale should be used individually to measure the appropriate area it is designed for and each subscale should be scored and analyzed separately.[32] Additionally, scoring in this scale does not include high- or low-empathy scores or categories. Instead scores fall on a continuous scale for normal populations. Figuring out how to measure empathy is an incredibly important aspect to figuring out whether or not reading fictional narratives can prompt us to feel empathy and to grow that capacity.

So the next question is how tests for empathy have been conducted specifically as a result from reading fiction. A variety of different measures are used in order to quantify the high number of fluctuating variables that need to be accounted for. These fluctuating variables include print exposure or how familiar one is with narrative fiction (how well-read individuals are),[33] personality (and how likely one is to be attracted to fiction or nonfiction reading),[34] gender (women read more fiction than men),[35] and one's imaginative capacity to get lost or transported into a narrative.[36] All of these factors can influence the ways in which one might be affected by reading narrative fiction. For instance, Jennifer Argo has suggested that readers who are highly empathic tend to read more fiction.[37] This would explain the reason why fictional narratives and empathy are positively correlated, but it would not explain what I am looking for, which is some evidence that reading fiction produces higher empathy levels in its readers.

One of the most popular measures used in psychology of fiction research is called the Author Recognition Test (ART).[38] One of the important factors related to how much reading fiction can influence an individual is one's overall familiarity with reading and one's comfort level in interpreting literature. Before the ART was developed, researchers were left to self-reporting surveys about how much people read and their familiarity with various authors. The ART provides a much more reliable assessment of how much exposure people have to print media. The test works like this: Respondents are given a list of names and are asked to check all of the names of people who they *believe* are authors of fictional works. Included in the list are several foils containing names of persons who are not authors. The score is determined by how many names of real authors the participant checks. Any name of a foil they check will be subtracted from the overall positive score. Respondents are told that there are several foils and that they must check only the names who they are sure are authors.

According to Raymond Mar, who uses this test extensively in his own research, although this is not a *direct* measure of how much one has read, it is a reliable "measure of how much exposure to print an individual has had, which has been found to correlate strongly with both reading and related behaviors."[39] The test has been shown to have better predictive validity than any other form of self-reporting questionnaire about fiction exposure.[40] There are a number of different versions of the ART now, one test to measure how much fiction people read, another to measure how much nonfiction is read, and a third to measure how much print media (magazines) people are exposed to. This test is useful to those doing psychological testing with fiction because the level of narrative exposure and the level of comprehension ability are significant variables that can affect the level to which narrative fiction might be able to influence a reader.

In addition to measuring previous literary exposure and empathy, researchers studying the psychology of fiction and narratives are often also interested in people's personalities. Most often, researchers want to guarantee that individual differences in personality do not strongly influence levels of empathy and a person's likelihood to be drawn to reading fiction. One of the most common measures of personality is the Big Five Personality Inventory. This assessment uses participant responses to forty-four items, each with a five-point Likert-type response scale (1 = *strongly disagree* to 5 = *strongly agree*). Participants respond to each question in accordance with how much the statement matches their personality. The inventory measures five main subareas of personality: openness, conscientiousness, extraversion, agreeableness, and neuroticism.[41] Although measuring reading and measuring empathy might not be exact sciences, psychologists have come up with several useful ways of measuring so they can look for the relationships between reading, empathy, the ways we engage the imagination, and possible moral changes in behavior.

7. THE EVIDENCE ARGUMENT

One of Currie's concerns about the studies relating fiction to empathy has to do with the correlational method and the heavy reliance on self-reports and introspection. As I outlined earlier, he says that there is *no empirical evidence* and, thus, we should just enjoy reading our books but not try to justify our pleasure with claiming that there is some sort of benefit. This concern is reasonable, but perhaps a bit shortsighted. Most of the psychological studies that have been conducted that try to show how reading narrative fiction can generate empathy are correlational. But Currie dismisses these as real evidence, so it is worth looking at the reasons why this is the case and what the obstacles might be to performing experiments.

Correlational studies are very common in well-respected psychological research. The problem is that correlation does not prove causation. Two variables that are correlated *may be* causally related but they may not be. A correlation only provides enough information to show that variables are related, but not enough to explain the relationship. So, reading fiction and increased empathy are clearly *related*, but correlational studies cannot show that reading fiction *necessarily* causes increased empathy. For example, Raymond Mar and his colleagues found in one study that "fiction was associated with the empathy task (the MIE), whereas nonfiction was not."[42] Further, they found "IRI Fantasy was also correlated with the empathy task, indicating that individuals who find themselves more easily drawn into narratives perform better than others when asked to infer the mental states of target individuals."[43] In a different study, Katrina Fong and her colleagues aimed to show how reading different genres might influence the level of interpersonal sensitivity one might have after reading. They found that "individuals who exhibited more exposure to fiction tended to have greater interpersonal sensitivity while individuals who had been exposed to more nonfiction did not show the same relationship."[44] In another study by the same researchers, while investigating the effect of genre on gender roles, they found that "fiction exposure predicted greater egalitarian gender roles, less endorsement of gender role stereotypes, and lower levels of sexual conservatism. In contrast, exposure to nonfiction did not statistically significantly predict any of our measures of sexual attitudes."[45] These are all really important relationships that have been found using the correlational method. They also regularly employ the use of validated psychological scales like the MIE test, the ART, and the IRI. The researchers themselves do not make claim to these findings being any more than correlations. But they provide an essential starting point for further controlled experimental research. Experiments will not be conducted without indication of correlations to begin with.

There are good reasons that there have not been more experiments linking the reading of fiction to empathic changes. For instance, it is difficult to control for the myriad of relevant variables having to do with the kind of fiction exposure readers have had, the level of emotional transportation readers experience, the kind of fiction people might be attracted to or who is attracted to different kinds of genres, outside influences on empathy, and the sleeper effect (how empathy might change over time after one reads a book or engages in an experiment). Researchers also cannot control for the ways in which readers identify with various characters. One reader might identify with a main character, and a different reader might connect with someone else in the story. All of the things I wrote about above, in terms of accounting for what empathy is, ways of measuring empathy, and the way researchers attempt to control for different variables, lead me to believe that through the use of controlled experiments we will have some solid empirical evidence that reading fiction can increase empathy.

8. CONTROLLED EXPERIMENTS ON EMPATHY

Recognizing the lack of controlled experiments in this field, Dutch psychologists Matthijs Bal and Martijn Veltkamp decided to tackle the issue. They conducted two experiments in an attempt to show that reading fiction increases one's capacity for empathy. Their experiments took into consideration some important context, especially the work of Richard Gerrig. In his work on the ways readers engage with fictional worlds, Gerrig suggests that "while reading, people become transported into this narrative world, which has often been referred to [as] being lost in a book."[46] This notion of transportation is a key aspect of his work, which attempts to account for the ways that we tend to get lost in narrative worlds. He defines transportation as "a convergent process, where all mental systems and capacities become focused on events occurring in the narrative."[47] This notion of getting lost in a story is easy to imagine. Readers who are transported tend to lose track of time, lose track of their surroundings, and are deeply immersed in the world of the story.

Bal and Veltkamp used Gerrig's notion of transportation and hypothesized that only participants who are emotionally transported into the fiction they are reading will increase their capacity for empathy. Those who read fiction but are not transported will not experience an increase in empathy. They constructed their experiment using a control group that read nonfiction and an experimental group that read fiction. Hoping to replicate, as much as possible, the natural circumstances in which people read, participants completed the experiments from home on their computers.

The first of the two experiments conducted by Bal and Veltkamp used 66 Dutch college students as participants. Thirty-six of them read fiction and 30 read nonfiction. The working hypothesis of the experiment was that "fiction reading is positively related to empathy across time, but only when the reader is emotionally transported into the story."[48] Participants were asked to read either an Arthur Conan Doyle short story (*The Adventures of the Six Napoleons*) or a selection of articles from a high-quality Dutch newspaper (*De Volksrant*) of the same length. All participants were asked to write a summary of what they had read to ensure they comprehended the text fully. All of the participants passed the comprehension test. Emotional transportation was measured immediately after the participants read their selections using a scale from Busselle and Bilandzic. Bal and Veltkamp asked participants to answer three questions and respond based on a scale of 1 to 5 (1 = *not at all* to 5 = *to a great extent*). The questions were these: 1. "The story affected me emotionally" 2. "During reading the text, when a main character succeeded, I felt happy, and when they suffered in some way, I felt sad" 3. "I felt sorry for some of the characters in the text."[49] Using the IRI that I described earlier, empathy was measured immediately before reading, immediately after reading, and then again one week later. The results supported Bal and Veltkamp's initial hypothesis that "fiction readers become more empathic over the course of a week when they are emotionally transported into the story, while lowly transported fiction readers became less empathic over time. As expected, this was not the case in the control condition."[50] According to the researchers, this was the first real controlled experiment showing that empathy increases over time with emotionally transported readers and actually decreases over time with fiction readers who have low transportation.

Although conducting experiments on how reading narrative fiction influences empathy can prove to be a difficult task, researchers David Kidd and Emanuele Castano[51] conducted five additional experiments that all focused on how reading literary fiction improves both affective theory of mind (the ability to understand the emotions of others)[52] and cognitive theory of mind (the inference and representation of others' beliefs and intentions).[53] The experiments focused on affective theory of mind are the ones that I am most concerned with, since this is positively linked with empathy.[54]

In their first experiment, Kidd and Castano began by comparing literary fiction to nonfiction to test their initial hypothesis that literary fiction would "prime theory of mind."[55] In order to choose texts that accurately incorporated aspects of literary fiction, they used literary prize jurors to choose the books to be read for the literary fiction groups, selecting books written by award-winning authors. A fairly large sample of 86 participants read one of six short texts based on random assignment to one of the three fiction conditions or one of the three nonfiction conditions. After finishing the short reading, participants completed two tests to measure theory of mind (one to measure affective theory of mind, the other to measure cognitive) in addition to completing measures including the ART to assess fiction exposure, a transportation scale to assess transportation into the story, and a measure of mood. Results revealed that scores on the measure of affective theory of mind (in this case, the Reading the Mind in the Eyes test described earlier) were higher with the participants who read the literary fiction selection than with the nonfiction readers. Kidd and Castano also found that previous exposure to fiction had an influence on affective theory of mind scores, with more familiarity with fiction predicting higher scores.

After finding in the first experiment that reading literary fiction did have an influence on affective theory of mind, in comparison to reading nonfiction, in their second experiment Kidd and Castano evaluated the effects of literary fiction compared to popular fiction and not reading at all on affective theory of mind. Books for each condition were chosen in a similar manner to the first experiment. Participants in the literary fiction group read one of three excerpts from books that were finalists for the National Book Award, the popular fiction participants read one of three excerpts from recent bestsellers from Amazon.com, and a final group of participants read nothing at all. After reading, participants completed a cognitive theory of mind measure and a measure of affective theory of mind called the Diagnostic Analysis of Nonverbal Accuracy 2—Adult Faces (Faces).[56] This measure of empathy contains three sections in total: faces, voices, and postures. Participants look at a face, listen to a voice, or look at the posture of the person in the measure and indicated whether they think the person is happy, sad, angry, or fearful. Kidd and Castano found that participants in the literary fiction condition had fewer errors on this measure of empathy (were better at reading nonverbal cues) than participants in the popular fiction and no reading conditions.

The third experiment was a replication of the second experiment, aiming for the same results, except that Kidd and Castano used different readings for the literary and popular fiction groups. For the literary fiction condition they used three stories from a collection of 2012 PEN/ O. Henry award winners for short stories. Three stories from an edited anthology of popular fiction served as the stimuli for the popular fiction group. To measure affective theory of mind and empathy, the Reading the Mind in the Eyes test was also used instead of the Faces. Results found that Reading the Mind in the Eyes' scores were higher in the literary fiction condition than in the popular fiction condition, successfully replicating the results of the second experiment.

In their final experiment, which focused on affective empathy, Kidd and Castano specifically tested for the influence of individual variables such as the age and gender of participants and possible confounds, which are outside variables that are not being controlled for but change in accordance with a variable that is being controlled for and manipulated. This experiment used the same texts from the third experiment and had a literary fiction, a popular fiction, and a no-reading group. Again, using the Reading the Mind in the Eyes test, Kidd and Castano found that empathy scores were significantly higher for participants in the literary fiction condition and there was no difference in empathy scores between the popular fiction and the no-reading groups.

So, despite some concerns that empathy is too abstract to measure, there are several empirical tests that are able to measure the empathy that is associated with and is generated by reading fictional literature. There is also a large body of work in psychology that deals with perspective-taking more generally but does not use literary works as a basis of control or experimentation. For my purposes, I wanted to show the kinds of studies that have been done using real literary fiction, measuring as well as possible the kinds of empathic occurrences readers have. I also wanted to show that there are experimental studies that have been developed to measure these responses beyond just the correlational studies. All of these experiments have shown that our intuition that reading fictional literature makes us more empathic is empirically verifiable.

9. CONTROLLED EXPERIMENTS ABOUT THE SOCIAL BENEFITS OF READING

There are also empirical experiments that have been conducted using fictional literature to measure the development of social skills. I will talk here about two different kinds of studies, one having to do with the stereotypes of bookworms and nerds being associated with readers of fiction and nonfiction, respectively, and then another study that has to do with reading multicultural literature.

In an experiment conducted by Raymond Mar and his team, the researchers decided to see whether the stereotype of a bookworm (an avid fiction reader who does not socialize much) was really associated with the stereotyped lack of social skills.[57] In order to test this, they contrasted the stereotypes of bookworms (fiction readers) with nerds (nonfiction readers). Their hypothesis was that fiction readers could actually improve their social skills through reading fictional literature. Their supposition works conversely, as well, arguing that nonfiction readers can impair their social skills because both the structure and the content of what they read tends not to be about human relationships, intentional agents working from particular motivations toward specific goals, or dialogue. In this way, the content of narrative fiction tends to be a lot more like the real world than nonfiction is. That is, fiction tends to be centered on people who we imaginatively engage with, it follows a discernable temporal sequence, and it prompts readers to make similar kinds of inferences to those we make in the actual world about why people do various things or why people feel in certain ways.

Mar suggests that there are three general arguments for why there might be a positive relationship between fiction readers and increased social abilities. First, he suggests that "frequent fiction readers expose themselves to concrete social knowledge embedded within stories, which is then applied to real world interactions."[58] As I described previously, the structure and the content of fiction often resemble the actual world in that readers read about proper and improper ways of handling various situations and how different reactions tend to turn out. The second argument Mar suggests for why fiction readers might be more socially adept is that "frequent readers of narrative hone their social inference and monitoring skills, and that these improved skills are exercised in the real world."[59] Readers watch closely the ways that characters interact in their stories, and they tend to be able to make good predictions about the way that people act. The third argument is that "individuals who are very empathetic, and skilled at making social inferences, simply enjoy reading fiction more and are more likely to engage in this activity."[60] Thus it could be that those who have better social skills are drawn to fiction because it appeals to their already developed interest in relationships, social inferences, and empathy.

The experiment Mar and his team conducted used a number of the previously mentioned measurements like the ART, the IRI, and the MIE test. What they added this time was that they correlated these previous tests with an additional one called the Interpersonal Perception Task, which measures a person's ability to make accurate inferences about several interactions they watch on a video. Participants must pay close attention to nonverbal cues in order to get an accurate read on the situations. What Mar found was that exposure to narrative fiction is positively related to social ability, and exposure to nonfiction was negatively related to social ability. This is not particularly surprising, but what is different about this particular study is that it does not use an individual work of literature to measure from. It is, instead, based on the ART alone, which measures in a much more general way one's familiarity with authors and, in turn, *how much* fiction one reads. Further, Mar explains that fiction readers, "by reading a great deal of narrative fiction, may buffer themselves from the effects of reduced direct interpersonal contact by simulating the social experiences depicted in stories."[61] Despite the time one spends away from real others while reading, being a fiction reader actually supplements the social interactions one has because narrative comprehension has a tendency to help develop those social skills anyway.

Dan Johnson and his team also tried to understand some of the possible social impacts that reading fiction can have, especially having to do with the negative stereotypes that people have of different races and cultures. His research is specifically focused on how reading fictional literature can reduce both implicit and explicit prejudice against Arab Muslims, since "hate crimes against Muslims in the U.S. have increased by 6,000% from pre-9/11 levels in 2000."[62] In Johnson's first experiment, he divided participants into three groups who read either a full narrative, a condensed narrative, or an unrelated nonfictional passage (those in the control condition). Both the full narrative and condensed narrative passages were about a strong-willed Muslim woman. Whether or not participants read the full or condensed narrative, Johnson explains that each condition contained identical "counter stereotypical exemplars and exposure to Muslim culture, but the full narrative participants also received the richness of descriptive language, dialogue, and monologue."[63] The narrative was an excerpt from the fictional novel *Saffron Dreams*, by Shaila Abdullah, which describes a

Muslim woman who is pregnant, well-educated, and strong-willed and who gets assaulted in a New York City subway station. She is courageous and stands up to her attackers and rebuffs their ethnic and religious slurs. Both the full and condensed narratives end with the protagonist enjoying an afternoon in the park with her child, so there is a nice resolution to the storyline. Participants in the control condition read a short nonfiction history of the automobile.[64]

Johnson wanted to try to measure how much the fictional narrative influenced the feelings of identification and compassion that it had on its readers and to see whether reading the narrative influenced these feelings to a significantly greater degree than the condensed version or the nonfiction control group. After reading the respective passages, participants evaluated on a scale of one to five how much empathy they felt toward Arab Muslims as a group, based specifically on six descriptors: compassionate, sympathetic, softhearted, tender, warm, and moved.[65]

In addition to the compassion test, Johnson also had participants complete the Implicit Attitudes test to measure implicit prejudice toward Arab Muslims. That test consisted of seven block trials in total.[66] In the first block, participants completed twenty trials where they pressed the z key on the computer (all the way on the left) for a name they associated to be Caucasian and pressed the m key (all the way on the right) for a name they associated to be Arab. In the next block of trials, participants pressed the z and m keys, respectively, for positive and negative adjectives. The third and fourth blocks of trials combined both the names and adjectives with Caucasian names. Positive adjectives were still associated with the z key, and Arab names and negative adjectives were still associated with the m key. The fifth and sixth trial blocks were identical to the first and second trial blocks, but the letter key associations switched. Arab names and positive adjectives became associated with the z key, and Caucasian names and negative adjectives became associated with the m key. The final trial again combined the names and adjectives but with the new key assignments.[67]

Johnson found that participants who read the full narrative "exhibited significantly lower Arab-Muslim explicit attitudes than participants in the non-narrative condition, but not the condensed narrative condition. These results indicate that reading narrative fiction can reduce both implicit and explicit prejudice."[68] Additionally, participants who read the full narrative exhibited significantly higher empathy for Arab Muslims than participants in both the condensed narrative and

nonnarrative conditions. Johnson showed clearly that reading narrative fiction can help to reduce prejudice and has more social benefits than reading different forms of literature.

After this, Johnson wanted more evidence. With help from his colleagues, he conducted a second experiment that was similar to the first but one that used a variety of different measures. For this experiment, Johnson used a different scale to rate explicit prejudice toward Arab Muslims than he had in the first. The scale used in this experiment asked participants to rate Arab Muslims as a group from one to nine on stereotypical traits (*smart-stupid*, *aggressive-passive*).[69] To measure anxiety levels, participants also completed a questionnaire asking them to rate certain traits on how similar it was to how they would feel in a future encounter with an Arab Muslim. The options included items like *feeling awkward* and *embarrassed*.

Johnson also measured implicit prejudice. This time he used a measure that involved word completion. Participants completed a total of 30 word fragments each having a positive, negative, or neutral word completion. Johnson showed each participant a male face. Half of the faces pictured were of an Arab-Muslim man wearing a turban, accompanied by a word fragment. The other half of the faces shown were of a Caucasian man wearing a baseball hat accompanied by a word fragment. Depending on the association that the participants drew between the face and the word fragment, they would either complete the fragment with a positive or negative word.

Johnson connected the results of the first and second experiments and found that participants who read the full narrative, rather than the condensed narrative or nonnarrative, completed more of the word fragments with positive words instead of neutral or negative word completions. Specifically, those who read the full narrative completed more of the word fragments associated with the Arab-Muslim face with positive word completions, reflecting a decrease in implicit prejudice. Participants in the full narrative condition also showed significantly less stereotyping of Arab-Muslim individuals and significantly higher empathy compared to participants in the other conditions. With this, Johnson not only found support for his hypothesis that narrative fiction can help people relate to other individuals who are different from them without inducing anxiety, his experimental results also provided empirical evidence that readers can gain social benefits from reading narrative fiction.

10. CONCLUSION

This chapter began with a number of questions from Greg Currie about the legitimacy of the empirical research that was being done to "prove" that fiction can make us smarter, more empathetic, and more socially competent. I think that I have addressed the evidence question by describing the kinds of psychological experiments that have been done with actual literature. But the epistemological question still looms, perhaps. So how do we *know* that fiction benefits us? Well, first, one of the initial worries about fiction involves the kinds of things that we might learn *from* fiction. There is a huge amount of literature about this, but what I am interested in here is not so much what is *in the fiction* but what *reading* does for us. I think that what I have done here is shift the focus of the research from the book to the reader.

The kind of knowledge that can be learned from reading fiction is not real-world knowledge—knowledge of historical facts, descriptions of real places, or descriptions of real events—we have history and journalism for that, but it can be thought of as social knowledge or knowledge of how humans tend to interact with one another. The kinds of books one chooses to read have an impact on his/her knowledge of what people are like and how they act. The books that children read shape their view of what normal social relations look like. Stories shape the way children understand race, gender, and social and economic status, among other things.[70] When adults are readers, we too can be influenced by what we read and just by the fact that we are reading. When we read we do several things that are worth practicing, like sitting still for long periods of time, focusing on a single story for an extended amount of time, making coherent sense out of a text that requires focus and attention to make connections, and most importantly, we gain practice identifying with characters. People who are not well-practiced in identifying with fictional others can have a harder time identifying with real others, generating empathy for others, and understanding the motivations of others. Literary abstractions can also be much more descriptive in terms of causations and inner monologues and can provide justification for action than real life often does. Literary fiction should not be thought of as a poor representation of reality but instead as an abstraction of real life.

So Currie's worry that what we get from literature is not real knowledge is not a worry that I share. What we get from reading fictional literature is social knowledge. As clearly demonstrated throughout this chapter, psychologists have shown and measured in great detail how that works. The knowledge is effective depending on whether or not a reader is influenced by it. The same works do not impact all readers in the same ways, and some works may not impact a reader at all. Part of that may be a choice, but a large part is about whether or not the reader is equipped (in terms of skill for literary analysis) or emotionally ready (one might just flat out reject the perspectives given in the story) to take on the identification, the perspective-taking of the characters, or the emotional salience of the story.

A number of philosophers have written about the possible moralizing effects of certain novels. Generally, they argue that these books would have a particular moral lesson for readers. This list includes things like Martha Nussbaum recommending Charles Dickens' *Hard Times* in her book *Poetic Justice*.[71] Eva Dadlez argues this in her book *Mirrors to One Another* when she talks about how a number of the Jane Austen novels can serve as effective thought experiments.[72] Eileen John talks about the moral subtleties that are highlighted in Toni Morrison's novel *The Bluest Eye*.[73] Only one psychological study I found asked participants to read multiple chapters of a novel in order to measure empathic responses.[74] But my position on this is that no single literary work, no matter how great a work it is considered, will have the kind of impact that will be immediately measurable, because knowledge from reading is not merely about learning from content. The emotional potential of reading fiction is also not necessarily going to be immediately clearly evident or measurable.

So we need to remember the important distinction between the measurable empirical world and the humanities. Just because we do not measure things in the humanities in the same way that can be done in the sciences and social sciences does not mean that change does not happen or that learning is not real. I take it to be a dangerous mistake to think that only that which can be measured is thereby valuable to a proper education or life well-lived. I think that the measuring that I have described here is imperative to the ways that we might need to justify reading fiction in, say, school curricula, but it is also important to remember that reading individual fictional works only really makes sense within the context of reading in the big picture. Some readers are more prepared to be affected by what they read because they have practiced doing it for years. Some readers will be able to glean the lessons from Charles Dickens or Jane Austen because they have a scaffolding of skills to be able to actually get something out of it. Many readers just do not have those skills, and so reading these works will be an exercise in futility and frustration.

Measuring empathy, how much familiarity one has with a list of authors, and the level of emotional engagement or identification one has with a character allows academics to be able to prove the direction of causation within their samples. They can show trends, impacts, and differences. This is appealing for people who want to make grand claims about readers and fiction. Although I find some of these studies compelling, I also do not want to fall victim to the belief that this is the end of the inquiry about the benefits of reading fictional narratives. The information gathered with these studies allows me to show how readers can be impacted by narrative structure and content as well, but I still think that we should read more than we do and that narratives can change the way that we think of ourselves, our circumstances, and truth.

NOTES

1. Gregory Currie, "Does Great Literature Make Us Better?" *The New York Times Opinionator,* (June 1, 2013), http://opinionator.blogs.nytimes.com/2013/06/01/does-great-literature-make-us-better (accessed January 29, 2015)

2. Gregory Currie, "Literature and the Psychology Lab," *The Times Literary Supplement* (August 31, 2011), http://www.the-tls.co.uk/tls/public/article765921.ece (accessed January 29, 2015)

3. Currie, "Does Great Literature Make Us Better?"

4. Currie, "Does Great Literature Make Us Better?"

5. Although Currie doesn't cite it by name, he is referring to a 1994 study by Felix Post, who reports on diagnoses based on the *Diagnostic and Statistical Manual of Mental Disorders* (*DSM*) that he made of 291 famous men (and only men) derived from biographies he read of them. He cites that 48 percent of literary authors suffered from *severe* psychopathology whereas the rate of psychopathology in scientists, statesmen, and academics was significantly lower.

6. Currie, "Literature and the Psychology Lab."

7. Currie, "Literature and the Psychology Lab."

8. Currie, "Does Great Literature Make Us Better?"

9. Currie, "Does Great Literature Make Us Better?"

10. Anne Eaton, "A Sensible Antiporn Feminism," *Ethics* 117 (2007): 694.

11. Currie, "Literature and the Psychology Lab."

12. Currie, "Does Great Literature Make Us Better?"

13. Currie, "Literature and the Psychology Lab."

14. Currie, "Literature and the Psychology Lab."

15. Keith Oatley, *Such Stuff as Dreams: The Psychology of Fiction* (Malden, MA: Wiley-Blackwell, 2011), 13.

16. Oatley, *Such Stuff as Dreams*, 13.

17. See Martin Davies and Tony Stone, eds., *Folk Psychology: The Theory of mind Debate* (Cambridge, MA: Blackwell Publishers, 1995) and Martin Davies and Tony Stone, eds., *Mental Simulation: Evaluations and Applications* (Cambridge, MA: Blackwell Publishers, 1995) for a full account of simulation theory and Theory Theory.

18. Raymond Mar and Keith Oatley, "The Function of Fiction Is the Abstraction and Simulation of Social Experience," *Perspectives on Psychological Science* 3 (2008): 173–92.

19. Oatley, *Such Stuff as Dreams*, 32.

20. Oatley, *Such Stuff as Dreams*, 33.

21. Wayne Booth, *The Company We Keep: An Ethics of Fiction* (Berkeley, CA: University of California Press, 1988).

22. Suzanne Keen, "A Theory of Narrative Empathy," *Narrative* 14, No. 3 (2006): 208.

23. Keen, "A Theory of Narrative Empathy."

24. Keen, "A Theory of Narrative Empathy."

25. Amy Coplan, "Will the Real Empathy Please Stand Up? A Case for a Narrow Conceptualization," *The Southern Journal of Philosophy* 49 (2011): 44.

26. Coplan, "Will the Real Empathy Please Stand Up?"

27. Coplan, "Will the Real Empathy Please Stand Up?," 51. These results are described by Coplan based on a study by Shamay-Tsoory et al.

28. Lea Winerman, "The Mind's Mirror," *Monitor* 36 (2005): 48.

29. Simon Barron-Cohen, Sally Wheelwright, Jacqueline Hill, Yogini Raste, and Ian Plumb, "The 'Reading the Mind in the Eyes' Test Revised Version: A Study with Normal Adults, and Adults with Asperger Syndrome or High-Functioning Autism," *Journal of Child Psychology and Psychiatry* 42 (2001): 241–51.

30. Katrina Fong, Justin Mullin, and Raymond Mar, "What You Read Matters: The Role of Fiction Genre in Predicting Interpersonal Sensitivity, *Psychology of Aesthetics, Creativity, and the Arts* 7, No. 4 (2013): 370–76.

31. Mark Davis, "A Multidimensional Approach to Individual Differences in Empathy," *JSAS Catalogue of Selected Documents in Psychology* 10 (1980): 85.

32. Sarah Konrath, "A Critical Analysis of the Interpersonal Reactivity Index." In *MedEdPORTAL Directory and Repository of Educational Assessment Measures (DREAM)* (2013).

33. Keith Stanovich and Richard West, "Exposure to Print and Orthographic Processing," *Reading Research Quarterly*, 24 (1989): 402–33.

34. Oliver John, E. M. Donahue, and R. L. Kentle, *The Big Five Inventory—Versions 4a and 5,* (Berkeley, CA: University of California, Berkeley, Institute of Personality and Social Research, 1991).

35. Fong, Mullin, and Mar, "What You Read Matters."

36. Davis, "A Multidimensional Approach to Individual Differences in Empathy."

37. Jennifer Argo, Juliet Zhu, and Darren Dahl, "Fact or Fiction: An Investigation of Empathy Differences in Response to Emotional Melodramatic Entertainment," *Journal of Consumer Research* 34 (2008): 614–23.

38. The ART was originally developed by Stanovich and West (1989).

39. Raymond Mar, Keith Oatley, and Jordan Peterson, "Exploring the Link between Reading Fiction and Empathy: Ruling out Individual Differences and Examining Outcomes," *Communications* 34, No. 4 (2009): 412.

40. Linda Allen, Jim Cipielewski, and Keith Stanovich, "Multiple Indicators of Children's Reading Habits and Attitudes: Construct Validity and Cognitive Correlates," *Journal of Educational Psychology* 844 (1992): 489–503.

41. John, Donahue, and Kentle, *The Big Five Inventory*.

42. Mar, Oatley, and Peterson, "Exploring the Link between Reading Fiction and Empathy," 416.

43. Mar, Oatley, and Peterson, "Exploring the Link between Reading Fiction and Empathy," 417.

44. Fong, Mullin, and Mar, "What You Read Matters," 372.

45. Katrina Fong, Justin Mullin, and Raymond Mar, "How Exposure to Literary Genres Relates to Attitudes Toward Gender Roles and Sexual Behavior," *Psychology of Aesthetics, Creativity, and the Arts* 9, no. 2 (2015): 5.

46. Matthijs Bal and Martijn Veltkamp, "How Does Fiction Reading Influence Empathy? An Experimental Investigation on the Role of Emotional Transportation," *PLoS ONE* 8, No. 1 (2013): 3.

47. Bal and Veltkamp, "How Does Fiction Reading Influence Empathy?"

48. Bal and Veltkamp, "How Does Fiction Reading Influence Empathy?," 4.

49. Bal and Veltkamp, "How Does Fiction Reading Influence Empathy?,".

50. Bal and Veltkamp, "How Does Fiction Reading Influence Empathy?," 5.

51. David Comer Kidd and Emanuele Castano, "Reading Literary Fiction Improves Theory of Mind," *Science* 342 (2013): 377–80.

52. Simone Shamay-Tsoory and Judith Aharon-Peretz, "Dissociable Prefrontal Networks for Cognitive and Affective Theory of Mind: A Lesion Study," *Neuropsychologia* 45 (2007): 3054–67.

53. Simone Shamay-Tsoory, Haim Harari, Judith Aharon-Peretz, and Yechiel Levkovitz, "The Role of the Orbitofrontal Cortex in Affective Theory

of mind Deficits in Criminal Offenders with Psychopathic Tendencies," *Cortex* 46 (2010): 668-677.

54. Simone Shamay-Tsoory and Judith Aharon-Peretz, "Dissociable Prefrontal Networks for Cognitive and Affective theory of mind: A Lesion Study," *Neuropsychologia* 45 (2007): 3054-3067.

55. Kidd and Castano, "Reading Literary Fiction Improves Theory of mind," 377.

56. Stephen Nowicki, "Manual for the Receptive Tests of the Diagnostic Analysis of Nonverbal Accuracy 2," Department of Psychology, Emory University, Atlanta, GA (2010).

57. Raymond Mar, Keith Oatley, Jacob Hirsh, Jennifer dela Paz, and Jordan Peterson, "Bookworms versus Nerds: Exposure to Fiction versus Nonfiction, Divergent Associations with Social Ability, and the Simulation of Fictional Social Worlds," *Journal of Research in Personality* 40, No. 5 (2006): 694–712.

58. Mar, Oatley, Hirsh, dela Paz, and Peterson, "Bookworms versus Nerds," 698.

59. Mar, Oatley, Hirsh, dela Paz, and Peterson, "Bookworms versus Nerds."

60. Mar, Oatley, Hirsh, dela Paz, and Peterson, "Bookworms versus Nerds."

61. Mar, Oatley, Hirsh, dela Paz, and Peterson, "Bookworms versus Nerds," 705.

62. Dan Johnson, Daniel Jasper, Sallie Griffin, and Brandie Huffman, "Reading Narrative Fiction Reduces Arab-Muslim Prejudice and Offers a Safe Haven from Intergroup Anxiety," *Social Cognition* 31, No. 5 (2013): 581.

63. Johnson, Jasper, Griffin, and Huffman, "Reading Narrative Fiction Reduces Arab-Muslim Prejudice," 582.

64. Johnson, Jasper, Griffin, and Huffman, "Reading Narrative Fiction Reduces Arab-Muslim Prejudice."

65. Johnson, Jasper, Griffin, and Huffman, "Reading Narrative Fiction Reduces Arab-Muslim Prejudice."

66. Anthony Greenwald, Brian Nosek, and Mahzarin Banaji, "Understanding and Using the Implicit Association Test (IAT): I. An improved scoring algorithm," *Journal of Personality and Social Psychology* 85 (2003): 197–216.

67. Johnson, Jasper, Griffin, and Huffman, "Reading Narrative Fiction Reduces Arab-Muslim Prejudice," 583.

68. Johnson, Jasper, Griffin, and Huffman, "Reading Narrative Fiction Reduces Arab-Muslim Prejudice," 584.

69. Johnson, Jasper, Griffin, and Huffman, "Reading Narrative Fiction Reduces Arab-Muslim Prejudice," 588.

70. Jeanne Tsai, Jennifer Louie, Eva Chen, and Yukiko Uchida, "Learning What Feelings to Desire: Socialization of Ideal Affect Through Children's Storybooks," *Personality and Social Psychology Bulletin,* 33 (2007): 17–30.

71. Martha Nussbaum, *Poetic Justice* (Boston: Beacon Press, 1995).

72. Eva Dadlez, *Mirrors to One Another: Emotion and Value in Jane Austen and David Hume* (Malden, MA: Wiley-Blackwell, 2009).

73. Eileen John, "Subtlety and Moral Vision in Fiction," *Philosophy and Literature* 19, No. 2 (1995): 308–19.

74. Gregory Berns, Kristina Blaine, Michael Prietula, and Brandon Pye, "Short- and Long-Term Effects of a Novel on Connectivity in the Brain," *Brain Connectivity* 3, No. 6 (2013): 590–600.

Conclusion

Reading as Good-for-Nothing

I believe that when future generations look back at our time they will see us as a culture that was obsessed with measurement and assessment (and social media and legal blame, but those are topics for another book). In days past we have taken pleasure in all kinds of things for which we never bothered to seek proof or measurement. People read because they liked it. It was a fulfilling pastime, and well-educated folks tended to do it more than others. But now we want scientific evidence to justify the time given over to reading. We want reliable institutional assessment measures that guarantee the efficacy of the lessons taught in schools. We want to know the academic measure of where each child stands on a numeric scale beginning in kindergarten, more often than not before the child can even read. Taken to an extreme, children are measured, scored, and compared in their first minutes of life when they are assigned their first Apgar score. From then on they are put in comparison groups, and parents are shown graphs that measure their height and weight as compared to others their age. Inevitably, those height and weight scores are replaced by grade points, SAT scores, and class rankings.

But what we don't measure for children are things like creativity, problem-solving skills, empathy for others, joy, perseverance, and the development of a healthy, balanced personality. The college where I teach is finding how difficult it is to measure resilience through a four-year study. These are all traits that most people would say they value, but they are not the ones measured, not the ones funded, and not the ones valued by our educational system or the larger culture.

Nelson Goodman, in his book *Languages of Art*, discusses the notion of truth and how we use it differently in reference to both science and art. He suggests that we be careful not to relegate the arts and the knowledge that comes with our experience of the arts to be associated with something other than truth. Rather, he suggests, "the difference between art and science is not that between feeling and fact, intuition and inference, delight and deliberation, synthesis and analysis, sensation and cerebration, concreteness and abstraction, passion and action, mediacy and immediacy, or truth and beauty, but rather a difference in domination of certain specific characteristics of symbols."[1] What we have done is just what Goodman warned against: We have associated truth with science and measurement and have neglected the activities that are associated with the arts, with feeling, and with pleasure.

The difference between the humanities and the sciences is key here. The sciences measure observable phenomenon. The humanities seek to find meaning and interpretation. In William Deresiewicz's book *Excellent Sheep: The Miseducation of the American Elite & The Way to a Meaningful Life*, about the changes in American higher education, he argues this: "the scientist seeks to be objective and appeals to the impersonal languages of numbers. The artist speaks from individual experience and appeals to our own individual experience. Humanistic knowledge isn't verifiable, or quantifiable, or reproducible. It cannot be expressed in terms of equations or general laws. It changes from culture to culture and person to person. It is a matter not of calculation but interpretation. When we engage in humanistic inquiry—when we think about a poem or a sculpture or a piece of music—we ask, not how big it is, or how hot it is, or what does it consist of, but what does it mean. We ask of a scientific proposition, 'Is it true?,' but of a proposition in the humanities we ask, 'Is it true for me?'[2] We must not forget that the skills we learn in the humanities are not the same as the inquiries we make in the sciences. And with reading, practicing understanding the experiences of others, especially when it is well thought out, descriptive, compelling, and interesting, we get better at, well understanding ourselves and others."

Greg Currie says that we should stop trying to justify what goes on in literature and our possible meaningful (and measurable) interactions with it and just move on. Despite the fact that I do believe there are measures to show how fictional literature affects us, perhaps part of what Currie says is right. Perhaps we should stop trying to justify it. We should not stop because of a recognition that it isn't really beneficial or because we haven't quite come up with the right measures, experiments, or rubrics, but because we see an inherent value in the humanities, their methods, and their impacts.

In a recent essay on value, Susan Wolf argues that we have developed a too limited notion of value, one that is too closely tied to a notion of usefulness and benefit. She argues that we have become too used to a welfarist account of value that measures a thing's perceived value with its benefits for someone. She explains that we should think more about the "good-for-nothings" that are artworks or written texts (including some philosophy) that don't really benefit anyone except the artist or author themselves. Normally, for something to be considered good, she says, "it needs to be good *for* someone or something whose welfare is enhanced by it. Good-for-nothings are works that do not necessarily benefit anyone or are in any particular way useful. Good-for-nothings are good in themselves, good examples of their kind. They are good works of art, literature, history, philosophy, or whatever. Wolf explains that "we are rightly grateful that these works were created; we rightly admire them, appreciate them, and take pains to preserve them."[3]

There are a multitude of examples of good-for-nothings, often related to the things we associate with intrinsic value. These are things like human life, music, and literature. Some philosophers have argued that pleasure is good in itself (like Plato in the *Protagoras*[4] and Epicurus who argued that pleasure should be the primary measure of ethics), while others condemn it since its excess often leads to pain and thus deprives us of future pleasures. What seems to be happening, however, is that for a large host of reasons there has been a shift to keep and value that which is measurable and to discard and devalue that which we cannot measure. (Mostly, I assume, these reasons have to do with the cost of higher education, the desire for constant assessment of students, programs, and teacher effectiveness, and the need for educational systems to justify their budgets.) Wolf argues that "insofar as we try to understand the value of good art, good philosophy, good science, too exclusively in terms of their potential to benefit us, we are looking in the wrong direction."[5] Of course art, philosophy, science, literature, pleasure, food, and music all have some (measurable) benefit. But it seems particularly shortsighted to focus exclusively on the measurable outcomes of the experiences we have with those things. As a professional philosopher, I regularly have to defend the value of a college philosophy degree, and in my case at a relatively expensive liberal arts college. I go to both students and parents prepared with articles, graphs, and statistics showing how well philosophy majors do financially, how well they do on graduate entrance exams, and how well they do in law school. What I omit and diminish is what my real love of philosophy is about: getting excited about new ideas, thinking through a problem in a new way, learning about big systems, and the way ethics, epistemology, and ontology go hand in hand (like in Plato). The questions I deal with in philosophy are interesting in and of themselves, and they are ultimately very helpful in the practical world. But these are not measurable benefits that are sellable to consumers. So I stay quiet about them.

Wolf warns us against this instrumental or welfarist kind of value. She does not think it shouldn't be recognized at all but that we should be careful not to forget about the good-for-nothings. She says that if we don't mention this other kind of value, we might stop noticing it is there. Indeed, she says, "the more entrenched welfarist conceptions of value become in our language and in our thought, the less likely it is that we will even recognize the possibility it is there."[6] If we stop talking about valuing good-for-nothings, we will forget that they are good in themselves. If we stop reading for pleasure, uninterested in the sort of benefit it might have, we will miss out on a world of information, perspective taking, empathy building, and character building that we cannot get anywhere else.

I had a conversation with a friend recently about canning tomato sauce, which I do every year. He said that he tried canning but added the costs of the tomatoes, spices, and canning jars and lids and then divided by the number of jars it would produce. He decided that there was no way that canning could be as cost-effective as buying tomato sauce in the grocery store. He said he could not imagine why anyone would do it, especially considering the time and effort involved that he did not even include in his calculus. I told him that I can tomato sauce because I like the way it tastes, I like knowing where my food comes from, I have great memories of my mom canning, I like teaching my children how to cook, I love the smell, and I like cooking the rest of the year with my own sauce. It is not cost-effective if you only look at it for materials and labor, and it is not something that I would want to advocate that everyone should do. But it has value for me and it is something I value spending time doing with my family. This is not an argument that everyone should do it or that everyone should value it, but it is a recognition that I find value in it that goes well beyond the product.

But what about reading? I have spent considerable effort in this book to justify and demonstrate the benefits of reading. In the end, I believe the benefits of reading can, at least partly, be accounted for by Wolf's alternative notion to welfarist value. Reading might not have a measurable outcome that can be tested or graphed. I think that we are in grave danger of so often touting the measurable benefits of reading that we might forget to notice that it can be fun, relaxing, and pleasurable. It is a way to connect with others about shared experiences and interpretations, and it might just make us smarter or more capable. But that should not be why we do it.

NOTES

1. Nelson Goodman, *Languages of Art: An Approach to a Theory of Symbols* (Indianapolis, IN: Hackett Publishing Company, 1976), 264.

2. William Deresiewicz, *Excellent Sheep: The Miseducation of the American Elite & The Way to a Meaningful Life* (New York: The Free Press, 2014), 160.

3. Susan Wolf, *The Variety of Values: Essays on Morality, Meaning, and Love* (Oxford: Oxford University Press, 2014), 68.

4. See Plato, *Protagoras*, line 353e.

5. Susan Wolf, *The Variety of Values*, 73.

6. Susan Wolf, *The Variety of Values*, 83.

Index

About the Author

Sarah E Worth is professor of philosophy at Furman University. She has published widely on aesthetics and the philosophy of literature, including articles in *The Journal of Aesthetics and Art Criticism, The Journal of Aesthetic Education, The British Journal of Aesthetics, Contemporary Aesthetics, and Philosophy and the Contemporary World*. She lives in Greenville, South Carolina with her husband Bill and twin sons, William and Charles. She makes jewelry for fun.

Pet Sitters!

Heart to Heart

Pet care